Déjà Vu with Quixotic Delusions of Grandeur

Déjà Vu with Quixotic Delusions of Grandeur

MEMOIR

MARC SAPIR

Dedicated to Moi,
who suggested that I should write my life story,
and in remembrance of Oliver Sacks

TABLE OF CONTENTS

FORWARD TO THE
REVISED FIRST EDITION

Issuing a revised edition soon after the initial release of a book requires explanation. Leaving the most frustrating reason for last, let me detail content changes. In the essay titled: The Death of Hal Carlstad, I write about my effort to convince Kaiser Permanente to send my friend Hal home despite his requiring high-level hospital care (that was 17 years ago). Now the January 2024 issue of the Annals of Internal Medicine publishes research by Levine, DM et al.: *Acute hospital care at home in the United States: The early national experience.* 2024 Jan; 177:109. The Journal Watch, General Medicine newsletter summarizes the research: "In a study of 5,000 patients who received hospital care at home, outcomes were favorable." This information updates that story.

For decades, alongside many thousands of others, I have worked advocating major health care system reform, in particular a free Medicare for All program for the US. Due to space considerations, I previously dropped out writings on that effort, but I've decided that I ought include at least something on our endless battle with market politics, so much a part of my life. A brief piece has been added to Part VI.

To the oral essay by William I have added a photo of William with Ella, the "call and response" side-commentator in his essay. I've also added several other photos: two accompany the story of Ara

Belle Kingsby, a cartoon from the Mad as Hell Docs touring group, one of management level staff from the Center for Elders' Independence, a Halloween photo from the old (defunct) Central Clinic of Alameda County in 1991, and one of me talking to the great Argentinian writer Jorge Luis Borges in a Buenos Aires restaurant (he was, unfortunately, already long dead by then)…

Importantly, this revised edition is being printed and distributed through IngramSpark, the print-on-demand company which is a spin-off from the Ingram Book Distribution firm. Though I own the rights as the actual publisher of the book, the earlier edition was printed by Barnes & Noble Press (also a print-on-demand operation). Barnes & Noble Press distributes books they print via BN.com. However, most independent retail booksellers worldwide buy their books through Ingram's distribution network. Once I had published the book through Barnes & Noble Press, Ingram would not be distributing the book. I had to present IngramSpark with a different book with a new ISBN. This revised edition is now available to independent small booksellers worldwide.

MS February 28, 2024

INTRODUCTION

Myth-making: In the mammalian beginning there were sight, sounds, smells, tastes, touch and aversive pain. And all of a sudden there bloomed imagining and imagination. And once hominids recognized their imagination, they gave birth to florid language. Soon imagination and language combined to create culture and these three forces formed—along with material categorization and calculation—INTELLIGENCE. We call it intelligence because the conjured images allowed them/us to create and to plan; new worlds were built from tools motivated by creative imaginings—thought experiments. Now, neither inevitability nor fate seemed to govern their world. They could envision and effect how to overcome many adversities, and use the forces of nature and living things to their own purposes in a calculated way. And they did so in a process that expanded like a shock wave over the millennia and then a tsunami after the invention of the steam engine and then the cotton gin; and capitalism exploded therefrom, right up until today; and beyond our earlier wildest imaginings.

On November 1, 1967 I joined with nine other anti-war activists to sit-in and disrupt interviews by the Central Intelligence Agency (CIA), diligently recruiting Stanford students to become spies, provocateurs, academic researchers, literary and newspaper editors, assassins and murderers. The US was already two and a half years into its devastating war of aggression on Vietnam to prevent her independence (excluding the 17,000 Green Berets that JFK sent in earlier). Preventing Vietnam's self-determination was indeed explicit US policy. It was no secret that President Dwight Eisenhower had stated that if the US allowed the free election agreed to in the 1954 Geneva Peace Agreement between the French and the Vietnamese, Ho Chi Minh, a communist and nationalist, would surely win 80% of the vote. So the US appointed a dictator (who then lived in the US) to rule Southern Vietnam and—abrogating the Peace Accords—our government made plans for conquest.

Our 1967 sit-in was successful—both in stopping the interviews and in shining a light on the outrage of Stanford University casually sponsoring recruitment to a government apparatus already well-known for undermining and overthrowing other governments around the world—from Guatemala (Árbenz—1954) to Iran (Mosaddegh —1953), from the Dominican Republic (Bosch—1960) to Cuba (Castro, eventually 500 failed assassination attempts after 1959) with Vietnam then in the mix and many more interventionary wars of aggression to come henceforth.

I was just one of many young people who had realized several years before 1967 that the US planned to unleash catastrophic levels of death, suffering and chaos on Vietnam to prevent that free, fair and monitored election that was guaranteed in the France-Vietnam Geneva withdrawal agreement of 1954. I had desperately written letters to Congress on this subject beginning in 1963.

Before and subsequent to that CIA sit-in—over about a decade in toto—Stanford University students (with significant faculty and staff collaboration) developed an exceedingly potent anti-war movement. It numbered into the thousands at various times. My memoir only sparingly covers that movement, how it grew rapidly and had a great impact on the university which railroad mogul Leland Stanford founded.[1] But I believe a core truth about that moment in history is this: young people were outraged to learn and understand that US imperialism, despite lip service to freedom, democracy and justice for all, was not the least bit interested in democracy, justice or equality as it powered its way throughout the world. That outrage was further compounded by the direct experiential evidence that that same outward-facing imperialist logic also dominates and prevails through-out our culture, our institutions, pedagogy and language. This became clear when we/they discovered that the board of trustees, the owners and governors of Stanford University, were, mostly, war profiteers and war promoters, whose belief in human rights and even democracy within the United States and on campus extended no further than protecting their investments, public images and power. The 60s gener-ation learned who these folks were—and still are today—behind their masks (to quote Bob Dylan's "Masters of War"); worse, that they are not only the very motor of imperialist power, but, despite their wealth and power, they are simultaneously us (as Americans). Calling them the power-elite (C. Wright Mills), the ruling class (Marxism) or any-thing else cannot diminish their role in our own lives and our identity as a nation and people. So long as their ideas and methods dominate (as they do), no categorization can separate us from them given their hold on contemporary mass culture. Mass culture binds us to them and their ways of thinking and acting in too many hidden ways. Feel-ing this inescapable attachment is, in my view, the root of contemporary American rage, whether it be rage of the racist neo-fascist Right, of random mass murderers and road ragers gone ballistic, or of those who demand we free our people from the anti-social relations of Capital to build a livable civilization.

---

1 Lenny Siegel's Disturbing the War—The Inside Story of the Movement to Get Stanford University out of Southeast Asia 1965–1975 (Pacific Studies Center) is a well-documented presentation of that movement.

I open with an introductory note about Vietnam to highlight that a good deal of my own identity developed there, through six years at Stanford, and then further evolved after my graduation from medical school. However, readers will see that the memoir rumbles and rambles far and wide, travels far beyond my own life from zero to 80+ too. I ask that readers keep this introduction, including my opening paragraph, in mind—particularly when my writing jumps away from my life and work and into the spheres of social evolution, physiology, physics, medicine, phenomenology of the mind, neurology, death, education, literature and so on. Seek the unifying thread.

Woodcut by myself, circa 1968, that appeared
in a peace/arts newsletter on campus.

My own particular life began back in 1941, so by the time I got to Stanford in 1964, my so-called "formative" years were far in the rearview mirror. Nonetheless, the person who I became and remain was significantly molded by those Stanford years—the infamous 60s. I do not thank Stanford for the medical degree that I earned there, though it has done me well in life for its "status". Despite my warm relationships with several faculty who I worked with closely and thought of as mentors, friends and comrades, the university itself tried more than once to punish many of us for our activism and for exposing them. I do thank Stanford for that combat, and for teaching us (all of us who were there then) more than we had imagined we might learn about the corruption of the so-called Ivory Tower. These institutions, supposedly independent of the state, claim to be guided by the high ideals of advancing knowledge, progress and human culture; and to training young minds to be critical and honest, moral and incisive—and not merely technicians. But their managers and owners teach us something more: how their institutions are fundamentally wedded to the propagation and dominance of capitalism and capitalist ideology, above all else. They remind us also of the hubris that came along with our evolution as an inventive linguistic species with profound imagination. Onward, as the time for correction grows short.

PART I

The Skein of Life

GUNS

On a balmy October afternoon in 1971, I found myself on my back on a street in South San Francisco, my left shoulder blade pinned to the curb. I had tripped on that curb and fallen back, but I didn't notice any pain because there was a lanky young man with an unsettling ferocity in his eyes standing over me, pointing a handgun at my face. So close was the gun barrel that he couldn't possibly have missed me had he pulled the trigger. I was 30 years of age, also lanky in build—a little over six feet tall, 170 pounds. He was probably about 21. We were not well acquainted. Unlike the tales that go around, my whole life did not flash before my eyes. That was 50 years ago, so I don't remember what went through my mind. But if I thought anything it was back to June of the previous year when four unshaven, un-uniformed, slovenly dressed—which is to say disguised—cops had jumped out of an old jalopy one night in the middle of a residential street in Palo Alto and all four leveled their guns at me simultaneously from outside the four car doors. They had broken a window in the home of John and Rusty Keilch where my then wife Carrie, nine months pregnant, and I were temporarily staying. I was just about to graduate from Stanford Medical School. I went outside in the dark night to scare off what appeared to be thugs...with a shotgun. I survived, but now a year later this was becoming a bad habit from which I might not survive repetition. This young white guy was no cop, but a troubled, heroin-addicted, Vietnam veteran.

As I lay with my back pressed to the curb, maybe I thought thoughts about death. But luckily someone else, a friend, a comrade, perceived the seriousness of allowing even a few more seconds to pass. From across the street, at a window at the home where several of us had been meeting, a shot rang out from a .30-caliber carbine and the young man over me crumpled to the ground. Remarkably, as if in a 1950s shoot-out western, he had been shot in the arm actually holding the gun, which fell to the pavement. The bullet, it later turned out, entered at his wrist, went up his forearm, then exited below his elbow and entered the right side of his lower chest, tearing and lodging in his liver. When he died a week or so later while hospitalized, it was not due to the direct effects of the wound, which he had survived after part of his liver was removed. The police/coroner medical report stated that because his immune system was badly weakened by drug addiction, he had developed a severe infection and sepsis and was unable to fight it successfully, even with antibiotics. The shooter, a young Colombian in the US without papers, was, surprisingly, not arrested or charged with any crime. Instead, he was disappeared. Rumor had it that he was simply deported, and not killed/disappeared after the fashion of the wanton murders of activists by Latin American government death squads with US training and support in the dirty wars then going on. What/who he really was and what happened to him then I will never know.

Were I able to remember either of these young men's names I would surely tell you, especially the young Colombian fellow who saved my life. But I don't. However, I have no trouble remembering the events and circumstances that preceded and post-ceded this particular brief moment in time half a century ago, which I will here relate to you.

The meeting which I had been attending was that of the South San Francisco collective of Venceremos, a multi-ethnic organization in the Bay Area of about 300, mostly young, radical Leftists who foolishly believed that a working class revolution was imminent and would overthrow capitalism and imperialist aggression such as the Vietnam War. Very heady and very wrong, apparently. Venceremos was born out of a Bay Area organization called the Revolutionary Union when RU's leadership found themselves divided over how to proceed. I was, at the time of that spat, living on the outskirts of Detroit, in an intentionally segregated (by Henry Ford) town named Inkster so that his white workers at the Ford Motor Company's Dearborn plant could live in Dearborn nearer the factory in an all-white, racism-promoting suburbia that excluded Black workers. I was there as a medical intern at the Wayne County Hospital situated on a sprawling county property with its own Post Office called Eloise, Michigan, just adjacent to Inkster across Michigan Avenue. With my wife, Carrie, and our infant daughter, Erica, I rented a small house in Inkster only a block or two south of the hospital property. Besides the three of us, two other couples had jumped at the romantic challenge to move from California to Michigan to work in and with the largely Black "industrial proletariat" in the Michigan auto plants. And we also had my female German Shepherd, Cocaine. But about six to eight months after we arrived in Michigan, when the RU honchos in the Bay Area had their big blowup and decided to separate into two groups, the six of us also divided. Carrie and I decided to stay with the group we knew centered in the S.F. peninsula and we formed a collective from friends we had made around the Detroit area. We allied with the peninsula group both because it was led by the people we knew well and had affection for and because their calling their new organization Venceremos (Spanish for "we will win") was emblematic of their decision that a majority of members on the leading committee (the Central Committee of Venceremos) had to be ethnic minorities and women (that is, the principle of "third world" leadership). The co-chairs of Venceremos were Stanford English professor Bruce Franklin and Aaron Manganiello, a Latino leader out of the Brown Berets organization, who was a personal friend. The other group was soon to call itself the Revolutionary Communist Party. It still exists. Led by Robert Avakian, son of an East Bay judge, it is visible but largely ineffectual in achieving any significant political reforms, so far as I know. RCP is quite good at yelling and writing "revolution, revolution, revolution" (it's actually the name of their newspaper and their book store(s)) as if the word might materialize the deed. Venceremos, on the other hand, went belly-up in a short time in early 1974. I had quit over a year before that, though I had also become attached to and would marry a member of the Venceremos Central Committee, Sheila Thorne, both of us divorcés. She also left Venceremos before it collapsed. We are together still, over 50 years later, with four children, six grandchildren, and two great-granddaughters, Grace being the first and Alison the newborn (August 2022). I wouldn't say our marriage has been "graceful" but we are blessed with Grace nonetheless; and these five decades have been an exceptional ride.

Before I met Sheila I got to South San Francisco sans Carrie via a circuitous route. Those were heady times and the hundreds of radical activists in and around Stanford were often supporters and defenders of the Black Panther Party for Self-Defense. The Panthers—as a community self-defense and "serve the people" organization—were being regularly shot down by police in many American cities. In my view some rather exceptional, honorable and moral human beings like Fred Hampton, the Chicago Panther leader murdered by police while he slept in his home, had had their lives cut short. Just as now there were also many well-armed right-wing militias which were fiercely anti-communist. And in 1969 we, the RU, called ourselves a communist organization.

Having decided that it would be important to have surgical skills in that tumultuous and murderous environment, I chose to enter a residency in Gynecology and Obstetrics after my internship year at Wayne County Hospital. I particularly found the idea of providing medical care to birth mothers, mostly healthy, bringing the joy of new life into the world very appealing. The hospital I chose for residency was Lincoln Hospital of the City of New York, in the heavily Puerto Rican South Bronx. Lincoln was affiliated with the Albert Einstein Medical College (similarly to how Wayne County Hospital was an affiliate of University of Michigan Med School). Moving to New York was like going home since I had lived my early years in the Bronx; and after college I had lived on Morris Park Blvd and worked as a research technician at Albert Einstein. However, Lincoln hospital was in turmoil, one reason I chose it. A birth mother had died due to negligence. The Young Lords Party (a Puerto Rican organization, but allied with the Panthers) had then occupied the hospital and with support of community, many hospital workers and doctors in training, they won certain demands, including the firing of the department head of OB/GYN who was a racist. The new chief was a progressive and supportive guy amenable to paying attention to actual community needs and department improvement. Though aware of my political activism, he let me into the program.

In June of 1971 back in Inkster, Carrie and I bought a used Ford Econoline van, packed up our stuff and our daughter and drove to New York. There, to my surprise, she declared that she had loose ends back in Detroit and had to return for a while. The "while" never ended, for the next thing I heard from her was a theatrical, absurd "Dear John" letter that she was leaving me (that she was involved with another fella she knew back in California—who she would later marry and have her second child with). This sudden fracture of my second marriage after only two years was a crushing emotional blow, but in my distraught state I flew back to Detroit and was able to convince her to let me be the parent who would tend to our daughter's development.[2] Having kids had been my idea in the beginning. She agreed that I have custody.

In reflecting back on that time it's pretty obvious that beginning an intense, highly demanding surgical residency with a very high-risk patient population, living alone in a new environment with a one-year-old child, and grieving the loss of my marriage added up to an unworkable situation in several dimensions. I had lived six years in California and one at Inkster and had no social network in New York. Although my parents did still live in Yonkers, I was not going to become dependent upon them at age 30 and with an MD degree no less. I decided by the end of July that I would have to quit the residency, where I already faced many middle-of-the-night complicated deliveries. I was constantly waking up senior residents and attending physicians for advice on difficult breech deliveries or shoulder dystocia or fetal distress, young mothers who had often had no prenatal care and simply showed up in labor. I decided to move back to the place where I had friends and comrades, the San Francisco peninsula.

When I returned to the Bay Area I asked to join Venceremos, and when that was agreed they asked that I move to South San Francisco (SSF) and join that collective, whose members—young men and women—were mostly Latinos. Several had been Brown Berets members. I agreed and rented a garage apartment just below the San Bruno mountain, and applied for my California medical license. Yet, you'll recognize that this lengthy digression tells you less than nothing about the soon-to-be-dead-guy with the gun pointed at my head in the street on the autumn day in 1971.

Among the members of our SSF collective were a friendly fellow named Fernando and a young woman, maybe named Elena. Elena was the girlfriend of the soon-to-be-dead, Vietnam vet heroin addict.

---

2 At that point she was moving back to California and I would be in New York.

The vet was not a member of Venceremos and, with his addiction, he wouldn't have been welcome.[3] He got it in his head that Elena was cheating on him with Fernando. It's right out of a bad telenovela of course, but no such relationship between them existed. She could not disabuse him of his paranoid suspicion which is, in a sense, understandable. He's white, an addict, and not in the organization that his girl hangs around with endlessly. At any rate, on that day he gets high, perhaps on meth or cocaine or something in addition to H, and he shows up at the door of our meeting at a quiet house on a quiet street with a gun, demanding that Fernando come outside. It seemed to me then that he might kill Fernando as he began to chase him around in the street screaming. *He's got nothing against me and I'm white*, I'm thinking, as I run outside and across the street, getting between them to try to both distract and calm this fellow. And that's where you first came in on this tale.

If that's anticlimactic I'm glad, because I could have ended up dead, which would be more climactic and I would never be writing these words nor have had such a full life. I don't know what happened to the Columbian shooter, a handsome, slender and calm fellow himself, but a friend told me that he was such a good shot because he had military training—whether by the Colombian military or the M-19 guerrilla fighters or the FBI I have no idea.

---

3 The media propaganda that the anti-war movement spat on or otherwise denigrated Vietnam veterans was a lie concocted to discredit the Left. Not only were the Army and Navy etc. roiling with anti-war sentiment and activists, who fomented actual insurrections within the military, but organizations like Venceremos were particularly proud of veterans who joined the movement. This young man with PTSD and addiction, however, was not a likely candidate.

DENIAL 101

Did you ever kill someone? No, I don't mean murder. There are lots of ways and reasons to kill someone aside from murder. Sometimes we kill people out of sympathy to help them out of pain and suffering, sometimes out of desperation, or neglect, or negligence, or ignorance, a misunderstanding, or by a mistake at a crucial moment—like taking our eye off the road while driving and plowing off a cliff or into a tree or into another vehicle or a pedestrian. Sometimes we kill someone we love by driving them to desperate acts, even suicide. Even when a death outcome was desired by the dead person, friend, lover, patient, comrade, the events and moments that lead up to a death—or near death—are moments that tend to live on indelibly in our minds forever—or at least until we too succumb. Killing and murder can be so very, very different in the eyes of one's culture, and yet it's hard to escape the knowledge that death is the ending in both. Soldiers in war face this terrifying reality all the time. They are encouraged and required to kill people; it's sanctioned murder, and thus not considered murder. But since it is "killing", it's a major cause of postwar mental distress—PTSD. Also, if we become too terrified or preoccupied by death, life becomes very difficult to endure. Denial is a special prerequisite for a species with high cognitive capability and long and deep memory. Our friend, BG, was preoccupied with death. Her mother had died by suicide and that apparently sealed her own fate. On the other hand, denial and blocking out death and pain and suffering creates its own complications.

For over nine of my approximately 46 years practicing primary care medicine I cared exclusively for frail and disabled elders, so I do have more than a few tales about dying to share, though I am not a big fan of death. I wrote about some of these in *I'll Fly Away*, my unpublished book of essays about people I cared for and knew quite well during the time I worked for the Center for Elders' Independence.[4] Most deaths I attended were as witness and comforter. Fortunately deaths I didn't try to prevent or even helped along were humane moments, almost always predictable if not specifically intended, and occurring in concert with the wishes of the people (or their families and friends when the patients were no longer able to communicate) because, obviously, in the end death can usually not be prevented without immense, even immeasurable suffering. I was a helper and supporter, but nevertheless I'm glad I wasn't a hospice doc. I'm sure that would have weighed heavily on me, to be primarily/ centrally working with dying. Working with the dying was not my main role at the Center for Elders' Independence, nor in life's chain, not by a long shot. At CEI, improving and maintaining quality of life was our constant goal. Our charges were part of a social environment that thrilled many if not most of them. But if you do geriatrics you do have to do some sympathetic palliative care when that's the best you have to offer under the circumstances of life's ending.

In the 1990s I wrote an essay about my earliest physician encounter with a dying woman named Ara Belle Kingsby and her large African American family. Ara Belle and her family taught me a lot in my early days doing geriatric care. Ara Belle Kingsby's is the lead story in my book (*I'll Fly Away*) about participants in the Center for

---

4 Several of those essays from my book, *I'll Fly Away*, will be found later in this memoir.

Elders' Independence where I was medical director for those nine years, and so I decided to include it (later) in this memoir. But my involvement in dying and almost killing (both intended and unintended) started way back when I was a child. Maybe this will be a familiar story for you also. I might have killed my whole family by accident when I was about nine years old. That's hard to forget.

Max Gustin, my maternal grandfather, was a Polish immigrant (with a "typically vivid" New York Polish-Jewish accent) who followed the standard route into the US through Ellis Island, first surviving in the Lower East Side tenements and then moving up economically in NYC. From a sweatshop worker in a shirt factory he became a shirt designer and later honed his design skills as a shoe designer. He married Sally Lookstein, she born in Manhattan into the prominent Milgrim family, and they moved to Harlem, then "upscale" as compared with the tenements of the Lower East Side communities that lacked toilets, sewers, heaters. You can imagine tenement life—having to run down four flights to get to an outhouse or hole in the ground out back. So Harlem was truly "uptown". Exactly how Max parlayed his design skills into the founding and ownership of Gustinettes, a growing shoe manufacturing concern, I have no idea, but obviously he was both a talented designer and also ambitious.

During much of the 20th century many African Americans considered owning a Cadillac to be an important status symbol of the American Dream come true. Max had that fever also.[5] Not only did he own Cadillacs but he had an arrangement with a New York dealer to trade his in each year for a new model. One summer Max asked my dad if he would drive the new Cadillac up to Loch Sheldrake in the Catskills where the Gustins had a spread. Perhaps Max and Sally

———————————

5 I wonder if this originated in Harlem?

found the drive stressful (there were indeed many curvy, dangerous aspects to the infamous State Route 17). Given that the Catskills were a "playground" where many people drank alcohol while attending shows by front line performers at ritzy hotels and drove recklessly, there were not infrequent deadly accidents. Perhaps Dad was picking up the new Cadillac directly from the dealer for Max.

On the return drive back to the city in the Cadillac, it was night and lightly raining as we drove through Bridgeville or Hurleyville or some other town like Woodbridge with bridge in the name. Though young, I was sitting shotgun because I was prone to car sickness, my mom and sister in the back seat. But I was fidgety, unhappy with what was playing on the radio, and didn't know how to change the stations. I badgered my father to change the radio station for me. As luck would have it though, this main street through town took about a 15-degree angle to the right just as Dad was leaning over the radio in this car with which he also was not familiar. I heard a horn and Dad swiftly jerked the wheel, swerving to the right, but we had grazed an oncoming vehicle. The Cadillac had significant cosmetic (though no functional) damage. This was before the days of seat belts and airbags, of course. Had my kvetching resulted in a head-on collision, who knows what the outcome might have been. Fortune, and Dad's quick reflexes, shined upon us that night, but I have no idea how my father dealt with his father-in-law, Grandpa Max, whose brand-new Cadillac had just taken a "shellacking". I don't remember being punished, but feeling responsible was plenty of punishment. These are things kids don't forget if you know what I mean?

So there was no murder or even killing in that case, but later—perhaps on that very same Cadillac night, though I believe it was a different year—we came upon the scene of a car crash on Highway 17, flashing ambulance and police lights aplenty. My mom pushed my head down between my knees so I couldn't see the scene. Maybe there were dead bodies; maybe there was blood; maybe there were dazed and bleeding people sitting on the side of the road. Or not. I don't know. I didn't know. But that imposed "cover-up" that my mother insisted upon never left me. I'll leave it to the reader to decide if the fear resulting from the imagined or the fear from seeing actuality are more traumatic to a child. All I know is that the event was seared into my memory, though I saw little or nothing. I vowed never to overprotect my children or anyone else in that way if I could help it.

Before I let go of death for now, there are certain deaths burned into my memory that I want to touch on briefly. Let me tell about Tony Sanchez, a farmworker from Hollister. During the years I was doctoring for the United Farm Workers union in the Salinas clinic, Tony and his wife were among my patients (and friends). They had great trust in me as their doctor and asked that I continue to care for him even after the closing of the Salinas clinic and my return to working in San Jose. Although they lived in Hollister (47 miles south of San Jose), I felt I couldn't say no. Then Tony had a bad heart attack and so he was admitted to the Intensive Care Unit at San Jose Hospital. I hadn't cared for hospitalized patients this sick for a few years. I consulted a cardiologist, of course, but I can't remember why Tony didn't have a coronary artery bypass graft (stents wouldn't be approved for another 15 years).

I think Tony may have refused bypass surgery, but I also think his heart was too electrically unstable at that moment. He was having the kind of irregular heartbeats (frequent runs of ventricular extra beats) that are an ominous indicator of potential electrical collapse. Tony was put on intravenous lidocaine, the medicine used to try and stop the ventricular irritability. The lidocaine drip didn't annul his frequent premature ventricular contractions with runs of tachycardia, so the dosage was continually increased. Tony died of a cardiac arrest within the first few days in the hospital. I felt terrible. I didn't know if I had done something wrong. Maybe he had too much lidocaine? Maybe some other course of action should have been followed? I had not taken care of a patient that sick in an ICU since I was out of training. Had I somehow betrayed this family—people who I felt close to—by my inexperience? I asked this of expert physicians. The answers were no, no, and no. No matter how hard we try, death will overcome. Yet the feeling of responsibility still hung over me like the Cadillac radio episode.

Around the time I drafted this essay almost 20 years later—with a great deal more experience with seriously ill hospitalized patients at CEI—I found it necessary to tell one of my dear patients, Helen T, "I have to let you go". Helen was not actually conscious at the time. She had had a stroke, was on a ventilator, and she was in respiratory and cardiac failure. The pulmonologist had, himself, thought there was little to be done and advised moving her out of ICU to a ward bed, still on a vent and still unconscious, which we did. But I get ahead of myself. Who was Helen? A somewhat private and withdrawn African American woman at 96 years of age, Helen was quiet when she attended the adult day health center; sometimes she declined to get on the van and come into the center on her appointed days. Of average height, weight and build, she had a pleasant face and soft voice. She was obviously intelligent, a good communicator when she spoke. And of note, she was a talented artist who painted. When the day center activities staff discovered this they had her regularly painting. Her idiom was watercolors and she was quite good, capturing the feel of a situation or environment. She did not use fine point brushstrokes and though her format was a form of portraiture and still-life, there was an impressionist quality to her style as though she had studied the French impressionists. Before she became acutely ill, her with-drawn tendency caused us some concern. Getting her painting regularly at the day center helped her become more interactive. And so one day I brought in a photo of our cat, Cali, curled up asleep in a wicker basket of clean clothing collected from the dryer.

Cali, the cat, in clothes basket watercolor by Helen T.

I asked Helen if she might paint me a copy from this photo. I also offered her $50. She kindly agreed and produced a fine watercolor, which I framed. It hangs on the wall at the midpoint landing of our stairs right behind the cat scratching poll which is now the property of Max, the cat. Max, at two, is the second cat after Cali. Cali contracted a rare form of leukemia. Jack (aka Jax) got an osteosarcoma, which is a very aggressive form of bone cancer. He had the leg amputated and lived another year before the tumor recurred and metastasized.

Helen had few relatives still living or in contact. But she had two very bonded and loyal young men who she had brought up as their grandmother. Although CEI usually developed very close relationships with families of participants, for some reason I was not familiar with her two grandsons and they had not been at family meetings, which were part of our protocol. Even before she suffered the stroke and a lung blood clot that put her in the ICU on a ventilator, I had visited her at her home in East Oakland as we needed to have a relationship with her grandsons and brief them on her condition and care plan. I met one of the grandsons. He was a bit suspicious then about her relationship to CEI and this white doctor. When she got very sick he had some difficulty accepting that she was in serious trouble and might die. Helen had made herself "do not resuscitate". She did not want prolonged machine ventilation. But her grandsons hadn't been involved in her decision and did not understand her rationale aimed at avoiding prolonged suffering, nor that she herself had made the choice. When she was hospitalized, they were very loyal and visited her regularly, though she was not aware of them. Eventually, the reality they saw convinced them that her end-of-life decisions made sense, even though this was very hard for them. They gave their permission for me to carry out her wishes.

After she was out on the ward, I visited Helen for a day or two, held her hand and talked to her. She was unresponsive. The last day of her life, when we were alone without nurses or her grandsons, I sat with her a while and then I looked at her and said, "Helen, I'm going to let you go. I know you understand and that it's what you want." I said goodbye, took her off the machine and told the nurses we were discontinuing artificial life support.

Several years after Helen's death, my father-in-law, Bruce Thorne, reached his hundredth birthday and the whole family flew out to Chicago for the celebration. His wife, Marianne, had died quite a few years earlier after a stroke. Despite his age Bruce remained cognitively intact, though he'd been suffering a number of physical maladies (whose details escape my memory) and was having more frequent hospitalizations. He was then living in a continuous care community in Lake Forest, Illinois run by the Presbyterian church. Evidence that he was still pretty lively though can be gleaned from the fact that he had a much younger girlfriend, who impressed Sheila with her savvy.

But over the next year plus Bruce suffered several falls and more medical setbacks, and was in and out of the hospital and the nursing home there. Then to assisted living care, then back to independent living but requiring supportive care from nurses on an ever-increasing schedule. Often rehabilitation staff were working with him as well. Eventually, on a visit by Sheila, he told her that he had had enough of the struggle and could not bear even one more round of hospitalization, decline, pain and struggle, ever weakening. He stopped eating by his own choice and died at peace—at 101.

Sometime earlier, back in his 70s, Bruce, a retired investment banker, decided to take up oil painting. He would generally paint from photos that he himself had taken during his and Marianne's travels in the wide world. His paintings, in my view, were quite good and he painted a lot over the next 15 or so years. He gifted three paintings to Sheila and at least one of his others ended up on the wall or offices of a bank somewhere in Chicago. Unsurprisingly Bruce, from an elite Midwestern Protestant family was a Republican (though not in today's fascist mold). He was a country club guy and they had a second home in an exclusive community in the Michigan upper peninsula, Huron Mountain, where Blacks and Jews were not permitted to join. But, in some strange imagined world in my mind, Helen—the withdrawn, quiet, but intelligent African American woman—and Bruce are having a conversation about their painting styles.

Seated man in robe and turban by Bruce Thorne.

DAD

Born and bred in New York City, my dad, Bob, was a traditionalist, brought up in an immigrant Jewish family in Brooklyn. He didn't get along with his father; and his mother, after delivering four children, suffered from diabetes and then strokes, and she became an invalid. The details of her disabilities from her stroke are not known to me, as she died before I was born and my father didn't talk with me about her or his relationship with his father. I know for sure that in 1939 standard medical practices didn't recognize the importance of exercise, blood pressure control, weight control or diet in diabetic patients. Insulin had been discovered by then but I don't know if she had any access. There were no oral medications.

My partner since 1972, Sheila Thorne, had tuberculosis as a child in the 1940s and there was no oral treatment for TB either. Instead of daily walks to keep her lungs expanded and well oxygenated, and to allow her to experience the world around her—its sights and smells and people and more—she was put to bed where she couldn't expand her lungs nearly as well to get good oxygenation (the TB mycobacteria—like many pneumonic bacteria—are happiest in dormant lung tissue). Luckily an early antibiotic (streptomycin) had been found to be effective against tuberculosis and she received regular injections and was cured. But injections and total bed restriction were inevitably traumatic for a young child. So between Sara Neidich and Sheila the primitive nature of the "science" of medicine not so long ago is apparent.

My dad was the youngest of the four Neidich-Sapir children and the only boy. I was told by my mother that his loyalty to his mom and dedication to her care was a major factor in his hostility toward his own father, who didn't do much in the way of being a supportive caregiver for a disabled wife. The family went from relatively prosperous to near poverty in the Great Depression when their chicken farm in Coney Island went bankrupt. In between, Grandpa Morris devolved from a Russian-Jewish-Socialist immigrant to a Republican dandy who played chess with the governor. Dad quit high school two or three years in and left home to work as a bicycle courier on Wall Street in Manhattan, though he'd still come home and help his mom. Working then gave him independence, but looking back retrospectively I think his leaving high school contributed to his early death. Despite high intelligence, being an avid reader, having good insights and being a man with a warm, sharing character, his lack of "credentials" compromised his life options even in that era (he was born in 1910). Much later, after many travails including his second heart attack, he went back to school, got his GED, his teaching credential, then became a secondary school teacher. He did his student teaching at Rikers Island, in the youth prison out in New York City's East River of all places, and came home at night shocked by the terrible conditions and brutality young people, mostly Black youths, were being subjected to there by prison guards. (The Black prison guards, he said, were the most brutal toward Black kids.) His first actual teaching job was at a public high school in Mt. Vernon, just north of the Bronx, where most of his students were also African American. Later, he moved to the Hawthorne Cedar Knolls school, also in Westchester County, a school exclusively for children with serious psychological problems (but not mental deficiency). He died suddenly before truly establishing a mark for himself.

Mom was by then a psychologist at Hawthorne Cedar Knolls. Bob was good at everything he did, and well appreciated by his students at Mt. Vernon and at Hawthorne Cedar Knolls for his warmth, patience, support and teaching skills. His death at 62 was a shock to the kids he mentored, as well as us. Dad was no ordinary shop teacher for he could teach inner city kids—and later the emotionally troubled youths—to make almost anything out of almost any material, and he had them learning with a wide variety of both hand tools and machine tools, which I will explain.

While still a youth back in Manhattan, Dad was befriended by a couple of brothers, the DeWitts, socialists who owned a successful machine tool company that must have been sizable. They offered him a good job. He had also met Mom, Selma, at a hotel beach on the lake at Loch Sheldrake in the Catskill Mountains one summer when he was the lifeguard there. He was a powerful swimmer who could swim the length of a pool effortlessly in just a few strokes. Dad, Bob, had mechanical and drafting aptitude and a knack with machinery, design, drawing and craftsmanship. In 1939 the DeWitts were contracted by Spain's Republican coalition government resisting the civil war provoked by the Rightist army led by Generalissimo Francisco Franco. The insurgents had the backing of Hitler's Luftwaffe Air Force, which reigned death and destruction on government forces, irregulars, towns and civilians all over Spain. Pablo Picasso's famous mural, *Guernica*, is based upon a German bombing massacre of Spanish civilians and partisans alike.

The Spanish government needed to repair their artillery and anti-aircraft weapons in the field. They contracted the DeWitts to provide mobile trucks equipped with lathes, drill presses and other machines and hand tools needed to service their heavy weapons. Dad designed these trucks, including the heavy machine equipment that could be easily accessed in the way lunch trucks and some RVs have side panels that fold down or out. Meanwhile, the Roosevelt Administration was ostensibly trying to stay "neutral" on the civil war in Spain, failing to defend a popularly elected government—although, with Hitler's rise to power and destruction of the Weimar Republic, a major war in Europe was obviously on the horizon. The US neutrality may have been a factor in Franco's victory. It also may have encouraged Hitler, who would soon be invading many nations. History books talk about Britain's Neville Chamberlain capitulating to Hitler's rising reign of terror and conquest in Europe, but essentially Spain was Hitler's early military intervention—before Germany invaded the Sudetenland, Czechoslovakia, or Poland. And little is made of the US failure to join forces with the Spanish government or the Russians in opposing the German role. The Soviet Union, our future ally in WWII, did materially support the democratic coalition government. Despite the US "neutralism", thousands of Leftist and other internationally minded Americans joined brigades fighting in Spain against Franco—the best known of these being the Abraham Lincoln Brigade. Hemingway's *For Whom the Bell Tolls* captures the feel of that war. My parents were able to gain the necessary visas to go to "neutral" Belgium, where secretly Dad supervised the construction of the contracted—but contraband—trucks in a warehouse. The work crew was Russian. This was 1939, two years before my birth.

From my mother's telling, these Russian workers related tales of widespread drunkenness, corruption and orgies inside the Kremlin walls; and of much fear of Stalin's wrath and paranoia. As far as I know, my parents were not members of the Communist Party in the US and were shocked to hear these accounts (whether true or false). The leaders of the CP in the USA aligned their international policies with the Soviet Union's. Those policy ties became absurdly obvious when the Communist Party, which had been staunchly anti-Nazi, suddenly changed its policy to neutrality when Stalin signed a mutual (though short-lived) non-aggression pact with Hitler in 1939. This policy shift made absolutely no sense for US communists since Stalin (just as Chamberlain and Roosevelt) was simply trying to stall a Nazi attack to buy time. However, this foolish CP policy caused great confusion and consternation in the Communist Party and would later be used, after the war, to claim that the Communist Party in the US was little more than an agent of the Russians. Led by Wisconsin senator Joe McCarthy, the paranoia aroused by the Red Scare and witch-hunts against communists in the US gravely wounded the trade union movement's militancy in the 1950s, justifying the McCarran-Walter act. The Smith Act made it illegal to even be a member of the Communist Party or espouse communist ideas and ideals, despite that the CP was not calling for the overthrow of the US government. During the presidency of Donald Trump (2016–2020), Trump's fawning over Vlad Putin—who he proclaimed he "trusted" to tell him the truth—was not less provocative than the CPUSA following the "Soviet line" (off again/on-again about Hitler), but no one in Washington, D.C., so far as I know, has made this comparison.

Not so ironically, the ruthless legal brain of the ruthless Joe McCarthy was Roy Cohn, a closeted gay New York lawyer who hypocritically espoused extreme homophobia. Before he died of AIDS, Cohn worked for and taught Donald Trump everything he knew about subverting the law.[6] Cohn told Trump to always stay on the offensive and never give an inch even when you are caught in a lie, a deceit or criminal behavior. No less a truly evil man than J. Edgar Hoover, Cohn was beautifully portrayed in Tony Kushner's remarkable masterpiece play, *Angels in America*, about the AIDS epidemic which took Cohn's life just about the time he was disbarred for his egregiously unethical behavior.

Despite the fact that the Soviet Union would sign that mutual

---

6 This relationship is nicely elaborated in my cousin Jim Zirin's book: *Plaintiff in Chief—a portrait of Donald Trump in >3,500 law suits.*

non-aggression pact with Hitler, the Soviet policy of materially supporting Spain's government against Franco in the civil war was better thought out than the US isolationist position. But Roosevelt apparently believed that the US had to stay out of Europe to defeat the strong isolationist movement here as well as to prepare the industrial base for war production.[7] Thus, we only entered the Western Front in Europe at Normandy many years later when the Nazis were on their last legs, having been badly mauled in Russia; both Roosevelt and Churchill were content to let the Soviets bear the brunt of Nazi aggression when Hitler repeated the fatal mistake of Napoleon and invaded Russia. The US, meanwhile, mounted a naval campaign against Japan in the Pacific. The American hands-off policy regarding the war in Europe contributed to the Russians losing over 20 million dead. It also allowed the US to become the only great power left standing after the war had devastated all of Europe, the Soviet Union, Japan, China and much of North Africa. Unquestionably, without intentionality, the Soviet people did help US imperialism's coming world dominance by defeating Hitler. They had no choice.

Not being a historian, I can't weigh in on the impact of the Russian role within the Spanish government, but, unlike some of the socialists and anarchists who rebelled against the Spanish government in which they had participated, the Russians didn't turn against the coalition government there. They backed out of Spain only when the war against Franco had become hopeless and governance chaotic.

In her later years, before she became demented, my mom, Selma, claimed that FDR's people had secretly approved Dad's little Belgium project. I never heard about that growing up and Mom tended toward grandiosity, so it could easily be false. My inclination is that it was not true, but even if true, it was a meager gesture. Meanwhile, the

---

7 I have no way to evaluate whether or not that was the whole story.

US refused to allow Jews fleeing Hitler to enter our country during Hitler's expulsion period (before the genocide was in full swing). I think FDR's failure to do more for Spain was both a moral failing and a political blunder. Hitler was in no position to mount a serious attack on the US no matter what we did, even with his submarine fleet.

As I say, to my knowledge, neither of my parents were ever members of the Communist Party, but as I was growing up in Yonkers I learned from their social gatherings with their friends that several of those friends had been in and around the party. At the same time, my folks never concealed their hopes that I not become a communist. As my friends and family know, I never joined the old US Communist Party, but that was mostly because in the Vietnam War era when I became a radical anti-imperialist activist that party's main role was disreputable, holding back the anti-war movement, allying with AFL union leaders. From George Meany on down, those leaders didn't strongly oppose the war. Meany was under the sway of and in cahoots with the CIA, through the American Institute for "Free" Labor Development (AIFLD) and other US government front groups.[8] That opportunism turned off the young activists of the New Left that grew out of the civil rights and anti-Vietnam War movements. The activists avoided anti-communist rhetoric, but most considered the CP to have by then become either largely irrelevant

---

8 Despite the fears of communists and communism instilled in our people, this tale of Communist Party conservatism and collaboration within the capitalist state is not unique to the US; Fidel and the Cubans who fomented and led the overthrow of the Batista government of Cuba were long resisted in their quest by their own CP. After WWII the Italian and French communist parties became mainly electoral social democratic parties that worked within the "system". Later communist parties, such as the Chinese—after Mao's death—and Vietnamese—after Ho's—transitioned their countries into full-fledged capitalist states and economies under one-party rule.

or an obstacle to be worked around. For example, with the peace movement demanding the US bring its troops home from Vietnam, the CP members in coalitions persistently argued that ending the US aggression was too radical a demand for American workers and we should only carry signs saying "stop the bombing" of Vietnam. They actually insisted that marchers not be allowed to carry signs that demanded withdrawal of US forces (but were rebuffed).

Dad's field artillery repair trucks were turned into ambulances as the Spanish government was vanquished by Franco and Nazi air bombardment.

I became an espoused communist on my own, anyway.[9] And so did thousands of others. I guess the lesson is: don't tell your kids your fears about what they should not do or become. Just teach them accurate history, good values and work habits by example and collaboration; then let them find their own way. I remember how my dad, typically American I think, preached that he didn't care what I did with my life as long as I worked hard to be good at whatever that was. "If you become a garbage collector just make sure you're a good one," he'd often repeat I'm thankful for that advice and support. Of course that mantra was about living one's life in general, not propounded in a political context. When I became aimless in college, stopped going to classes my third year at Brandeis and wanted to drop out, my parents drove up to Massachusetts distraught and convinced me to seriously get to work, if only to not disappoint them. Maybe they frightened me, but mostly I think I didn't want to let them down.

Sadly, my father's work in support of the elected popular Spanish coalition government went for naught. When he and the others in his work crew drove the trucks through the night secretly across the French border through the Pyrenees mountains into Spain, the government was already collapsing in bloody military defeat. The trucks were delivered, then stripped of their machinery and used as ambulances.

Shortly, my parents learned by cable that Dad's mother, Sarah, was dying, and they returned to New York by ship as quickly as they

---

9 I gave up calling myself a communist around 1984–1985 after resigning from the Communist Labor Party headed by Nelson Peery (see later). I didn't any longer think the model fit. I also came to the conclusion that as strong as Marx's analysis of capitalism was, his ideas about inevitability and the upward spiral of history, about the concept of democratic centralism and other precepts, were just as idealist as the thoughts of other philosophers and thinkers he was focused on critiquing.

could. Sarah Neidich succumbed shortly after their arrival. Presumably, or so I was told, had his mother not failed and had his Spanish project gone better, Dad was planning to go to China to help in the war against Japanese occupation. But I don't know if this is true, or if it may be a figment of my imagination. Back in my 30s and 40s I held the brilliant Canadian thoracic surgeon, surgical instrument designer and tuberculosis survivor, Norman Bethune, as a hero. Bethune did serve in China as a surgeon on the Long March, before dying of sepsis from an accidentally self-inflicted finger wound during surgery, so maybe a faulty memory conflated Bethune and my dad, two people I admired.

When I was born in July 1941, five months before the Japanese Navy and Air Force decimated the US Naval Fleet at Pearl Harbor, my parents moved, as they had been planning to, into an apartment in a newly opened housing project developed in the East Bronx by the Metropolitan Life Insurance Company. In those days the Parkchester community was a "step up" for most of those who moved in there. Later it became just another one of the urban "projects". Much later, I think it was toward the end of high school, I took some friends to show them where I had grown up (till age seven). I hadn't thought this through well enough. In a minor altercation, we were chased out by a group of Black kids, who probably viewed us as a white invader gang. They didn't give us a chance to explain, before they bloodied one of my friend's (Walter's) nose. Nothing serious though. Sometime around my birth—for reasons I have no way to investigate—Dad decided to leave the DeWitt company and opened his own retail store in the South Bronx on Bruckner Boulevard selling machine tools, mostly to contractors and construction firms I think. I vaguely remember the store and the cobblestone paving of the street and the overhead highway heading for the Triborough Bridge. I was no more than seven when the store closed and I was too young to know or understand why the Sapir tool company failed precisely at the time when my parents bought our smallish three-bedroom suburban house in Northeast Yonkers, about 15–20 miles or so to the north, close to the Bronx River Parkway. I had just finished 1st grade in Mrs. Layton's class in public school in the Bronx when we moved. I do remember feeling stressed by the many changes. Though I had loved my warm, supportive kindergarten teacher, Mrs. Ward, I didn't have that kind of bonding with Mrs. Layton, who I think of as brusk, and with the end of 1st grade and my seventh birthday coming up, my future felt insecure.

On the other hand, I had apparently become a fairly independent youngster because even at six I was allowed to cross a street at a traffic light and walk to school on my own, a distance of a few blocks. And my mom was fond of telling a story of my independence: how she would take me shopping with her and when she shopped at Macy's nearby in Parkchester I would spend endless time riding up and down the escalators on my own while she shopped. Except one day I flat-out disappeared and she became very distraught. Perhaps the police were notified. But I already knew how to find my way home walking and showed up shortly afterward, to everyone's great relief. I was only five or six.

I do remember a painful adventure I had at that age. Another youngster had shown me a door that had come unhinged at the bottom of a steel overhead street light pole. It was not far from our building and there were no streets to be crossed. One day while on roller skates I decided to follow the blacktop paths to revisit this magical place. When I went to open the heavy door, it came off its hinges and landed on my thumb. The door probably weighed 15–20 pounds and boy did that make me howl in pain as I skated back home. The (subungual) hematoma under my thumbnail caused the nail to fall off some days later. In medical practice this type of trauma—bleeding under a finger or toenail—is commonly seen. We relieve the painful pressure of blood under a finger or toenail by drilling or burning a small hole through the nail so blood can escape. There are nice tools to drill the hole, but some old docs like me use the ancient technique of heating an unfolded paper clip end over a flame until it turns red, and using that to burn a hole without putting much pressure on the nail. It's fairly painless and gives immediate relief when the blood oozes out.

As far as our leaving Parkchester, I later wondered why a young family would take such a precarious step as to buy a home just as their business failed. I have no answer for this question. I mentioned before that Dad was a traditionalist and a loyal husband. He believed that he had to be the proverbial breadwinner and show that he was capable of making life work out well for his family. Additionally, though an intellectual, he was a high school dropout whereas Mom had a four-year college degree. So maybe these factors motivated him to buy a home so as to prove himself. Or maybe there are pieces to that puzzle that were not revealed to me—personal, political or cultural elements. It was the late 1940s, and a lot of white people aspiring to the middle-class life were moving to suburbia now. At the same time the anti-communist witch hunt was in full swing, driving the Communist Party underground, and the party essentially dispersed, which was practically self-annihilating at this point, though it regrouped in the civil rights era despite the loss of thousands of members, including something like 1,500 Black members who left in a group around 1960 and accused the party leadership of racism (according to Nels Perry, who was part of that Black Block). My parents always insisted they had never been members, but even so, all those former communist friends may have been part of the "undergrounding" of the party in response to the imprisonment of several party leaders under the Smith Act and the coming execution of the Rosenbergs. For example, my folks told us of the Emspak family who lived in our neighborhood. The father had been a key leader in the United Electrical Workers Union. And he was then in prison for nothing more than just being a member of the Communist Party. Young Frankie Emspak, the son, was in my sister's class in school; and when I attended PS 15 in Crestwood (Grades 2nd-4th, then 7th-8th) myself and others would sneak through the property of an old grouch (who frequently yelled at us to stay off his property) on LaSalle Drive. We'd pass down behind the grouch's home and then through the Emspak's and then down a friendly wooded trail a couple of hundred yards, over a creek, and would end up directly at our school. Without that shortcut through the grouch's and Emspaks' private property we would have had about an additional half-mile walk down to school.

When Dad's business failure came to a head in 1948–1949, my mom's parents, Max and Sally Gustin—owners of Gustinettes shoe manufacturing company—offered Dad a position as both a vice-president and as manager of their factory, which employed about 80 workers. The factory was then located near the East River in Long Island City (Queens). Dad had the social skills that stood him well with the workers (and he was pro-union). He had the technical skills to operate, tear down and repair the equipment, and the business skills that Gustinettes needed. Plus he was hardworking and determined to do well. He also went on the road to department stores in the Northeast and Midwest doing sales. I recall him flying off to St. Louis and other cities on TWA's Constellation, a unique plane design with its three upright tail fins across the back. But in the end the stress and frustration from working with the entire difficult Gustin clan was his downfall, and also contributed to his early death. Due to top-heavy management salaries (at least five family members were on management salaries) and, later, rising competition from international corporate investments in the shoe industry (such as the General Shoe Corporation which my Uncle Howie, who was married to Mom's younger sister, Doris, joined), Gustinettes, after a move to Paterson, New Jersey, would also fail about 13 years later. By then I was in college. Before I was off to college I spent a couple of summers working at Gustinette's myself. The first summer I was responsible for promotional mailings to their customers nationwide. I also set up the payroll. People were paid in cash that I counted out and inserted into tiny manila envelopes with the breakdown details, like withholding, written on the outside.

The second summer, much to my joy, I got to work a stamping machine in the factory, stamping out leather soles. This was a very powerful machine run by an air compressor. You'd get an order of how many soles and their sizes and the shoe model, and then find the right molds, line up the steel blade one at a time that met the order requirements, place the mold blade down onto a sheet of leather, grab the machine handle, align the flat press surface over the mold and push a red button: "boom", it stamped out the sole and you were ready to reposition or remove the mold and the new sole and get ready to stamp again, always trying to align the blade to cause the least wastage of good leather. I loved this job and got pretty good at it with speed and efficiency. Of course, it was like playing at being one of the "workers". It might not have been so enjoyable after a year or three or if my dad wasn't the floor manager's boss. Frank was bound to treat me well. Dad and I even went fishing for flounder with him in a small boat on Long Island Sound a few times. But I was proud of my work and the other workers treated me like one of their own, impressed that I took their work seriously and did a good job. It never dawned on me then that I was actually taking a job from some other worker.

At 52, in 1962, my dad had his first heart attack. He had become quite overweight during my youth (going up to 235 pounds at six feet tall), had a lifelong meat-and-dairy-heavy diet—Mom reported that in their early years he'd often come home and chug-a-lug down a full quart of buttermilk in short order. He had plenty of work stress and a sometimes difficult, if loving, wife, and he did not keep up his exercise though he had been an athlete—a runner, a speed skater, a handball and basketball player. I was home from college when that heart attack felled him. I ran down from my room to find him lying in bed in terrible pain. He was pale. Like a young child, I pleaded with him not to die. He told me to stop bawling and "act like a man". Dad rarely castigated me, but that shut me up alright. This was a kind man who rarely rebuked, and in his painful state he was pointing out that I wasn't being very supportive or courageous (even if he couched it in male macho rhetoric, his pointing out my emotional selfishness was right).

In the 1960s, the procedure known as a Coronary Artery Bypass Graft (CABG) was still in the experimental stage. The first case was done in 1960, and in researching for this memoir I learned that it was performed at the Albert Einstein Medical College where I would, three years later, become a research technician. After Dad's second heart attack, later in the 60s his doctor, an internist, mentioned the consideration of this surgery as well as diet and weight loss. I was either in my last year of medical school or already graduated when Mom told me of this discussion and that they were both hesitant. I affirmed their view that it was a new procedure and so the risks were not yet clear. As in this early situation—and despite my radical left politics and personal risk-taking—I have always tended to be cautious and conservative about advising new techniques and medicines for my patients. I don't feel guilty about expressing that viewpoint to Mom, but it's certainly possible my father would have lived many years longer had he had a CABG then. Ten years later I would have offered a different opinion.

While Dad was recuperating from his first heart attack, Gustinettes declared bankruptcy. His share of the business assets were expropriated (stolen) by my mom's youngest brother, who had been what in the 1940s was called a "'juvenile delinquent'" child growing up. Mom, about 12 or 14 years his senior, had taken D under her wing when he needed support, and they were close emotionally, but, with his psychopathic tendencies, he paid her back by leaving us bereft.

In my early years in Yonkers I was adapting to suburban life. In some ways life was idyllic. We had about 30 children living on just one suburban block—girls and boys of various ages, kids born just before, during and after WWII. Although I often spent three weeks at a summer camp called Ella Fohs in Connecticut (run by the YMHA of the Bronx and directed by a good friend of my parents, Barney Lambert), our family would spend part of each summer vacation at the place Mom's parents owned in the Catskill mountains (the "Borscht Belt") in the small town of Loch Sheldrake. There was a sizable lake there and the Lookstein-Gustin clan actually owned two homes within a block of the water. The one closer to the lake was inhabited by my great grandmother, Sophie Lookstein (née Milgrim—the department store family) and some of her adult children and grandchildren. Up the block, Max and Sally (née Lookstein, my mom's parents) Gustin had a much bigger spread, close to an acre with a main house, a shotgun back house with four bedrooms and two bathrooms, a cook and gardener's cottage, a deep water well and pump house, a basketball court with one basket, and later a swimming pool.

The back house where we stayed was home to very unfriendly wasps, nested under the eves right by the room I occupied. More than one year I awoke in the middle of the night with a gigantically swollen and exquisitely painful lip or eyelid. That resulted the next morning in my dad opening up the fire hose on the side of the pump house and blasting the wasps nest to kingdom come. But, without fanfare, they returned to nest there the next year anyway. Just behind the basketball court, a wood of large, old, mostly deciduous trees and some pines flowed southward toward the highway about a third of a mile away. To the east of the wood was an endless field of wild bushes, many of which were wild blueberry bushes. Mom and us kids, cousins and maybe an aunt or two would climb a low fence and pick berries to our hearts content, although the lore was that all that open land was owned by a man named Fox or Wolf who would chase people off his property with a gun. We would all laugh hysterically about this because no one could ever remember if this grouch we never saw was a fox or a wolf. If we were out in the field picking berries when the town siren moaned and groaned its call every high noon, we would turn to each other and say, 'It's old Mr. Fox [or Wolf] calling out the police on us."

Max Gustin, my maternal grandfather, after designing shirts later honed his design skills as a shoe designer. Long after his death my mom donated one of his particularly flashy silver brocaded high-heeled shoes to the Metropolitan Museum of Art. I don't know if earlier in history American museums actually had major sections on modern dress styles, but by then they did. Miniature models of that sequined shoe were sold in the museum store. Too gaudy for my taste.

YONKERS

When I was in junior high school in Yonkers at PS 15, located in the Crestwood neighborhood not far from what is left of the meandering Bronx River, I had a group of friends (by today's standards you wouldn't call it a gang, but more a gaggle of guys) that hung out together, mostly playing baseball and bike riding around in the suburban hill community where we lived—we lived just above Crestwood—in Colonial Heights. Crestwood is on relatively flat lands along the west side of the Bronx River, separated from the river by the similarly meandering Bronx River Parkway. By then the river was not very broad, interrupted by ponds formed by an occasional small man-made dam. The ponds served as skating rinks in winter. One hundred and eighty years earlier George Washington had retreated up the river from New York City by boat/ship fleeing the attacking British, and then he defeated the Brits at White Plains. When the river became unsailable, I have no idea, but it was long before we arrived from the Bronx.

The Bronx River Parkway is an old-fashioned roadway in the sense that it meanders through trees and along the river. The speed limit was—might still be—40 mph, but it had a good surface and two lanes each direction, and the pleasant environment of the river— deciduous trees, some grassy areas, old stone overpasses. Colonial Heights, where we lived, and the adjacent Mohegan Heights, run along a north–south low ridge-line west of Crestwood. The heights were an interesting mix of old homes on a few widish boulevards lined by old maple and oak trees and a bevy of newer suburban cookie-cutter-patterned houses that dominated some of the sloping streets built into open spaces of grasslands, trees, bushes and poison ivy, wherever the scattered older homes weren't. My parents had bought one of the new development's homes on a corner lot at the intersection of Biltmore Avenue and LaSalle Drive for 24,000-plus dollars. Due to the steep downhill angle of our wraparound street corner, our driveway on LaSalle on the east side of the house was one story below the front door on Biltmore. So the garage led into our concrete basement, which my father partitioned into three rooms—a workshop, a furnace room and a larger basement area, that he paneled and floored and ceilinged with faux-paneling and synthetic ceiling and floor tiles. We had a ping-pong table. There were two stories above to the house proper. My sister Judy and I possessed the two rooms on the small second floor, a bathroom between us at the head of the stairs. The staircase was right in front of you when you entered the front door. The sloping of the shingled, traditionally peaked roof constricted standing at the very edges in my room. But it was a decent-sized room and with my bed up against one wall, and another bed against the opposite wall, there was good head clearance between them, probably seven to eight feet to the ceiling. Also on the wall between them I had a window looking out east over LaSalle Drive, the garage below and into the distance east over Crestwood. I had two other windows—north and south—as well—though they were in dormer nooks with my desk in the larger of the nooks. Had the beds not been there it would have been impossible to stand up against the walls, for the sloped roof left only about five feet of height at the wall's edge. My walls were covered in gray and white wallpaper containing a pattern of stylized bugles.

Our house was actually a small home by today's standards but the first floor had a master bedroom, a room we called the den (where we watched TV; it later became my mom's office), an L-shaped living room, dining room and a tiny kitchen. The dining area had a door that opened out onto the deck that topped the garage. That deck over a one-car garage was about as large as our living room. If I forgot my front door key and no one was home, I could always get into the house by going through shrubs on the side of the garage, climbing onto a three-inch-wide concrete ledge that was part of the fireplace chimney base and sidling along clinging to chimney bricks till I reached the deck fence, which I could easily climb over.

Mom and I in front of 60 Biltmore—
deck to the left, my room above (by Judy Sapir).

The window into the dining room was usually unlocked, which allowed me to reach in and unlock the door to the deck.

On the opposite corner a home like ours, but fronting on LaSalle Drive (while ours fronted on Biltmore), was being put up when we moved to Yonkers. It was purchased by the Lasco family, who had a daughter my sister's age—two years younger than myself—and my sister and Naomi Lasco became friends. Naomi's room on their second floor had a window opposite the one by my desk. Years later, having the prurient and voyeuristic mind of a teen, I would try—and fail—to watch her undress through the maple tree by the street across the way with binoculars. We were neighbors, and she was my sister's friend. Judy relates that in junior high she organized a dance party of under a dozen kids in our basement when our parents weren't home. I think I was dancing "cheek to cheek" with Naomi when my dad came down the stairs and sent everyone packing. I never even kissed this pretty girl.

Up LaSalle Drive from the Lascos to the north, another new home of similar stereotypic pattern by the same developer was going to be built a year or so after the Lascos'. It would be purchased by the Schwartz'. The construction of that house nearly killed one of the youngsters on our Biltmore block. Biltmore Avenue, upsloping gently (to the west) with a flat area in mid-rise where we played ball, arose by our house and went on for the length of three football fields with about ten homes on either side. It was only one long block. The first three houses (including ours) on our side of the street plus the last house up top were part of the patterned new homes development I've mentioned. They were of a conventional design for the late 1940s. We were lucky to have a corner lot which was larger, about 100'x 100'. The older five or six homes on our side of Biltmore were of a colonial style—stone-faced or brick, somewhat larger, and of varying architectural design.

Five houses up from us, in one of those older New England-styled houses, lived the Colby family. They had three sons. Richard, who was one of my friends, two years older than me, would later get his biochemistry PhD at Cal Berkeley and teach at a small New Jersey college. He was the tallest at about six-foot one and slender. John was a year younger than myself; and Gilbert was about four years younger. I would teach Gilbert how to play baseball. I thought of Richard as somewhat of a mentor, sort of an older brother. A couple of years ago, when Richard stayed at our house here in Berkeley while attending a reunion at Cal Berkeley (it was a Free Speech Movement reunion) he told me that he's been on the Asperger's autism spectrum his whole life, something I hadn't earlier realized, though I remember some of his personal quirks, like peeling every grape before eating it. That seems to me more like obsessive compulsive.

Gilbert was about five or six when the Schwartz home was being built. Richard, probably only about 11 or 12 then, must have been caring for him and they wandered into the construction site, which was not protected from intrusion. They were on the first floor when Gilbert fell through the yet-to-be completed stairwell. Flying head-first onto the concrete basement floor, he was knocked unconscious. Terrified, Richard picked up Gilbert in his arms and carried him all the way back to their home, two blocks away. Their mother, Shirley, put Gilbert, now conscious, in the car and drove immediately to the hospital in Bronxville where he was admitted, with a concussion. Miraculously, X-rays did not show a fractured skull or any other broken bones, and he did not suffer an internal hemorrhage that could have killed him. There were no such things as C/T scans and MRIs then to assess the internal state of his brain. Richard, the only Colby family member I remain in touch with, tells me that it was Christmas time and the pediatric ward was empty but for Gilbert. As a result he scored a slew of presents, many of them neither age nor gender appropriate, from total strangers bringing gifts to hospitals to help interned kids deal with their medical condition and hospital isolation in the holiday season. Thus Christmas should not always be shunned by Jewish kids.

According to Richard, Gilbert as an adult had a problem with facial recognition of people, which he attributed to his concussion at that early age. Acquired prosopagnosia from head trauma does occur, though it is rare. However, the brilliant neurologist-writer-geriatrician, Oliver Sacks, had congenital prosopagnosia (the inability to learn and remember faces), which he wrote about as a genetic loss of a small region of very specialized brain cells for facial recognition. Gilbert's accident lends credence to his own thought that his was the acquired type, despite it being less common.

But Gilbert, the youngest of three brothers, did get dementia before the age of 65, and it's not inconceivable that his head trauma contributed to that also. He has died.

When I was in junior high, or maybe back in 5th and 6th grades, our little gang of schoolmates—which the Colbys weren't part of—started to pay more attention to girls (and vice versa). We had a few little "off-the-grid" parties (like Judy's) when parents weren't around where we played spin the bottle and other essentially benign games. Unlike my sister's party, the girls involved here were our classmates also. One day when I was about 12 we learned that one of those girls in our crowd, Lois Kadan (who lived a few blocks from me), had been killed, hit by a bus while riding her bike on Central Avenue, a main north–south thoroughfare down off the hill on the western side of the heights. It was, inevitably, a terrible shock at the time. I hadn't known any other schoolmates who had died, and she was one of our crowd, just gone like that—a person, a life, a friend, a personality who touched us all, just gone.

Soon there was another death even closer by, but it wasn't a child and not as meaningful to me personally. The cantor of our temple and his family, with whom my folks were friends, had bought the home directly behind our property. Cantor Sam Kligfield had a warm demeanor and a beefy face. I recall, don't ask me why or how, he had a large mole on his chin with a hair or three. I was one of his students in his Chazonim Club. He always treated me with true kindness and my dad, who sang in the temple choir and was vice-president, had some high hopes that his only son, Mendel Abbe (that's my Hebrew name), might become a cantor. The Kligfield house fronted on Harvard Avenue, the next one-block-long street south of and parallel with Biltmore similarly running east-west. Because LaSalle Drive ran downward to meet the bottom of Harvard Ave., Harvard was considerably steeper than Biltmore and so it became the customary street for sledding after snow and ice storms. When icy it was fast, and avoiding plunging down a draw at the bottom at the intersection with LaSalle could be a challenge. You'd have to skid your sled around the corner or crash sideways into the curb at the bottom of the T-intersection—often being thrown from the sled. The Kligfields' backyard and ours abutted, interrupted only by a thin, low hedge. I can't remember how long after Lois Kadan's death it occurred but Kligfield's wife was diagnosed with leukemia or lymphoma. Then, lacking effective treatments (in the 1950s), she succumbed in less than a year. I believe she was 38 or 39.

Although my memory for early details is sparse, I can still conjure a few more uninteresting tales about my life in suburbia to bore you with. I've long thought that my parents' move to the burbs—which they probably believed was a way to enhance their children's opportunities, social environment and safety—actually retarded my own social development. In the period when I and my block friend Michael V were teaching Gilbert C and another youngster, Danny F, the skills of baseball and spending endless hours playing punchball and other games on the street, I remember my mom asking why I spent so much time playing with younger kids. I did spend an inordinate amount of time out playing even as I became a teenager. Outdoor play was the center of my life then. But I wasn't just playing with younger kids. I played with whomever was available. And I liked teaching the younger kids. Play is what kids do after all. Even if it's often aimless, purposeless fun, it has its developmental functions. As a clinical psychologist who would soon specialize in children with learning deficits, Mom surely knew this. But she was a typical overprotective Jewish mother. Meanwhile, suburban explorations and exploits were fairly limited to the domain of our local streets and our classmates.

My sister's view of the parent-child relationship she lived with is not so sanguine. Judy felt under-protected and emotionally under-nourished, even a little betrayed and belittled. She turned to me often for solace and comfort. I have to agree that my parents were male supremacist in some obvious ways. They made it clear that they thought I was the brilliant child in every respect and that Judy, whom I believe they loved as much, was just ordinary and average. They probably didn't even realize the sexism involved and I'm sure they said such things out loud at times, even to friends. They assured that Judy had opportunities and skills training, and went to college, but still thought of me as the repository of family brilliance who would make them particularly proud. Granted, I was a friskier kid than Judy, but we were both extroverts; and personality probably isn't the best marker for either ability or achievement. The later reality was that Judy, upon graduation from Syracuse University, turned down a scholarship to the graduate librarianship program at Harvard to get her MA in librarianship at Syracuse in order to get married (and assuage our parents wishes' that she do so). Our traditionalist-minded parents (especially dad) were unhappy that both of us were in sexual relationships and not married. I remember my Dad one day finally confronting me with the line, "It's about time that you make an honest woman out of Irene" (i.e. marry her). I was already a college graduate then. He probably thought that, in approving this idea, he was swallowing his pride at accepting a non-Jewish woman for my mate. But Judy, more conventional and middle-class-minded than myself, was never a slouch—intellectually, socially, or physically. Many years later, as a re-entry student, she graduated second in her law school class at George Washington Law having already brought up three daughters and then gotten rid of her otherwise good-for-nothing lawyer-husband who would not allow her to go back to school.[10]

The sad thing for me is that our parents' inattentiveness to Judy's emotional needs and their somewhat underplaying her creativity in comparison to my own maybe pushed her to become even more conventional, non-adventurous, and security-oriented. She became, like many, someone who usually prioritized personal survival and "success" as her sine qua non. On the other hand, I took enough risks in my life for both of us and I believe I was lucky to make it through (to wit my opening stories in this memoir), and yet I did survive.

Before my first wife, sweet Irene Giobbe, left me for a married fellow teacher with four kids, she would say: "Markie, you're going to either get yourself killed or end up in prison. I don't think you'll ever become a doctor." Risk-taking in the quest for justice was in my blood and temperament. Not that I was into drugs or criminal behaviors. I'm not of a mind to blame Selma and Bob, however, for Judy becoming a cheerleader in high school. I think that popularity was on her early agenda. Nothing wrong with being a cheerleader, but she was certainly playing the popularity game, something that didn't fit within my own identity, though I did want to be accepted and have friends. High school became particularly difficult for me socially speaking (though I realize it's a tough time for many/most teens) since I didn't enter puberty until I was about 16 and a half years old. By that age my mom, Selma, had been a junior in college at NYU, so her socialization must have been even more difficult than my own, something she much later admitted to me. So I can't complain.

---

10 When I say "good for nothing", after their divorce Peter, who worked for HUD, was later indicted for embezzlement of government funds and had his law license revoked.

SMOKE GETS IN YOUR EYES

My mom had that nasty habit: cigarette smoking. When I was already a doctor, she revealed that she smoked when she was pregnant, although I weighed a good seven-plus pounds at birth. Few people were talking about smoking causing cancer, emphysema, heart attacks or small babies prone to lung disease back in the 1950s. It was much later that we understood that second-hand smoke is even more dangerous than the smoke inhaled by a smoker. But at a very young age I nevertheless recognized smoking as a socially induced nasty habit and besides that, I literally couldn't stand cigarette smoke in the air. It was and remains very caustic to me, even nauseating. Surprisingly I can still detect a smoker in an outdoor environment from about a hundred yards away. When I was about 12 I kept bothering my mom about how bad her smoking was messing with my breathing and my peace of mind. She finally quit. She just stopped smoking.

A year or two before that our gaggle of guys started experimenting in ways that I wasn't myself happy about. One or two friends pushed me to try a cigarette. I was resistant—already repulsed by my mom's smoking at home—but I finally acceded to try it. One choked-up puff validated my repulsion. I have never touched another cigarette in my life; though I have occasionally smoked or eaten some marijuana. The marijuana smoke is caustic and irritating too, but at least it, and cigar smoke (my dad smoked cigars now and then), has an interesting aroma, and marijuana has that relaxing effect—unless you get paranoid as sometimes happens and did to me once. Be aware, now that marijuana is legal in many states, that while occasional use of weed is relatively safe, and there are several important medicinal uses, regular daily use of marijuana does have permanent negative impacts on brain function, thinking, brain size and probably lungs also.

But my crowd of guys' fascination with fire, smoke and matches wasn't limited to cigarettes; nor did we have access to marijuana back then so far as I know. My friends were looking for "teenage" trouble. One of them was the son of a cop. "There's a field of tall, dry grasses by my house," J told us. "You know it's part of that abandoned monastery where we play, jumping off rooves and such, and the owners are never around. It would make a really good baseball field. We just have to slowly burn down the grass and rake it out, and we can have our own baseball field. Ok?" That sounded good. Why not? Well, we all brought jackets to smother the fires and formed small teams of two or three to surround each burn area and put them out before they got too large. The tall grass was dry and the fires went quickly out of our control. Someone called the fire department and we ran away and hid in the bushes. The fire department put the fires out. This isn't California so the grass and ground weren't as dry or conducive to running completely wild out of control. The police and fire department folks found us easily enough, heard our explanation, gave a stern lecture, but no one was arrested or sent to Juvie, probably because we were all white and one of us was a cop's son. I can't remember if I told my parents what had happened or if the authorities even took our names and contact info. Maybe they did. The whole episode freaked me out. Had we been Black or Puerto Rican I can only imagine that we would have been treated much differently—taken off to Juvie. But if you need evidence that this was really about troublemaking, catch this. A month or so later the guys decided to do it again, and they did. I didn't show up. Exact same outcome. Including the impunity.

Of the 30-plus kids on Biltmore Avenue, only myself and Michael V were part of that school-based boys group. But we 30 on Biltmore Ave. boys and girls of stratified ages, were like a club. Sometimes we'd have 20 kids or so of all ages and genders in a punchball game mid-block where the street was level. Although the games overflowed into front yards and bushes, there was no danger of breaking windows or causing significant damage when we were using a plain old Spalding pink rubber ball (used to be called a "spaldeen"). Occasionally the game was Ring-O-Leevie-O or Capture the White Flag. It was the kids that made Biltmore Avenue an actual, almost urban, neighborhood, even though, to my mind, none of the parents were people who worked in factories and there were no ethnic minority families on our block. But I missed the railroad trains that went by Parkchester across Tremont Avenue where footbridges crossed over the sunken railroad tracks, and I'd lay in bed at night in Yonkers listening for the distant train whistle wailing away cruising through the villages of Eastchester and Tuckahoe below to the east on the other side of the Bronx River.

Of course Biltmore had its eccentrics. Two houses up from ours on our side, also in a similar house, lived the Jorgensons. Johnny Jorgenson was a year older than me. He was somewhat self-isolating from most of the kids. He was in a different school year from everyone else, while most other kids had at least one or a few others in their school class. He was tall, maybe six-foot two at a pretty early age, and slender. Most of the families on our block were Jewish. The Jorgensons were not, but that didn't explain Johnny, because the Miller kids next door to us were also not Jewish and were part of the block crowd and friends of Judy and me. I hung out with Johnny once in a while when other friends weren't around to play with. He wasn't much into ball playing or team play. I remember him once showing me a covered jar. He had captured various insect species and put them into the jar just to watch them fight and kill each other. That image, his espoused intent to enjoy the power to create antipathy, left an indelible memory. *What's with him*, I thought. But he wasn't mean to me, not that I can remember.

Then we all learned that Johnny was indeed a seriously disturbed youngster when he got caught for a dangerous unprovoked activity. I think he was alone when he was grabbed by the cops after throwing rocks at cars from an overpass onto the Bronx River Parkway. One car's windshield was shattered. No one was killed. Why would anyone do that? After that I stayed away from him altogether.

Surprisingly, although there were about 20 homes and families on Biltmore, there were only two or three grumpy folks who got to yelling when kids got on their lawns or otherwise invaded their "private" property during play.

When my father had that first heart attack, it was evening. Three houses up lived Ruby Friedman, a physician and friend of my parents, with his wife, Ruth, and their two kids, Muriel (another of my sister's classmates and friends) and Danny, three years younger. Their home was one of the more attractive older stone-faced houses I've mentioned. I don't remember it being particularly large. Before the Friedmans moved to Biltmore, the house was owned by the Landwear family. Like Muriel and Naomi Lasco, Faith Landwear was also my sister's age. She too had a younger brother, Bobby, who became infamous because he liked to pee on fire hydrants, like a male dog. I guess he saved our fire hydrants from permanent corrosion when their family moved away.

The Friedmans became fast friends with my parents. Occasionally Dr. Friedman doctored me. Ruth, my mom's age, was still alive and hosting bridge parties into her 90s. When Mom was about 90 Judy and I decided she'd become too mentally confused to live alone there on Biltmore. Mom had collapsed during a bridge game at Ruth's and was hospitalized. Instead of a physical malady, the etiology was determined to be mental. We weren't able to get her to move down near Judy in Maryland just then, but that fiasco is a riotous tale I'll save for later. Back around 1962 Ruby Friedman rushed over to our house when Dad had his first heart attack. Some years later Ruby Friedman was diagnosed with Amyotrophic Lateral Sclerosis (or Lou Gerhig's disease), which causes progressive paralysis, then death, but never damages the intellect or the sensory side of the nervous system. Theoretical physicist/cosmologist Stephen Hawking may have lived longer with ALS than anyone with that disease. Because of the computer era and advances in neurology, neuropsychology and neurosurgery he was able to communicate his brilliant ideas in physics by just thinking them, right up to the day of his death. Ruby Friedman however had an aggressive case of ALS and, totally paralyzed, died in a few years, leaving another widow on the block to join Mom.

Two houses further up from the Friedmans, Shirley Colby (mother of Richard, John and Gilbert) became the talk of the neighborhood when she sold her "invention" to Pillsbury. Shirley had perfected a biscuit dough that could be sliced up into discs, packaged into a cylinder and frozen, ready to be twist-popped open onto a pan for bakeable biscuits. Her husband, Charles (he and Shirley were good friends of my parents also), had both a minor neurological disorder of some type and some emotional flatness. But he was a quiet, intelligent and kind man, so far as I recall. I think he did some gardening, but I don't remember how he made a living.

Directly across the street from the Colbys lived the Solomons in another stone house. From their family arose one of the block's great tragedies when the Solomon father committed suicide right there in the home. He shot himself in the head and was found in a pool of blood by one of his children, Norma if I recall. I don't think anyone else on Biltmore was even known to own a gun (though my father once told me that when he picked up the cash for Gustinettes payroll at the bank in Queens, he carried a gun in a concealed shoulder holster to defend against robbery). I don't know why Solomon was so despondent at that point. I had seen and greeted him a few times but not really had much interaction with him or his children. Norma Solomon was his oldest daughter. She was a year younger and a grade behind me. But after her dad died—I think I was maybe a junior and she a sophomore in high school—I hung out with her during that summer, when I did not go to camp either as a camper or a counselor.[11] We didn't have a particularly intelligent interaction that I can think of. Norma's greatest notoriety on the block was her ability to turn her eyelids inside out to show her pink mucosa, have them stay that way and then quiver them. It was unforgettably strange and grotesque. It didn't impress me as a particularly useful or interesting skill, but it was how she got attention. I can't say why she interested me, as she didn't seem to have any strong opinions or take stands on anything like racism or war or politics, which were beginning to be a focus of my attention. Perhaps it was the combination of her being nice-looking with an attractive, petite figure, and my desire to help her get through the terrible loss of her father, or my wanting to explore what that felt like (at that point my dad had not yet had a heart attack). Bad enough that Mr. Solomon died. But the details were shocking. I don't think Norma opened up very much about her feelings and loss. We did talk about it and her family a couple of times and that exhausted the subject. Of course, in her own mental life this tragedy couldn't have flown out the window so easily. We smooched now and again, but that was all. I wasn't a particularly precocious lad. In fact I didn't have sexual intercourse with any woman until I started dating my first wife and classmate, Irene, during my third year at Brandeis at the age of 20.

---

11 I forwent summer camp, which I truly loved, for a couple years, embarrassed by my still pre-pubescent state.

Growing up through public school in Yonkers, I had childhood crushes on various female classmates—Linda and Janet in grade school and then one or two others. However, my youthful infatuations did not involve actual relationships, other than that we were young classmates who might chatter in passing. Just a head trip. One interesting sidelight is that neither Linda nor Janet were Jewish (and I later went on to three marriages to not-Jewish women, though Irene converted).

From an early age I loved music and I tended to fall head over heels for musical girls, beguiled by those with the most mellifluous voices in the school choir. Myself and my classmate Rupert Waite were the most prominent male singing voices in junior high school. I was proud of that, but not of much else as elementary school and junior high school flew by, as time tends to do. At 16 I was still a pre-pubescent, baby-faced kid about five-foot five tall. In 8th grade I was one of the shortest kids in the class, just over five foot. For the 8th grade prom, my parents actually got me fixed up with the daughter of friends of theirs, Leah Weissman. She was a very pretty girl, and very intelligent. A parent drove us to the dance. We sat in the back seat. I had no idea what the appropriate behavior would be in this situation. We didn't even share a good night kiss given how this all came about and who was driving. Leah did not attend the same schools. I don't think I ever saw her again, though I wished then that I might have a reason to see her again. She was smart and friendly as well as attractive. We are in 1950s territory here. If it sounds that way that's because it was the 1950s.

TIME SLIDES BY

By now if you're still here I suppose you have a lot of free time on your hands or you're one of my grandkids wanting to know Popo's whole story. I too want to know my "whole story" so cut me some slack. We all know that timing in life is exquisitely important—but maybe time neglect is valuable also, equally important and necessary for human sanity and growth. Humans need to understand timing in a cosmic sense because time, as Einstein realized, isn't fixed. Technology and the protestant ethic and spirit of capitalism have fetishized time efficiency (from Taylorism to Deming to Skinner). In truth there isn't usually a good reason to be rushing around in the ways we do, acculturated to time efficiency as a moral good. Mitch McConnell's nasty criminal Republicans understand that if they do nothing and make sure nothing gets done they can become more powerful. Sure emergencies and exigencies require us to be prepared to act quickly. As a doctor I know that sometimes time is a matter of life and death, yet consider that people who don't ever waste time may actually be drained of something human. I suspect that to never "waste" time puts us at risk for self-immolation, like an imploding collapsing star at the end of its natural life. In this modern age we call this "burnout". That isn't to say that I encourage anyone to wile away their life contemplating their navel. Not under the influence of marijuana, depression or paranoia does the passage of time preemptively save the soul. I know a few people stuck in that latter morass and I worry about them because they spend all their time worrying about worrying. Nevertheless, since it's important for humans that we be actors in our own lives and world, and we do need to find our center to do that, we should avoid being ruled by artificially imposed constructs like time efficiency if we can help it.

In the 1960s every kid who said "Hell no, we won't go" to fight your dirty war of aggression against Vietnam was staking out their sanity by what they wouldn't do with their time. Those who went under "force of arms" (so to speak) occupied their time on killing fields, shaking in their boots, killing their officers or just hanging on for dear life. Whether or not they noticed it, those who died or were permanently scarred by Vietnam, had had the possibility of considering whether to just "waste" time instead of being so abused and life-destroying, even though that meant being locked up for two to three years in some cases. Muhammad Ali had his heavyweight championship taken from him and he was prevented from fighting for four years due to his draft refusal. But in that process he was transformed into one of the most important figures (and heroes) in US history, a well-deserved notoriety beyond his boxing prowess and entertainment skills—though of course, like the rest of us, he was not without his faults and frailty.

When I took a year off from medical school in late 1965, I sort of wasted a year, but I learned important lessons then also. I found myself without grounding, without a community or organization, then separated from that which I had helped to develop at Stanford. I ran a regular anti-war newsletter (Opposition West) for the Bay Area Peace Organizing Committee which attempted to coordinate activities of peace groups throughout our region. And I pasted into it valuable articles about the movement, the resistance and the war as well as local calendars and events. It was printed up by a progressive printer, Forest Crumpley, whose shop was in San Jose. But, although there were member organizations from all over the Bay Area, distribution was limited to a few thousands copies. We got it out to the peace organizations and at various rallies, marches, and anti-war actions.

I had applied for conscientious objector status and was denied it, though my sincerity in opposing war was, at that point, unquestionable. My college roommate, Saha, not having been oriented by the National Lawyers Guild to never talk to the FBI, had related to the investigator his belief in my deeply held religious opposition to war and violence. I think old Rabbi Green and Cantor Kligfield back at Genesis Hebrew Center where my family were members said the same thing. But of course, I was an activist who needed to be taught a lesson about power in America. After denying my conscientious objector claim, the draft board wrote me a nasty letter claiming I hadn't told them my new whereabouts. I had proof in the form of certified letter receipts to the contrary.

The editor of *the Stanford Daily* at the time I applied for CO status was himself a strong opponent of the Vietnam War. A secretary or a student volunteer working in the undergraduate Dean of Students office tipped Mike Sweeny off that Dean Smith had given the FBI an earful about my anti-war activism and role in the student movement. Details I don't know, but Smith obviously was talking against my being granted CO status. Sweeny told me what he'd heard from his source, which was not complementary toward my sincerity, and I then published an expose in *the Stanford Daily* about the university's collaborating with FBI investigation of anti-war students. Having broken the story, Sweeny then added an editorial. To my great surprise Dean Smith "resigned" and was replaced the following week, though Stanford kept him around until he swung an important position at a small college.

Early on after LBJ escalated the war, I had become involved for a time with CNVA (Committee for Non-Violent Action). They were a small group, but sported cultural leaders like Ira Sandperl, who I met at Roy Kepler's progressive bookstore in Menlo Park, and folksinger Joan Baez. I believe they were a couple at that time. This group carried off some small civil disobedience actions at the Oakland Army Base, scaling the fence and getting arrested. I attended as an observer but was not arrested.

After my CO application was denied, I told my draft board to go jump in the lake. I could prove I had updated my new address to them, having kept a copy of communications I sent them. I angrily informed them that if they drafted me I'd just become another garrulous organizer against the war within the army. Draft me if you want to, I dared them. You have my address. I never heard from them again. Of course, after a year I did go back to medical school, which renewed my medical student deferment. But, along with some hundreds of medical students at Stanford, University of California San Francisco Medical Center, Johns Hopkins and Harvard, I pledged that I would never serve in the military in Vietnam no matter what. That pledge and the list of signers was published by us in an ad in *The New York Times*. To my knowledge, no one who took this pledge violated it, although I know a couple of signers later became Republicans. Before that, during my leave of absence year I seriously contemplated moving to Canada, and I took a trip to visit the medical school at Edmonton, Alberta. Then I decided not to move, but to stay and fight harder against the war while becoming a doctor.

But back to time: every time some politician or president or thief who's ripping off the world's citizenry of billions of dollars like Jeff Bezos, Bill Gates or Elon Musk starts talking about the importance of training our kids in math and science, I cringe and shake with anxiety. For me, Mario Savio, a leader in the Free Speech Movement at UC Berkeley around 1964 (while I was a Stanford med student). was prescient when he prescribed the need for people to instead throw our bodies on the cogs and wheels of the great machinery of capital and bring its state and powerful institutions to a grinding halt (because their main social role was maintaining inequality, the dominance paradigm and capitalist power over human life and culture). That is, Savio cried out to stop the time-clock of money time. Money wants to turn the amazing natural experiment known as Homo sapiens into just more cogs and wheels and productive machinery, using much of our time against actual social progress, while disguising all technical progress as socially beneficial. Some is, but a lot isn't. Technological progress unfortunately became the code phrase for money-making about two centuries ago. Many academic friends—even now as we are aged—still don't recognize that science and technology are morally neutral and can only be praised to the extent that they escape from the profit center mentality to be employed solely to benefit the rights and lives of all—with equanimity. If we cede control of our brilliance to the market, all bets about where that lands are off.

In contradistinction to a social agenda, money and its human subjects have largely thrown the idea of social evolution and progress (as a fundamentally moral question) to the wind and smashed it on the rocks, trashing the evolution of thousands of species, of nature, and of human civilization. Many scientists and other academics look at themselves and say, "No, I haven't done that. My work has great social value." But how many of these today take a stand like most of the scientists on the Manhattan Project atomic bomb development team did. Once the Nazis had surrendered and they were no longer a threat to develop atomic weapons, those scientists signed a petition to President Truman insisting that the government immediately begin negotiations with the Russians to ban all nuclear weapons development and end their Manhattan Project. Unfortunately Truman had no interest in doing this and Robert Oppenheimer made sure that the almost completed bomb would be finalized. The effort by the scientists was thwarted.

Money, having no animacy of its own, represents, for humans who see it as godlike and all-powerful, the denial—not just of morality, but of mortality also—through an attempt to merge their lives with things and inheritance and the perceived[12] security blanket of immortality. Eat your heart out Ponce de León. Because death is so intrinsically a part of life itself, this unique system of denial (money-making and property accumulation as a social measure of human progress and achievement) is socially suicidal, if only because death and human impermanence are logically and philosophically inescapable and so must be consciously integrated into life's journey.

"Getting ahead"—before the age of reason—amounted to learning how to survive. Since the advent of capitalism, however, a connection between survival and wealth and power—once the province of only monarchs and elites (as Shakespeare elaborates)—has been integrated into common culture. This perspective intimates that dominance, supremacy, property and wealth accumulation protect those who have these from ignominious death and historical irrelevance. Ironically, now in September 2021, Republican governors, senators and congress-people cavalierly spread this self-destructive mythology of desire and dominance to their anti-social, anti-vax, anti-science, anti-democratic supporters. Meanwhile they themselves load up on all the benefits of science and technology and medical and public health support that their class position and status allow so they may gain maximum protection from a terrible COVID-19 death. Trump himself was saved by early treatment with a monoclonal antibody. Over 2,000 mostly un-vaccinated Americans are dying now, again, every single day so that the powerful may deny their own death wish.

---

12 The nature of "perception" will become a core theme in this memoir.

Broadly speaking, money's "agent promoteurs" have turned human nature into a joke by creating social constructs that imprison even the freest people in a cultural straitjacket of compulsive buying of (and attachment to) things we don't really need and distractions which shape us and make us look, feel and behave like the people we actually shouldn't want to be. The money managers have sworn on their lives and promised to their teachers to use their Skinner box training to turn us all into fat rats, or impoverished mice, to the benefit of the fat cats. This translates into a form of material, cultural and moral enslavement. Basta ya!

But letting death sleep alone for the moment, let me tell you briefly about wives I thought I knew; and how two taught me to stop thinking I was so brilliant and capable of understanding human nature; how they disabused me of thinking I understood them or how to achieve meaning in life with them. Each in her way taught me, if only because teaching and sharing are intrinsic to our social nature. I learned a lot about myself from wives, even the one who was most indecent and duplicitous.

I got married three times in my life: to Irene Giobbe, Caroline Iverson and Sheila Thorne. Irene and I were bound closely together for our senior year at Brandeis, young classmates who made a connection, but we stayed married only two and a half years from April 1964 until late in 1966 in California. Carrie, who swooned at my feet after I spoke at an anti-Vietnam War event at Stanford in 1968, pursued me, dumped me, pursued me again, married me at an anti-war building occupation at Stanford in 1969 and then deserted us (myself and our daughter) just two years later. Sheila and I have been life partners since mid-January 1972. Such a time span seems to this frail mind inconceivable, unfathomable. How did we do that? Were we in denial and trying to hold back death? Had we learned our lesson or was some cosmic force involved holding us in its embrace?

I know from my work at Center for Elders' Independence that demented people sometimes think they haven't grown old and that their kids are still children. It's a confusion, but we are all still children when we die. To think that such an outlook is just the propensity of the "feeble-minded" brain addled by beta-amyloid plaques and tau protein tangles is another one of those delusions we ought to combat. These three women I got married to had very little in common except for something they weren't: Jewish—though Irene converted. And one other thing: they got married to me.

Growing up I relied greatly upon my mother for guidance and I confided in her, but she did tend to be a dominating figure. When we moved to Yonkers I was a pretty frightened seven-year-old. In 2nd grade I was very insecure trying to learn how to read. My teacher (I think her name was Ms. Marshianno) was supportive and friendly, but it didn't help. Mom responded by reading to me most nights. She helped me overcome my fear of failure and slowly she showed me how to grasp what I was seeing on the page. I caught on quickly then. Mom would go on to become a clinical psychologist specializing in working with children with learning problems. When she was about 80 I asked her if her decision to become a psychologist and focus on this field had to do with my struggles at age seven. To my great surprise she did not even recall that I had had a bad time learning to read—a typical example of how our memories are selective. I think she wanted to believe that I was innately brilliant. Everyone is, but we are easily scared away from believing it unless we have the support and nurturing.

I didn't realize that I was uncomfortable with the overprotective (or something like that) maternal style of many Jewish women until I noticed that I wasn't usually attracted to Jewish women even if they were physically attractive. I think it was a style thing, a kind of loving aggression that seems characterological within Jewish culture. Of course, not all Jewish women share the trait and there are a number of other cultures that tend to train women to be domineering in the way they love their children—see below. It's a delicate balance. Mothers do have to be authority figures for young children, after all, just like fathers.

To try to compare the women I married is obviously both inappropriate as well as unfair to them. Comparisons like that would derive from my own egoistic perspective on life and emotional attachments than actually relate to them. But since I was married to three women my mind inevitably compares these women anyway. Realizing the outrageousness of this, however, causes me to tell you that you won't read a comparison here. Moreover, to compare over 50 years of a full and intense real life with Sheila Thorne to a couple or two-and-a-half-year adventures is absurd. But I do want to write about Irene and Carrie some before I get back to the rest of my real life.

GOOD NIGHT IRENE

Irene Giobbe, who died at the age of 50 of liver cancer, was determined to break free from the chains of a constraining Italian Catholic family in Somerville, MA, near Cambridge. We were the same age, born within a month of each other into very different families. She was one of the five children of a well-known local doctor (Ciro Giobbe) in Somerville and had been sent to a traditional Catholic parochial school where she was subjected to the usual overly rigid disciplining and harshness of ruler smacks and authoritarian demonstrativeness by intimidating, and undoubtedly cowardly, nuns who go along to get along in their chosen asceticism. Nuns submit to conformity (i.e. to the Church and God) and then they must teach and try to enforce it on their charges. Often it doesn't work out as planned.

At home Irene's mother, Libera (Zoli), was a typically loving, shrill and demanding Italian. Irene was seemingly mellow, obedient and responsive, but she had a soul on fire. In her senior year in high school she met and dated a Harvard student. He was African. Her parents were not pleased. Whose idea it was for her to apply to college at Brandeis, where the student body was 85% Jewish and there were another 3% (100 Wein scholarship students) imported rich kids who were from Third World countries? I have no idea. But given the family and the Church, one might imagine it was Irene's. Also, she could get a scholarship and she could avoid the cost of room and board if she lived at home. And Brandeis had a good reputation. In my first year at Brandeis (1959–1960) I took the basic inorganic chemistry course. I was, after all, a pre-med student, though actually hoping to do medical research. I remember not liking the chemistry professor, Kalman, not studying much and not doing well in that course. Locked in an emotional funk, I did not even study for the end-of-semester final exam in mid-winter. I remember walking the dorm hall praying—instead of studying—though I already considered myself an atheist, for a snow storm that would close the campus. Snow had been forecast. To my great amazement and joy, a powerful blizzard hit the Boston region that night and the winds were so vengeful that deep snow drifts buried cars and forced the closure of the campus, which was on hilly terrain, and the cancellation of my chemistry exam. I studied enough for the rescheduled exam to just get by with a C. Strangely, I had done well in chemistry in high school and I actually liked the subject.

Chemistry was a course with a lab once or twice a week and Irene and I were lab mates, sharing the same equipment and table space. She was friendly and sharing and attractive, but the idea of getting together with her never crossed my mind. There was no electricity between us, just neighborliness. I was then trying to adjust to the exigencies of a very new way of life away from home. I had some women friends on campus (Irene was not one of these), but no intimate relationships. I think Irene was then commuting from home in Somerville, which would have probably meant three buses and two transfers and perhaps an hour each way.

I'm sure I must have occasionally passed Irene on campus and said hi over the next two-plus years, but it wasn't until late in 1962 that I stopped her, conversed and asked if she would like to go out with me some time. I believe I invited her to that year's Gilbert and Sullivan performance where I played bassoon in the show's orchestra. It turned out that her interest in science matched my own. Irene would go on to become a high school biology teacher here in the Bay Area in Milpitas, then East Palo Alto and—after our divorce—at Half Moon Bay or San Mateo. She had a keen sense of humor, was fun to be with, always had a sparkle in her eye and a little smile on her lips. When she smirked it was miraculously without hostility. She was sharp-witted, quieter than myself, but not passive, and we hit it off together. Neither of us—both of us were 21 by then—had had relationships involving sexual intercourse. We were virgin "twins". I was lucky to have a studio apartment with its own exterior door to the quad courtyard by my senior year. The university had no prohibitions concerning such relationships. I was also fortunate to have a wonderful, understanding and supportive roommate, Sahadevan (Saha) Amarasingham, a Sri Lankan Tamil, as a roommate. Saha and I would become lifelong friends. My mother would tell him he was like my brother, and she treated him as such. When Irene's father died suddenly during our senior year, the sage Saha, a couple of years older than I, advised that if I wanted to fortify a strong relationship with Irene going forward, it was important that I attend Ciro's funeral. I did. And of course Saha was right. Thirty years later when I was medical director of the Center for Elders' Independence I would advise the other doctors in our program of the importance of attending, when possible, the funerals of each of their patients, and I did likewise do that out of respect for the families and the value of the lives of the deceased.

Irene was also an artist. She painted. When we first moved to California in June of 1964, Stanford provided us an apartment in what was called Stanford Village, old WWII military buildings on the same property as the Stanford Research Institute in Menlo Park. Our apartment was a studio, but it was large, perhaps 30 feet in length and 15–20 feet in width. Irene adorned the walls with her figurative paintings. The only one I kept when she left is a day-dreamy representation of me sleeping on my side lying on our couch, with many of her other paintings with African and plant motifs painted into the background on the wall behind me on the couch. She represented me as a friendly looking sleeping lion with a big dark curly mane. Coincidentally, while I work on this memoir, our daughter Joanna calls and asks if she can have this painting, but it's all that I have to actually remember Irene by, and I decline. Also Sheila likes the painting, which hangs in her study.

Thirty years after Irene's death, Joanna's younger son, my grandson Moises, upon viewing an actual small photo of me from those years back then, with a head of bounteous dark curly hair, would exclaim, "You had a Jew-fro, Popo." The "lion on couch" painting hangs on the wall of Sheila's study at a right angle to our 45-inch TV screen. Sheila says, "It fits perfectly." It is full of warm colors that match the room. A portrait painting of an Egyptian man, in a traditional white gown and a head wrap, beautifully executed by Sheila's father after he took up painting upon his retirement from investment banking, adorns the wall opposite the TV. I imagine this man alive, his eyes gazing at the TV screen in puzzlement, or perhaps he notices me, as the lion, in Irene's painting. The husband of our dentist, Zarrin, is named Siamak, a Persian name that means lionhearted, so perhaps he too has a place in Irene's painting.

Irene's painting of me snoozing on the couch
at Stanford Village (as a lion–1964–1965).

Irene and I had no children—by choice. Of course we were only married two and a half years so that might have changed. But having been through the 1962 Cuban Missile Crisis where we seemed terrifyingly close to nuclear war, having been born during WWII, known of the Holocaust, brought up in the era after the terrible conflagrations and then lived our childhoods through the straitjacketing McCarthy All-American purge era—and now the Vietnam War which the US had forced upon the world was raging—the idea of bringing children into such a world seemed callous and selfish. We were young and not yet willing to accept reproduction as both a biological and social imperative in the grander scheme of life's river. Irene would say, did say, she had plenty of kids to work and play with as a teacher and didn't need any of her own.

Maybe had we gotten deeper into the heritable biology of life and evolution she might not have fallen in love with another teacher at the Ravenswood High School—Austin Meek. No doubt the fault was to a great extent my own. By then I had become essentially monomaniacal about the imperative of resisting and ending the US war on Vietnam. I was balancing medical school and meetings at night and protests and planning for these battles day and night. I was rarely around for her, even though she was supporting me with her salary and doing the cooking. We did not have any heated arguments but Irene was clear, after I took a year's leave from medical school, that she had come to believe I would never finish med school. As I wrote earlier, she thought I might end up in a prison cell, or dead. Certainly she might have been right, but predicting the future is dangerous business, as you can see, for she died 30 years ago and I'm still pecking away here. Although she was not a passive person, Irene had decided to not be the kind of shrill, assertive, demonstrative woman that she had experienced growing up in her mother's household. I was not listening to her quiet shout-out for rescue of our marriage from my monomania. For her, our marriage was a convenient way to escape the provincialism of her family and the Church, but she had not yet decided to love me unconditionally given my determination in life to fight for justice, and there was nothing more unjust at that moment in history than the Vietnam War aimed at asserting American dominance. The two sides of this coin didn't fit.

Earlier we had had some counseling sessions through Stanford's health assistance program with a young psychiatrist who was a post-doc at the hospital. I thought he was helpful and we had stopped seeing him together by the time Irene had become involved with Austin. But she had been seeing him on her own. I was stunned to learn what was going on. The young psychiatrist had me come back and meet with him alone. At that time he told me, "You really have to let her go. She is having serious suicidal thoughts and is at risk of suicide. It's related to feeling guilty about betraying your trust and also to her Catholic background which magnifies that sense." Ironically, Irene had converted to Judaism which had pleased my parents, but had irritated me. She didn't ask my opinion before she went to my parents and got started. I trusted the young psychiatrist's words that Irene was thinking seriously of suicide. I had no choice but to take it seriously. I gave up the thought of trying to change what was happening.

After they both divorced their current spouses (me, in her case), Irene stayed married to Austin Meek just barely four years. We remained in phone contact on friendly terms during their marriage and after it failed, though she never discussed Austin with me. Once, Sheila and I visited her where she lived in a mobile home park up top of Skyline Blvd above San Mateo. Instead of a husband by then, she had her red Chevrolet Corvette parked in her driveway. I had never thought of her as acquisitive, but she told me it was something she had always wanted. Everything about this story makes me sad. Later she found a relationship with an electrical engineer and she had gone back to school in a new field—I think chemical engineering—but she must have given that up when she became ill. I lost contact with her then, in the late 1980s.

I found out about Irene's death only by chance—that she had moved home to her mother's with a cancer diagnosis, then died there in Somerville. In 1993 I was attending the annual conference of the National PACE Association in Cambridge, MA (related to my work with CEI—itself a PACE program). Being near Somerville made me think to call her mother to ask her whereabouts. Zoli answered and expressing suprise responded: "Who is this?" "It's Marc, Irene's first husband." "Oh, Marc, I'm so sorry to tell you that Irene passed away of liver cancer last year. She was here living with me."

I hopped on a local bus to Somerville and visited Libera (Zoli) Giobbe, who I had perhaps not seen since the funeral of her husband. She gave me a copy of Irene's obituary from the March 26, 1992 edition of the local Somerville paper. Damn, but they had many facts of her life demonstrably wrong and, in particular, the obituary did not mention either of her marriages. To their Somerville readers, neither myself nor Austin ever existed. But Zoli Giobbe, by then close to 80, did tell me something comforting when I visited: "I told Irene back then she shouldn't leave you," she said. "I told her you were a good person."

Like myself shedding my parents, Irene had tried to escape far away from her domineering mother. Certainly it was kind of Ribera to tell me she told Irene she shouldn't have divorced me, but that also made me feel guilty; for it seems I had betrayed Irene's trust to the extent that, in her moment of greatest need for support, she had returned to the care of the mother she had hoped to escape from. In my mind's eye I envision an argument between them there in Somerville: Zoli insisting that divorcing me was the wrong thing to do (and of course against Catholic teachings as well). I hope I would have taken Irene's side of that argument, even though the divorce was a disorienting body blow that weakened my self-confidence and made me susceptible to Carrie's "charms" not long after our divorce.

THE BRIEFEST CONVERSATION (1970)

(written 2007)

Somethin's happenin' here!

*("For What It's Worth", song by
Christopher Cooper/ Buffalo Springfield, 1966)*

Handcuffed, in the back of a police cruiser, dark of night, despondent. It's now late April 1970 in placid residential Palo Alto, California. ***What it is ain't exactly clear.*** I am about to graduate with an MD degree from Stanford Medical School. ***There's a man with a gun over there.*** In my state of mind, it feels like I might never be crossing that river, nor any stage, getting any degree diploma, going anywhere except up a lonely river. ***Tellin' me I got to beware.***

Again, moments in our lives we never, ever forget. ***Children, what's that sound, everybody look what's goin' down.*** Details stand out.

The cruiser drives off toward the holding cell at the police station. Not speeding, languid. Just me and the driver, a middle-aged Palo Alto cop, in uniform. I can't contain my demoralization. "Looks like that's the end of my medical career," I let out, sad and frightened, from the back seat. He turns his head partly toward me. I can see his face through a wire screen. "Don't worry," he responds paternally.

"It'll work out ok." His reassurance calms me, even if I don't then understand what he means.

What was "it"? I have to start with what "we" were. Radical activists, communists, revolutionaries. Supporters of the Black Panther Party. Enemies in J. Edgar's book and soon to be enemies in the pages of the House Internal Security Committee of the 92nd Congress. So, targets of COINTELPRO.

Still, this friendly, sympathetic cop was so reassuring. He was also right that a situation ripe for disaster "would work out ok." At 66, I've been practicing medicine for almost 38 years. The cop, I wish I knew his name and face, knew more than I did about what had happened that night, about what put me in his custody. But beyond those facts, I was able to walk away because I was/am white, a well known local figure, had a hotshot San Francisco criminal trial lawyer, R.J. Engel (a supporter of the political "movement"), and this was Palo Alto, not Philly or DC or Chicago or even SF. Had I been Black or Latino, I would not have been in the back seat. I would have been lying in a pool of blood on the sidewalk. I am certain of this, but you be your own judge.

On that late April night in 1970, the "Red Squad" of the Palo Alto Police Department (we could only guess that this plot was hatched by the FBI) had decided to entrap leaders of a young but rapidly growing local communist movement then called the Revolutionary Union (RU). RU was local to the Bay Area but already had hundreds of members—from high schools to colleges, from youngsters to oldsters, from the streets to the factories, people of various ethnicities. I had joined several months earlier. One leader, a target the Red Squad probably had in mind, was Stanford English professor H. Bruce Franklin—an expert in Herman Melville and science fiction, who later became the first tenured professor ever fired by Stanford for his political activities. Bruce and his wife and three young children lived in Menlo Park. The second targeted house was that of John and Rusty

Keilch, in Palo Alto, although several other people lived there at the time—including my wife, Carrie, and I. The Keilchs now live just down the block from where I sit in Berkeley. John is retired from the UC Berkeley planning department. Rusty has an important role in public health. I wasn't a leader in the RU and so probably wasn't the intended target. Carrie at that time was almost nine months pregnant. I was 28. She was 26.

The police action in Palo Alto involved a car full of undercover drug squad cops, unshaven, dressed as thugs in army surplus jackets, who would cruise the neighborhood and break the windows of our house with slingshots. The cops knew we were (legally) armed. It was no secret. Our organization was prepared to insert its members between police and the local Black Panthers anytime the authorities took a hankering to provoke a shootout with militant Blacks in East Palo Alto or East Menlo Park. We did so in preventative actions. Panthers had already been killed in San Francisco and other cities in incidents incited by the police. Aware of our brashness, the cops hoped that an over-response to a provocation might lead to either a shootout in which the police would triumph and/or the arrest of the key people they were after. A shootout would likely allow them to decimate the entire organization. The media would focus on the lunacy and criminality of any group who would cause a shootout with police in a community neighborhood, perhaps ignoring any police provocation and misconduct.

What I've written here about the police intentions and behaviors isn't speculation. There were taped police radio recordings of conversations between elements of the police. Through discovery in my case, investigators obtained documents that detailed the whole operation. This was COINTELPRO. The real thing, a disguised, coordinated military preemption.

When I heard the small rock(s) crash through the front windows of that house on Cowper Street, I was inside with a group of people socializing around the dining room table. We thought it was gun-shots. I did not know that the weapon used to break the windows was a slingshot, but imagined that someone was firing a 22 or pellet gun at our house. We were then opposed in the mid-peninsula area by heavily armed and organized right-wingers. In part because we had become a major political force with thousands of supporters and with the potential to elect people to local positions of authority through totally legal political organizing (with day care center parents, street people, factory workers, students, you name it), we had every reason to believe the posse comitatus and other Rightists would attack us. They had promised to do so and were as upset as old J. Edgar that there was so much open communist influence in local politics at that point. When the rock(s) came through the window, I grabbed a shot-gun that belonged to the house from a rack over the front door and after assuring there was no one just outside, I slipped out the front door. An old beat-up car was languorously rolling through the inter-section 150 feet away. My mind whirred. *What is this? Who are these people? Why are they not fleeing the scene of their crime?*

It never even crossed my mind that this was a police entrapment. All I wanted to do was scare away whomever was attacking us. I was certain that if they saw I had a big gun they would burn rubber and be gone. I walked into the middle of the street behind them and showed the shotgun. They did what I expected—tearing away at great speed. But then the whole scene changed, became more threat-ening. When they reached the end of the next block, the car did a squealing 180 and headed back toward me accelerating. Seeing this, I barely had time to get out of the street and duck behind a large enough tree to conceal my position in the dark of night. The car slowed and moved back just in front of the house. All I could think of at that point was that my wife was in the house, eight and a half months pregnant, and these guys seemed to be playing for keeps. Whatever they might be up to, they weren't even frightened off by my showing a 12-gauge shotgun, obviously a powerful weapon.

I knew how to shoot guns, but I had no military training, and maybe what I did then was just plain foolhardy. But in the hopes of again scaring them off and preventing them from attacking the house with guns or firebombs, I came out from behind the tree, showed myself and walked to a position about 30 feet or so to their rear and to the side, and stood there silent with the shotgun, pointed downward.

For the longest five or 15 seconds, nothing happened. It was too dark to see the occupants well. I was now sure they were aware of my presence and I had to make the next move. I decided to raise the weapon to further make the point that they ought to leave. The shotgun never got beyond 15 degrees from vertical. All four doors of the vehicle broke open in unison. Four crouching men emerged, one at each door with a pistol pointed directly at me. The two thugs on the far side had their pistols braced on the car roof. "Police, drop your weapon!" someone shouted out at the same instant they emerged. I believed then that they were cops, though the idea had never entered my mind until I heard those words. I believed they would shoot me if I didn't drop my weapon. I did as they said. In only a few seconds time five regular marked police cars came screeching around the corners from three different directions. We were under siege. The plot became apparent. Meanwhile neighbors from several houses across the street had come out into the warm spring night to watch the drama. The witnesses would testify at my preliminary hearing on charges of assault on a police officer with a deadly weapon that I had not raised the gun and had not pointed it at the officers—though of course no one knew they were "officers".

The shotgun lying at my feet, I was immediately arrested. Meanwhile, the attack at the Franklins' house in Menlo Park had gone even worse for the police with no arrests and no shootout. I found myself in the back of one of the police cars, totally incredulous as to what the police had done, their risking my life and their own for a political agenda probably orchestrated from D.C. We weren't bank robbers, drug dealers, terrorists or violent criminals of any type. We were political activists working to achieve changes we believed in—an end to the Vietnam War, racial justice, and a more egalitarian society for all. But we also believed the problems our nation faced, and faces today, weren't accidental "mistakes" but the predations of money, and imperialist power, in quest of political economic dominance in the world. Acting on those beliefs made us "the enemy".

The judge in my preliminary hearing (felonies go to full trial only after a decision by a judge from a *preliminary hearing of evidence* or on indictment by a grand jury) was a Reagan appointee. Although my lawyers had abundant evidence of the illegal conspiracy by the police and neighborhood witnesses swore that I had not committed the crime of which I was accused, the judge bound me over for trial. Stanford, however, did not block my graduation and I was allowed to leave California to begin my internship so long as I swore that I would return for trial. Shortly, the case got to the DA (down in San Jose where I would later settle with my family in 1973). He reviewed the file and was immediately aware that this case could not go to trial, for my lawyer was prepared to make the political conspiracy by the police a cause célèbre, and I was a doctor with a wife at term pregnancy. The evidence of both my innocence and of police misconduct were overwhelming and the DA dropped the charges.

I believed at that time that I had almost been murdered by the police. I urged my lawyer to file a damage case against the Palo Alto Police Department. As a criminal lawyer, RJ had more important things to do, so he gave the case over to a young woman lawyer in his office. He wasn't happy with my request. We asked for $50,000 in damages. My new lawyer also did not want to go to a civil damages trial. When the police offered $250 she urged me to settle and both sides told me I probably wouldn't win in court as any judge would favor the police. I accepted the settlement as a victory, in principle vindicating my own behavior, and gave the little money to the lawyer who charged me nothing else.

I doubt that the drug squad police had collective clarity on my identity before they cuffed me that night. Maybe that confusion—or an awareness that they didn't have the right target—helped save my life. But, had I been Black or Latino, what destiny? The statistics are clear.

These days (2007) I talk with a friendly county sheriff's deputy who I know at work. A year or so ago we discussed a particular patient with psychological problems who I fear may easily be shot by police some day. The deputy, a Latino, explained that uniform police policy is that cops can draw their weapons only if they feel there is a credible threat. But once they draw their weapons there is a training-policy reason why they shoot, and they shoot to kill. The only defense required of police who murder—even if the victim is unarmed—is that they believe they were in mortal danger. There is a circular logic to this training guideline which turns cops, even the nicest guys, into killers. If they draw their weapons they must later say they felt threatened. If they don't say it they are guilty of misconduct, having drawn a weapon without good cause. If they draw their weapon they are more likely to shoot because drawing their weapon is evidence they perceived mortal danger. Shooting someone is evidence they were in danger (even if they were not). Though individual racism persists in general and in police conduct, today's cops are being trained by this institutional racism; they are programmed to kill anyone as a part of their job, although most believe they are protecting society when they do so. Those rules on police use of weapons are murderous rules. Under today's uniform police training guidelines the 1970 situation would have been different. I would have been shot, even being white.

Medical student or not, standing in the street that night in April 1970, with a shotgun, believing these cops were right-wing thugs, and my pregnant wife inside that house, I was, in fact, a danger to

shoot those disguised cops. The police actions had made me dangerous, though I have never intentionally physically harmed anyone in
my whole life. Nevertheless, that kindly paternal older cop who drove
me to the new modern police station electronically equipped to coordinate military operations, was right—I would be ok—and I haven't
forgotten his kindness and humanity.

As I write these words, June 11, 2013, there has arisen a huge scan-
dal over the US government's National Security Agency secretly
obtaining unlimited access, and storage of, the telephone and e-mail
records of millions of American citizens. We have gotten to the point
that almost all human interactions can be monitored by government
and industry, and criminal activity can be imputed simply from
random linkages that may not represent anything even approaching
crimes or intention to commit crimes. It's been obvious for decades
that the storage of information about people is likely to lead to serious police-state misconduct. Though the felony charge against me
was dismissed and my innocence of that charge affirmed, I know that
any time a cop searches my name in a national database of past criminal records he/she learns that I was charged with assault on a police
officer with a shotgun. Many cops will conclude from that a possible
danger to themselves. He or she is likely to misunderstand and mis-
interpret what transpired because the full facts will not be disclosed
on their computer. Although charges may be dismissed, computer
files are not purged. These databases in criminal justice are, in part,
the way that the entire African American male community has been
criminalized, regardless of innocence or the triviality of a person's
interaction with the police.

Head Trip—Antecedents to drowning in the sea of troubles (composed in 2013)

DÉJÀ VU—ENLIGHTENMENT THROUGH REDUNDANCY

*(And if you thought the Trump ascendancy in 2015
was happenstance, consider these thoughts.)*

forgotten memories and musing

Clustering thoughts: identity; self-delusion; where we are as a species; musicality, synchronicity and social evolution—from the Maya to Oliver Sacks to the love of science and music to multiple personalities and the deconstruction of the human mind; tai chi,(bending bows and hanging in the balance); experiential and didactic learning; War and Peace—*what Leo Tolstoy understood about human nature, culture and mind; the mind and the mind's eye (the 21st century's reawakened neurological under-standing); imagination and lack thereof; my one act: wherein God or some facsimile speaks in various guises; and the redundancy: the meaning of death in relation to consciousness.*

TRIBUTE TO SELMA: MY MOTHER, SYDELLE GENEVIEVE GUSTIN

Genevieve, my mom's middle name, lived her last nine years in a senior apartment building in Rockville, Maryland, one of several such places that make up the "Smith" operation. It is called Ring House. The residents of the Rockville Smith building are seniors and for all intents and purposes, Jews. Beyond the beauty parlor, choir, library, computer and workout centers, the Smith place has many Jewish cultural and religious activities. I've never heard of a Jew named Smith, but who knows? Maybe Smith was just a developer of senior apartments, or his grandpa got named Smith when he arrived at Ellis Island.

Mom's Smith "Ring House" is a high-rise sitting on a many-acred piece of land also occupied by a Jewish synagogue, preschool, and a pond with geese. I used to wheel Mom out to the pond and relax there with her, both of us watching the geese and an occasional parent claiming a child from the preschool. Behind the high-rise residence there is also an assisted living facility and a nursing home.

Before she lost her mind, Genevieve[13] was a very outgoing extro-

---

13 I never thought of my mom as Genevieve during her life, so calling her by her middle name makes little sense. But her name on her birth certificate wasn't Selma either, but Sydelle, which she never used.

vert. After she lost her mind she became even more flamboyant and provocative. Though an accomplished professional woman with well-deserved recognition for her achievements, Genevieve's self-assessment went beyond self-promotion to irritating name-dropping and assertive political commentary, with which I often disagreed. She made sure everyone knew she entered NYU at age 14, but between the two of us she later admitted it was very hard being a 14-year-old trying to be accepted socially among young adults much older than her. She felt awkward and out of place. Though attractive, I imagine she had no dates or guys chasing her at that age, long before she met my dad. I mean, my God, sex would have been statutory rape and besides, she probably looked and acted her age, 14.

Though congenial, social, loving and generally respectful, adult Mom, to my thinking, was kind of like an overcooked steak, hard to chew and hard to swallow when it came to a long-term relationship. Mom had many friends and colleagues who did find her endearing, supportive and interesting. She did have a broad knowledge base. Sometimes Sheila, my wife, says, "You're just like your mother" (not meant as a compliment). The feeling can be mutual, though I think I know what she means. I was close with Genevieve and also careful to keep my distance after graduating college. Nonetheless, her professional advice (unlike her Clintonian-liberal status-quo boring politics) was usually spot-on. She was a clinical psychologist and professor at Bank Street College specializing in, and pioneering some modalities in, working with children with learning disabilities.

Living thousands of miles away, I didn't get to visit her much in those later Smith years, usually once or twice a year. As her demential decline progressed, my sister, who lived nearby and took over her finances and management, had to employ progressively more health care aids to attend to her. Genevieve had declared, when lucid, that under no circumstances did she want to end life in a nursing home. By the time she entered the Smith place, I think Genevieve was almost 90. The place wasn't a Continuing Care Community (CCC) where, upon enrolling, one signs away essentially all earthly goods of value including much of one's bank account in return for being allowed to transition back and forth into assisted living or a skilled nursing facility as needed, and in-home support is provided throughout the rest of life. Although the Ring House high-rise was on the same property as these other medical care buildings, the places with differing levels of care were operated independently. Despite not providing any personal care, Ring House's senior apartments were exorbitantly priced at many thousands of dollars a month. However, their outreach and PR department were good enough that vacancies were filled quickly with the elders of well-heeled families whenever someone died. They were a successful business operation—probably still are.

Since Ring House wasn't a CCC, it would have been quite costly to use those other levels of housing next door as Mom declined or had problems. Moreover, as I said, she had declared that she wasn't going to end up in a nursing home, and that was that. So we used the money gained from selling her house—the modest suburban home where I grew up on the hill near the Bronx River, which had cost 25,000 dollars in 1948 (but sold now for half a million). That provided Genevieve with home care that increased until—in the last several months of her life—caregivers worked around the clock because she couldn't do much of anything for herself. By then, Mom was being cared for by a very understanding, sensitive and competent ad hoc group of five or six African (Ghanaian) women—nursing assistants with families both in the US and West Africa—who Judy paid through their coordinator and leader, Mami.

Mom was six weeks short of her 98th birthday when she died, not unexpectedly, with end stage dementia. I had visited her just a few days before her death. By then I too was old, 74—and 14 years since retiring from caring for disabled elders near the end of life. In working with disabled elders, I coined the phrase "titrating death" for what that experience was like, because we, the staff, were so involved with program participants that rarely did anyone die in a sudden turn of events. In fact, if a family member or friend of a staff member suddenly died—for example, murdered on the street while working, as happened to a UPS driver related to one of our own van drivers—it was a much greater shock, as if they were our own kin. Unexpected deaths disturbed the sense of rhythm we had become used to: a pattern of decline, decay, and acceptance of death.

On the evening of my departure from my last visit with Genevieve, Sara and I went up to her apartment. She awoke and, to my surprise, she recognized me even while groggy. I gave her our permission to check out. "It's ok, Mom," I said. "We'll be fine," I told her. "Don't worry about us." Three days later, Sara called. "She's died," Sara said, relieved.

Eight years earlier, about a month or so before we'd moved Mom south from New York, she had suddenly decided that she wouldn't let me drive her down to Judy's. Damn! We'd arranged a party in Maryland for her birthday. We'd planned it in her honor, and several of Sara's kids and grandkids would be there. "You're going to force me to stay there, not let me come home," she said when I arrived in New York. Well, it wasn't really like that, since she'd already planned to move and she'd visited the Smith place and approved it, but this day she refused to get in the car. So after explaining I was going to go without her, I took her car and drove down to Maryland. We'd have to put our heads together and figure out how to deal with this conundrum, her blind obstinacy.

Unsurprisingly, Genevieve didn't like the idea that I was taking her car away, even though her license had been suspended (after she failed the driving test performed after I reported her confused state), and so she started shrieking at me. I used my most convincing, filial and genteel approach, urging her to come along, but to no avail. She was pretty paranoid by then—she'd even accused one of her best friends of stealing her outdated disabled person car placard from her—and as soon as I drove off she called the police, which she told me she'd do, and reported that I'd stolen her car, which technically speaking was true. Luckily, the cops didn't stop me before I crossed the George Washington Bridge into Jersey. I got to Maryland sweating all the way, my eyes glued to the rearview mirror on the Turnpike, just waiting for the flashing lights and the siren's sound. I kept thinking, *If I am stopped now, I've crossed state lines while allegedly committing grand theft auto. Could this get to be a federal case?* But the local Yonkers cops didn't do the APB thing. I wasn't stopped, though they did eventually catch up to me (by phone) at Sara's house in Maryland. It took us several days, conversations, time and trouble, and faxing documents to clear up that we had power of attorney (thank goodness Genevieve had prepared for this kind of thing by giving us power of attorney). Did she anticipate the need for preventing her later-to-be-demented self from having her kids thrown in the slammer? Unlikely, but it's always good to have your mother watching out for you in any case.

There are other chapters to be told, but I'm not up to it at the moment—being tired and old myself. Just to entice you though, here's one vignette titled: Saha tells of the environment of bliss in suspended animation. Saha,[14] my beloved Sri Lankan-born long-time college roommate, lived in Silver Spring, MD, the next town up the road from Rockville where Mom was. He visited her occasionally. Even though not everyone at Ring House sitting around their lobby and the outdoor patios had dementia, he noticed that they all seemed to have come to a conspiratorial agreement to not remember much of anything about each other, the very friends with whom they con-

---

14 Saha died of heart disease at home in Denver in late autumn 2022.

stantly conversed. Though they talked and talked endlessly about current events at Ring House and in the newspaper, Saha reported that they apparently knew little of each other's lives.

And then there's the story of The Rats. That's how Genevieve almost got thrown out of the building. She barged into a tour group of new resident prospects to warn people to stay away from Smith's Ring House because of rats in the walls. The staff were outraged. But in the end a full investigation found that birds—not rats—had indeed gotten inside and nested in the walls. But that's another story entirely…

THE DIALECTIC
OF THIS MEMOIR

*"The greatest purveyor of violence in the world today:
my own government."*

MARTIN LUTHER KING JR.

Rage: I'm an old man. An American. Father, grandfather, fool, pretender, physician, writer. Yet another opinionated, outraged male, a Jew, a doctor of many decades to the California working class. I have outlived my father, who died at age 62, by over a decade at this particular moment in human time (2013), in years lived, in calendar time of course, and in experiential time as well.

"But why does everything have to be about you?" some other fool will ask. Well, it's a memoir, damn it. However, let me declare this: I've never uttered that phrase in quotes as an epithet against anyone. Still, I've heard it said by others and to others. I don't like it. Those are cruel pejorative words to my mind and way of thinking. Cruel when invalid, but equally cruel when true, because they invalidate a person as much as any face slap or other humiliation, even if justly applied on the facts of the matter. Actually, although we can only live our lives through our own minds, even in a memoir everything isn't about the writer—in this case me. Anything we think or write or experience potentially provides recognizable resonances. And on the other side of the coin, sure, many things in this world aren't about you or me—or even us as a species. To believe so would be typical hubris of the human type. Consider that the monotheistic God syndrome of Western religious ideology is a form of anthropomorphism, taken to its logical conclusion.[15] However, the more important point, from my perspective, is this: everything within the frame of human culture is reasonably about us all in some ways. Even the cruelest calumny, even the most egotistical, even the most incredibly brilliant, resonant, heroic, creative and magical happenings. Because we are, after all, one social species, whose commonalities are important and worth exploring.

I've called this book a memoir, in part because I could not possibly write a linear autobiography from the beginning of my life to the present. I don't remember my life that way. Do you? Memory comes in tattered and constantly revised shreds. One thing leads to another, an endless stream of fragments as the mind unfurls. I think of memory like the hooks on a curtain rod in the hippocampus attach-

-----

15 The God syndrome has gotten us into trouble so often. People run around claiming only their unique he/him godhead is watching over them and our world. It's got to the point where almost every professional ballplayer points skyward upon each success, and thanks their God for their momentary success. Doesn't that mean that their God isn't so keen on their opponent(s)? Or that the opponents didn't make the grade as equally dedicated to supporting their own God? Or does it mean that my God is better than your God? This problem might never have arisen if all people identified the same God watching over them—even if he wasn't real. But there's the rub, humans—starting with the Biblicly anointed Jews—always relegate others' religions to lower status than their own. "For we are the chosen people of God" every sect says. And there being no limit to the number of unique Gods or religions that humans can and do conjure, competitive religious beliefs can be best understood as a holdover from tribalism and the striving for unrestrained dominance and superiority. At least that is the function of religion in the Judeo-Christian and Muslim eras.

ing the curtain of memories hanging there, recollections that are tied to themes and feelings and other experiences, a constructed continuity like in dreams remembered. Memories, although connected to our identities, aren't necessarily tied to a real timeline even though each memory claims a particular time stamp. It's even possible that the impressionist confabulations of our dreams patch things together—often in incomprehensible non-linear fashion—as counterweight to balance some of the fraudulence in our conscious constructions of our lives. Meanwhile, we also compare the world of ideas in our minds to the world of our lived experience. As a result any single particular revision and mis-recollection can cause a chain reaction deforming our histories like a heavenly body distorting the path of light or gravity wave.

This book represents not only experiences, but my head, my mind—thoughts, ideas, recollections. I'm sure it's full of semi-fictional recollections and constructions. Did you hear the tale about Ronald Reagan (before he had any signs of dementia) portraying himself as having played on his college's football team? The reality was that he had done radio broadcasting of their games. Oliver Sacks writes about this phenomenon (which is common), citing the research of Elizabeth Loftus who documented successfully implanting false memories in subjects' minds by "simply suggesting (repeatedly) to a subject that he or she has experienced a fictitious event".[16] I am intrigued by the concepts of truth and reality as they have evolved as part of our collective human understanding of our world. As individuals we remember, we forget, yet there always remains the human historical and cultural scaffolding, this vast body of social knowledge passed on from the human past since we first found language(s) in

---

16 *The River of Consciousness*, p. 119 hardcover edition, Knopf, 2017.

the social commons, in the gens, in the village square in the zocalo. Yet that cultural knowledge can be in conflict with the knowledge and frames of other cultures.

As individuals, we can't be sure why we remember some events so vividly and other events lose all traction. And yet every thought we have is unconsciously filtered through our memory bank and our culture's memory bank. Not only the minds of the demented play memory tricks. Each living person's mind constantly tailors and reconstructs memory to meet both the conscious and unconscious need to form coherent narratives. Neuropsychological research has proven this. It isn't my own idea. What often remains more obscure is the extent to which a nation's dominant culture (in our case American exceptionalism), conditions our own mental narratives.

I have spent much of my life fighting, in various ways, for truths that I believe(d) in even though these truths, like "We hold these truths to be self-evident, that all men are created equal…" sometimes shape-shift precariously into demons/into opposites as we learn more and more about actual American history and the men who issued these truths. In the Left subculture, the shape-shifting of "American exceptionalism" is exposed as the hubris of power lust. For American exceptionalism embodies a core ruse—the profound misunderstanding of our nation's role in human social evolution. Throughout the era of capitalist dominance, the US role in world history is projected as heroic in defiance of such actual history as the slaughter of the Indians and the legalization of human bondage. Our exceptionalism is conjured as actualizing national superiority and uniqueness. Of course, every culture is in many ways unique and exceptional, and so the very idea of cultural "superiority" is a vacant concept.

Cultures get very complicated in how they categorize and how their moral standards impinge upon ways of seeing the world. Do you know, for example, that some cultures actually see more, different, and differently demarcated colors in the visual spectrum from our own? The wavelengths are unchanging, but the social interpretation and thus how the brain "sees" and interprets color is culturally bound.

Early in the period of human language development and social evolution, mental constructs of the world took on mystical and mythical aspects. On the one hand, nature's patterns and distinctions were well observed—better than most of us can observe today—by early peoples; they studied, categorized and then integrated knowledge into their lives. Survival required it. They also formed cosmological stories of origins, survival, continuity and evolution. These stories were based upon observations that provided mental and social coherence—and still today can excite and capture the collective imagination of younger generations. Though somewhat reductionist, early narrative cosmology was based in the real—which plants (and animals) cured, which killed; but also the details of beauty and process: reproduction, change, death; which moon phases and planetary alignments heralded seasonal changes and vital cycles; which neighboring groups were friendly, which dangerously aggressive; which gods (as natural manifestations) protected us, menaced us, helped us; how to name and relate to our various kinship groups and so forth. These aspects of culture and social evolution passed down through generations.

As humans developed technical skills, this allowed for farming, stationary communities, excess food storage and the advent of population concentrations—as well as larger-scale warfare. The pantheism of natural forces then succumbed, replaced by a singular omnipotent human-like God, as monotheism. This facilitated new narratives that underpinned the rising religious "political" institutions—with the Church taking on the role of the state dressed in imperial robes. The Church, as state, imposed abstract ideological purity as well as embodying and exercising earthly forms of power. The alienation inherent in the coming into being of "state power" was violently magnified when the Church replaced pantheism with its own rules of governance that equated religious heresy and non-conformity with treason. Thus came the Inquisition and Dante's *Inferno*,[17] and also why the first thing the Inca did when they defeated an enemy group or tribe was to smash the icons and iconography of the conquered group, then substituted and taught their own religion.

Such ideal notions—represented by the Church—can not adapt to new ideas based in science. This set the stage for scientific thinking to challenge the Catholic Church's anthropocentric Ptolemaic views of the universe and solar system. Idealism exposes its own weakness when, inevitably, actual conditions don't validate its truths and so lead toward social incoherence and collapse. Nevertheless, the rule of Europe under the ignorance of the Roman Church and its Inquisition could only be replaced when a more prescient state religion rose to replace it. The Protestant reformation had some impacts in this direction, but it took the marriage between science and the rise of early capitalism, to provide a more durable state power. Therein, an entirely new religion was birthed.

The Renaissance exposed the extent to which idealist harmonic theology as state power could not manage reality. That was the era when the excommunicated Copernicus and others' scientific observations contributed to trashing the Inquisition by demonstrating the utility of artful investigation. Wonderful? Well perhaps, but we best not idealize the problematic marriage between science and the soon-to-be new state power, capitalism, which spawned its own forms of idealist despotism.

Certainly science and technique reveal the immense power and

---

17 Which is why the separation of Church and state are so fundamentally important to any democracy, though this principle is under strong attack today in the US, by the states of Israel, Iran, Turkey, the Taliban, and the Rightist movements in many countries worldwide.

capacity of the human mind, and the potential to sustain both life and quality of life. Yet, this rising religion of science captured by private enterprise also let loose many demons (for example, today's conspiracy theories and anti-science nonsense galore). How could this have happened? Yes, science appeared to relegate most earlier mythology—and by implication early "culture" and "social existence"—to quaint relic-hood. But in the marriage of convenience to capitalism's pseudo-"democracy", science and technology became subordinate to and agents of an unstable state power based upon inequality at its root. That contradiction sparks the spectrum of anti-science mythologies.

MISBEGOTTEN (2022)

The Venceremos organization existed only from late 1970 until winter of 1973–1974. And yet those three years seem like such a huge slice of my life. 1972–1973 was the period in which Sheila and I became lifelong partners; when, due to a tiff between us, I fled (with a health group) to Wounded Knee on the Lakota Indian reservation at Pine Ridge as a doctor. We were supporters of the American Indian Movement-led Oglala Sioux take-back of their land and rights; where I met Crow Dog, the medicine man; and Russell Banks, Leonard Peltier and others. It was the period when, in Menlo Park, Venceremos folks spray-painted anti-war, anti-imperialist slogans late at night on the Philco-Ford factory in which, by day, Sheila worked on an assembly line; a place where the workers were not even told they were producing systems for the war; where the in-plant secret newspaper Sheila and her factory friends put out exposing that reality, worried the company and the government enough that they had the FBI stand at the entry gate and inspect women's bags and purses at shift change—though they never found a paper on anyone.

In short, it was an exhilarating time and reflected the pulse of the reborn America—from the factories and high schools to the universities to the military, where draftees were throbbing with angry resistance, an American humming, though tamped down in public perception by media distortion of these realities. But Venceremos could not last long which was, in large part, due to a level of exuberance and adventure that was, sometimes, beyond foolish to the point of dangerous and absurdly reckless. Though I was not a direct party to the events I will now describe, it strikes me that this fiasco was somehow "pathognemonic" of why the organization would implode (with a little help from the FBI). Moreover, I may have unwittingly and unknowingly contributed to the sense of urgency that precipitated these events. Thus, I write about the misanthropy here with a twinge of guilty conscience.

When the disaster known as the Chino prison break unfolded, I had already left Venceremos. Venceremos stood in strong support of the Black Panther Party for Self-Defense. We recognized the importance of the Panthers to both the survival of Black communities and to any future prospects for a social revolution bringing actual democracy to the US. In fact, a movement faction that was particularly bound to the Panthers led by Miriam Cherry (I think she was Stanford faculty in religious studies) had quit the organization just around the time of the founding of Venceremos to become solely a Panther support organization.

Just a few months after I moved into Sheila's home on Willow Road in Menlo Park, the phone rang about 3 a.m. A Black Panther house in East Menlo Park-East Palo Alto was surrounded by police cars and there was a sense that murder by the cops could be in the offing. After all, everyone—not just us Leftist radicals—knew that Chicago cops had killed Fred Hampton in his bed, murdered Bobby Hutton in the streets of Oakland, killed George Jackson in a Marin courthouse and shot so many others. Sheila threw on some jeans, grabbed a shotgun, told me to take care of the boys, jumped in her 1969 blue Volvo wagon, and, alone, headed down the road east a mile, to the other side of the freeway (for all the reality of it, the other side of the "tracks"). Fortunately, quite a few people turned out quickly to the site of imminent confrontation that night and the cops backed off. Fortunately also, Sheila, our comrades and the cops also went home safe and sound.

In this climate, Venceremos had committed itself to support imprisoned activists and all political prisoners. Sheila was—or would become—Venceremos' contact to the wonderful Ruchell MacGee, a Panther and lone survivor of the George Jackson events, still imprisoned today, lawyering for others.[18] I never met Ruchell myself, but I remember driving Sheila up to Folsom Prison to visit him. One day, some months later, I told Jean Hobson—a Palo Alto mother of three late teen/young adults, and another member of the Venceremos central committee—that we needed to become more effective, more demonstrative—do more. I was no Venceremos leader at all, but I've always given out lots of opinions. Jean was a personal friend. I felt a sense of urgency. I remember Jean, who would later do some prison time herself for Chino, responding that she was working on that. I had no idea what she meant then. Maybe I thought she was just trying to calm me down (which she did). Yet, had I unknowingly given Jean both moral and morale support for one of the most poorly thought-out political gambits attempted in those times? It seems to me incongruous for this middle-aged, middle class, intelligent Palo Alto woman who had successfully brought up those three wonderful children to have been so thoughtless.

---

18 Ruchell MacGee (Cinque) was released from prison on August 4, 2023 at the age of 84. He died only 81 days after his release.

The newspaper of Venceremos was named *Pamoja Venceremos*. It had morphed out of a merger of the *Free U*, newspaper of the Midpeninsula Free University and the *Midpeninsula Oberver*, a movement newspaper started by former Stanford student activists. The broad anti-war and counter-culture movement had given birth to the Free U in downtown Palo Alto. If I recall, Pamoja is a Swahili word for unity or united. Venceremos is Spanish for we will win. Although most of the articles in the paper were written by Venceremos members, supporters were encouraged to submit letters and articles. Prisoners were particularly encouraged. Out of the blue from the California prison at Chino came "revolutionary" literate articles and praise from a prisoner no one had heard of extolling the efforts of Venceremos, the Panthers and others. He was, in fact, a white guy set up in this scheme by the FBI. I don't remember his articles, his name or anything about him at all but apparently some Venceremos members were enamored by his writing (no doubt not even his own) and developed a relationship with him.

Unbeknownst to most Venceremos members or to the leading committee, some folks developed a plan to break the guy out of prison on a day he would be taken out to a court appearance. Mr. heroic revolutionary was, in fact, a common criminal who had been offered God knows what benefits or relief to play this role. I later learned that Venceremos had an explicit policy that illegal activity like that could never be discussed, planned or carried out through or by the organization in any of its forms. Otherwise, such activity would implicate and destroy the entire organization. Thus, I only learned about these events from the news coverage. The plotters were apparently successful at stopping the police car in which Mr. X was being transferred. They released him from custody. But somehow they ended up with a prison guard on their hands as well and he was shot and killed. Why the FBI, who presumably knew of the plot all along, did not intervene before or at the point of attack has never been explained (so far as I know). Perhaps they were intent upon arresting a wider circle of collaborators involved in hiding ("harboring") the escapee—which they later did. Those involved were easily located, tried and convicted. Folks who "harbored" Mr. X afterward got lesser sentences. The young man who pulled the trigger was convicted of murder and sentenced to life. Bob Seabock was then 19 years old and the boyfriend of Jean Hobson's youngest daughter. He was in no sense a brash, angry, or apparently trigger-happy fellow, but a quite sweet youngster. Bob spent approximately 47 years of his subsequent life as a model prisoner. I wrote to him a few times. Later, at the initiation of another former Venceremos member, MN, I, along with others wrote to the parole board urging them to recognize that his release would present no danger to society and reprising that he was a model prisoner. Nevertheless, I surmised that being labeled as a "cop killer" he would never in this life be released from prison—at least not alive.

Forty-seven years is an almost unimaginable length of time for a young man to be locked away into old age. Nevertheless, I was wrong about him not ever getting out. As Sheila and I filed out of a classic film showing at the University of California's Pacific Film Archives in 2020, someone called our names. Mike Fox, who had been a young member of Venceremos just out of high school (and later became an EMT or paramedic), reminded us who he himself was. Then he asked us: "Do you know who this fellow with me is?" Neither of us did. "It's Bob Seabock, just out of prison last week." A stunner. I can't remember if we hugged Bob or shook his hand, too stunned to do more than congratulate him on his freedom. I apologized to him for giving up and not staying in contact or writing again on his behalf all those intervening years.

My giving up on Bob Seabock's chance of release wasn't the first time that I failed to do something because of demoralization or speculative conclusions. In the final analysis staying involved matters, even when we only do a little. What we do or don't do collectively summates and has impact. I have a storehouse of examples of how demoralization became a major force in social disempowerment.[19] We have not seen nor heard of Mike Fox, nor Bob Seabock, since that brief encounter.

However, despite Venceremos' policy that illegal activity not involve the organization, the fact that six or so members were involved in this dangerous and fatal folly where a needless murder occurred could no more be ignored by the organization or the public than it was by the FBI. Surprisingly, the latter chose to limit their arrests and prosecutions to those who were actually involved. Perhaps they were clever enough to recognize that having knocked a supporting pillar out from under the heady Venceremos, the structure would eventually collapse of its own weight. Or were there other reasons they did not throw out a wider net of arrests and use the propaganda against the leaders of Venceremos? No one involved in the Chino fiasco ever showed any willingness to talk with me about any of this, so I am merely reporting my thoughts. But I should say this: for the next year or so Sheila and I shared a mutual paranoia that, although neither of us were involved in those events, she—as a member of the leading body of the organization—could have been arrested at any time.

By then we were living in San Jose, having bought a small home

---

19 One example occurred in 1979 when Ronald Reagan was still governor of California. Medi-Cal insurance was then widely available to poor people in the state. Reagan announced that he was eliminating eligibility for the poor in general and would only retain coverage for pregnant women and the disabled. The newspapers (appropriately) made a big splash about this "taking away" of health care. The results were seen immediately. Even though the changes were not to go into effect until the beginning of the next year, applications for Medi-Cal insurance and renewals plummeted dramatically, precipitously. People simply gave up.

in the East Side Mexican-American (Chicano) barrio. Sheila was now working on the computer chip assembly line at National Semiconductor, and we had decided to have a child. Her first pregnancy with me ended in a miscarriage, but the second time, late in 1973, was the charm—that was Joanna. By the time that Sheila reached seven months and the prosecution of the Chino perpetrators was ongoing, it dawned on us that were Sheila to be imprisoned, there was some possibility (which we could not quantify) that she might deliver our baby behind bars; that without a "legal" father, the state might seize the infant and place her in foster care. So we decided to get married. Why not?

Thus we had a "shotgun wedding" of a new type, promulgated not by an outraged father of the bride to be, but by our fears of the power of the state. We sought a solution to the power of the state by gaining state sanction of our relationship. The strange tale of our actual wedding—from the night before through the ceremony by a Catholic priest—is reported later.

NOBODY KNOWS MY NAME[20]

(A sketch)

The Road Not Taken[21]

Two roads diverged in a yellow wood,
And sorry I could not travel both…(full text at [22])

---

20 Borrowed title from the book of essays with this title by James Baldwin.

21 (copied from a web page posted by the *Atlantic*) Robert Frost's poem "The Road Not Taken" is often interpreted as an anthem of individualism and nonconformity, seemingly encouraging readers to take the road less traveled. This interpretation has long been propagated through countless song lyrics, newspaper columns, and graduation speeches. But as Frost liked to warn his listeners, "You have to be careful of that one; it's a tricky poem—very tricky." In actuality, the two roads diverging in a yellow wood are "really about the same", according to Frost, and are equally traveled and quite interchangeable. In fact, the critic David Orr deemed Frost's work "the most misread poem in America", writing in *The Paris Review*: "This is the kind of claim we make when we want to comfort or blame ourselves by assuming that our current position is the product of our own choices…The poem isn't a salute to can-do individualism. It's a commentary on the self-deception we practice when constructing the story of our own lives." In the final stanza, we can't know whether the speaker is sighing with contentedness or regret as he justifies the choices he's made that shaped the narrative of his life.

Every day, people I know—or have known—are dying, leaving me behind to tell this tale.[23] But soon it will be my time, too, to join them. Meanwhile, the telling seems to matter, some-

---

22 And be one traveler, long I stood
And looked down one as far as I could
To where it bent in the undergrowth;

Then took the other, as just as fair,
And having perhaps the better claim,
Because it was grassy and wanted wear;
Though as for that the passing there
Had worn them really about the same,

And both that morning equally lay
In leaves no step had trodden black.
Oh, I kept the first for another day!
Yet knowing how way leads on to way,
I doubted if I should ever come back.

I shall be telling this with a sigh
Somewhere ages and ages hence:
Two roads diverged in a wood, and I—
I took the one less traveled by,
And that has made all the difference.

23 Just today (in 2021) I read that UC Berkeley epidemiology professor William Satariano died over a year ago. Though Satariano came to Cal after I had completed the one year epidemiology program in 1987, back in 1992 I was thinking to re-enter UCB as a DrPH student. I asked Satariano to adopt me as his advisee in the field of epidemiology of aging. Bill was friendly, but his declining my request, strangely, led to my becoming the first medical director of the Center for Elders' Independence in Oakland, a position I retained for over nine years. My work at CEI then became the greatest achievement and personal growth period in my 46-year medical career. Several essays appearing later in this memoir are about my experiences with elderly participants/patients at CEI. While the death of Satariano had little impact upon me emotionally, it brings to mind how shocked I was to learn—in that call to her mother in 1993, seeking news of her whereabouts—that my first wife, Irene Giobbe, had died of liver cancer two years previous at the age of 50. Sweet Irene died 28 years ago.

how, and so I will try to tell it with a bit of flare, anger, humor, love and perhaps a little imagination. My friend Fred is also a retired doc. He was a long-term emergency room physician at Kaiser Hospital in Oakland, CA, though I didn't know him then. We are peculiarly as different as night and day and yet not so different at the same time because we are both white American doctors who care about people and cared sincerely about our patients' well being. We are of similar age, both raised in New York State, and we also love to shoot basketball and talk a round of bullshit and politics on the court for a while now and again. You'd call Fred a liberal, I suppose. At one time in his life more conservative, he presently reads *The New York Times* regularly, attends daily lectures at Cal Berkeley on a wide range of medical, scientific and political topics and says he agrees with most of my views on politics. Fred admires me for my political engagement, but insists he's not an activist. He did help me leaflet people entering the YMCA once or twice, though, and he helped out as a medic for an event with Rev. William Barber II and the Poor People's Campaign at Glide Memorial Church in San Francisco in early 2020 before the COVID-19 pandemic hit.

Fred was a flight surgeon in the Air Force in the time of the Vietnam War. I was, like many non-Freds, an anti-war activist, a rebel and a resister fighting against what the Chinese then referred to as the "hegemonic" power of American imperialism in quest of world domination. Of course the narrative of our government was couched in high-flown principles of saving democracy not in domination. Saving democracy was also the anti-Axis rhetoric of the allies in World War II. The politicians carried it over into the postwar era— the Cold War against our former allies in the Soviet Union. But in backing and then replacing French colonialism in Vietnam and British colonialism and Zionism in Palestine, the US was validating the Chinese moniker, hegemonic power.

I begin this essay back again in World War II because I was, in fact, born during the early throes of that Great War, five months before Pearl Harbor was bombed. Naturally I don't remember that "day of infamy". But I don't remember the end of the war in 1945 either. Nonetheless I do know from reading that the government of my country, in 1945, obviously targeted the civilian population, fire-bombed and decimated Japan's 100 largest cities, by then mostly militarily defenseless, as prelude to wiping out the people of Hiroshima and Nagasaki with the first and only atomic bombs ever used in warfare. The bombings were purposeful—a geopolitical maneuver to block the Russians from invading Japan and ending the war that way a few weeks later. The Red Army had already destroyed the entire Japanese occupying army in Manchuria and marched unhindered into, and liberated, Korea from the Japanese. Hiroshima and Nagasaki were a message to the entire world that the US had this new weapon and no qualms about using it against major cities.

Though the "trench warfare" and poison gas of WWI (supposedly a "war to end all wars") had been, up to then, the most brutal slaughter of young men, it took a second "Great" world war to raise the bar to the targeting of major civilian populations as the penultimate terror tactic to subdue "enemy nations". Surprisingly, according to documentation by Bruce Franklin,[24] history reveals that that tactic was not specifically Hitler's—who favored invasion, conquest and gas-extermination of "non-pure non-Aryans". A particular irony is that before the US entered WWII, President Franklin Roosevelt had called on all sides and nations to refrain from civilian targeting. I was four years old when the massive firebombings of Germany and Japan began. As is often the case, however, the purposes dreamed up and the purposes achieved tended to diverge unannounced to human

---

24 In his books *War Stars* and *Crash Course*.

commonfolk—be those purposes noble or horrifying—particularly if the decision is not as innocent as the simply random choice of a path in the woods as in Frost's poem.

Perhaps my inability to remember most events in the early years of my life derives from being born Jewish in 1941. Günter Grass' young German boy in *The Tin Drum* was born into a Nazi family in the 1930s. He was so terrified by his social environment and his Nazi father in particular that he "refused" to grow and remained a small boy using his energies to wall out the dread. The makers of the film *Jojo Rabbit* (2019) may have had Günter Grass in mind when they wrote their screenplay, despite the lighter treatment of the subject, for Jojo was terrorized by his imaginary hero, Hitler, for most of the tale. Somewhat like Gunter Grass, Ariel Dorfman, in his remarkable novel *The Last Song of Manuel Sendero*, (written sometime after he fled the Nazi-like Pinochet matanza in Chile), featured an unborn child who refuses to be born into a human-constructed world of terror. Dorfman's fetus leads a rebellion of the unborn—a massive strike of refusing-to-be-borns.

My own childhood was not terrifying like the lives of Nazi and European Jewish children around 1940. I had it relatively easy. Yet the backdrop of *Kristallnacht* (1939) followed first by the Nazi expulsion of the Jews, then reversed with the sealing of borders to block escape by Jews, dissidents, Roma and other targets, the deportation to death camps and the Final Solution were part of my social environment, and, at every-moment, the threat was well understood by, and terrifying to, many parents and grandparents then.[25] That horror vibe was the surround sound of my early childhood. And in the foreground, not at all hidden, the overt anti-Semitic covenants and attacks throughout these United States had their own intensity. Fortuitously I was never directly impacted. This "social climate" (so to speak) was crystallized in Arthur

---

25 As I wrote earlier, this is how the cultural and social environment conditions the thinking, feeling and even memories of each individual.

Miller's only novel, *Focus* (1945) set in Brooklyn, NY. I was four then, so seeing the film *Focus* (2001, staring Laura Dern and William H. Macy) provided an intimation as to why my memories from those years remain guarded, repressed and pre-conscious. But I did grow physically—slowly, slowly but persistently. And I kept growing until I was about 20 and over six feet tall because the world changed and we Jews were first "allowed" to become white (if not Aryan). Then Europe's surviving Jews were handed (beware of Greeks bearing gifts, Virgil wrote in the *Aeneid* about the Trojan Horse) the land of yet another conquered, suppressible, dispensable indigenous tribe (the Palestinian people) in the land of Eden and the Holy Grail— by European colonialism (to a "people without a land", mind you, it was proclaimed). And, though my memory had been repressed, Zionism's apartheid policies eventually jarred it loose forever.

To forestall my awakening—though a choice perhaps made without this intent—my parents, good traditional, but very American Jews as they were, trundled me off to Brandeis, that Jewish academic mecca in Waltham, Massachusetts that was wed to the ignoble state of Israel, both born in 1948. At 17 I began awakening, but was surely not fully woked. I had just carried off a debate in high school where I defended Israel as a model egalitarian, even socialist society—what with the power of the Histadrut socialist-oriented trade union movement in politics and the utopian kibbutzim model of communitarian farming and rural life. You see, such gross distortions of actuality become ever harder to not-remember as time passes.[26] I had all my notes for the debate on 3x5 index cards.

---

26 It may be the mismatch between that ideal and the reality of Israel as an apartheid and settler colonial state that invests the Zionist polity with the ferocity with which so many Zionists attack their critics and would do anything including ethnic cleansing, genocidal policies and destroying the lives of other Jews to defend their lie that Israel is democratic and pacific, despite its aggressive settler colonialist Eurocentric arrogance.

So, it seems to me, that which I cannot remember in my early years turned out to be even more important in the flow of later human history than events which I can remember or participated in. But perhaps loss of perspective is something we all experience—sometimes, always, never. Denial, after all, as I wrote at the beginning, is a necessary human survival strategy, even though denial often serves to obliterate moral decency, empathy and even common sense. Alas.

My awareness that Israel was created as a reification of Western imperialism's atrocious dominance ideology to serve as a surrogate in the Middle East after the post-WWII dismantling of European colonialism would have to wait until years later. But in the meantime I was waking up nevertheless. I had boarded a charter bus in Northeast Yonkers at 17, headed to Washington, D.C. to join a civil rights march led by Martin Luther King Jr. It was 1959. There were only about 3,000 of us on that march. And now that I am writing this down, there were such premonitory signs in earlier years that I would adopt a religious zeal to fight injustice.

As a youngster I was not a particularly rambunctious or outspoken fellow. I think I was for a while somewhat a conformist because of fears of being isolated. But in 7th grade social studies when our male social studies teacher ridiculed another student before the class I became so incensed that I stood up and assertively accused the teacher of outrageous and inappropriate behavior. I was little more than five feet tall then. I then ran out of the class and all the way home. My mom had to go to school the next day to get me out of trouble and reintegrated. I don't remember any other negative ramifications.

Then there was a similar event four years later in trigonometry class in high school. The teacher was out and a substitute presided, a woman. The class became very unruly and out of control—spitballs, shouting, paper planes. At that point the teacher lost control of her own temper, as of the class. She verbally attacked one of the students viciously. I stood up on my desk and berated her and was sent to the principal's office, but I didn't get suspended.

I think I well remember these events both for their emotional intensity and because they presaged where life was taking me, who I was becoming. Just as the end of the McCarthy era released the pent-up anger and frustration that fueled both the civil rights and anti-Vietnam War movements of the 60s, the removal of the night terrors and the suffocating cloak of that era's anti-Semitism may have unleashed my own hidden fears, turning them to fury.

THE SAPIRS

When I was about 20—though it may have been earlier or later—after hearing my mom and dad have a huge yelling row I sat down with her on the staircase that led up to the bedrooms of both myself and my sister, Judy, and suggested they consider divorcing. "But we love each other too much for that," she'd said. I did not respond cynically with "You sure don't show it," even if that's what I was thinking. Had Dad had his first heart attack by then? I'm not sure but I'm sure that he had at least some scares with angina and had been diagnosed as high risk with high cholesterol and obesity. I was really worried that their angry screaming matches, his frustration with her kvetching, would cause his death. Ironically a lot of the screaming resulted from Mom pushing him endlessly on his diet, deriving from her own worries about his health.

My dad was both a gentle and gregarious man. Very likeable and engaging. He was a big man too at about six foot, weighing up to 235 pounds before he became ill. In high school he had run track and was a racing speed ice skater. He could play a tough inside game of basketball and ping-pong as well. He was strong far beyond my own strength in my prime when he was past his own. Dad had large, strong hands that could crush yours in a handshake if he chose to do so. I suspect that unless you were as close to him as Mom and I were you wouldn't be aware of his emotional vulnerability.

Bob had begun his adult life with energy and vigor, rebelling from a dandy of a father who, when he left Russia fleeing pogroms for

American dreams in the late 1890s, came out of the old country as a Jewish socialist, member of the Bund. Morris Sapir moved from the sweatshops of the Lower East Side Manhattan to soon enough owning a chicken ranch at Coney Island when my dad was young. Born in 1910, Bob (known as Izzie—for his middle name, Isadore) was the youngest of four children and the only boy. Morris by then had not only divested himself of socialist ideals but he hobknobbed and played chess with the hoi polloi, including the Republican governor.

I never knew my paternal grandmother—Sarah Neidich. I only know that after having four children she developed type 2 Diabetes and had one or more strokes that incapacitated her. In pictures she appears stocky—what Jews call zaftig—with an attractive face. According to my mother, Selma Gustin Sapir (born Sydelle), Bob played an important role as caregiver for his mother while in high school. He apparently resented the absence of his father, Morris, from the home, often out and about. The tension turned into a major row and Dad quit high school in his third year and got a job as a runner on Wall Street. By the time he was 18 or 19 he had landed a good job with the DeWitt Tool Company, owned by two brothers who were socialists. For Dad they were kindred spirits and he quickly learned much about large machine tools—their operation, their specs, their repair, their value and sales.

Dad's oldest sister was Kate Sapir. A tall, stately woman, who Dad looked up to as his big sister, they stayed close through the rest of his life. I didn't know it at the time, but my sister Judy more recently told me that Dad called Kate and spoke with her by phone almost daily; and Mother was jealous. Kate married a lawyer who was mixed up in NYC politics. My parents were not fond of Morris Zirin. Kate and Morris Zirin had one son, Jim Zirin, who also became a lawyer, and a Republican. Jim is a retired NY federal prosecutor and has written several books.[27] The one I've read is an interesting read: Plaintiff in

---

27 one is on the Bill of Rights.

Chief—A Portrait of Donald Trump in 3500 Lawsuits. Many chickens now coming home to roost are documented therein. The prominence of Roy Cohn in Trump's life and Trump's abuse of the legal system are salient features.

Aunt Kate was a high school principal in Brooklyn. They lived in a fancy Brownstone with a great view in Brooklyn Heights that we visited only a few times during my childhood. When I think of how rarely we saw them I have to imagine that either Morris Zirin was jealous himself and keeping Kate's family at a distance, or else Mom didn't want to deal with Morris, probably the former.

Dad's second sister, Florence, surely was a rebel, like Dad, for she married out of the Jewish religion—to the budding Polish-American artist, Theodore Roszak, who trained at the Bahaus and developed into a modern neo-abstract sculptor. Ted achieved great notoriety and won important and lucrative contracts, particularly for his outdoor steel-welded monumental sculptures.

Composition Alastor, 1931, celebrates Ted's love of music and his wedding to Florence. This, before his transition to monumental welded steel sculpture.

They eventually bought a four-story walk-up apartment home in Greenwich Village, which today is worth a fortune. Their only child, Sara Jane, herself a painter, inherited the building, but it's now occupied by Sara Jane's adopted daughter, Hannah, and her husband, Gabriel, as well as storage for Ted's remaining works and a first floor restaurant. Both of my parents had a high regard for Ted. I loved to visit them with our family of four as Ted would sit back in an easygoing way, smile through his bushy white mustache, and talk brilliantly and humorously about life. Ted had a good sense of humor and he was full of entertaining anecdotes. He enjoyed socially engaging when we visited and he always seemed lighthearted. Sara Jane would later tell me that he was not so easygoing as he might have seemed then. Some time after Ted died, Florence had a stroke and Sara ended up care-giving for an incapacitated mother herself.

Sara moved her mom to a house she purchased up the Hudson somewhere in New York State. I visited there once or twice but don't remember where it was. Judy and I are fond of Sara and we stay in touch with her. Her partner, Bruce Porter, is an emeritus professor at Columbia School of Journalism who has written several books, at least one of which, *Blow*, was turned into a movie and is about Latin American drug trafficking. I haven't read the book. Bruce and I have gotten along the few times we've been together, but in the past year he made clear that we don't see eye to eye politically, making a pejorative remark about W.E.B. Dubois and the Dubois quote I use in my email "signature". Two years ago I sent Bruce Porter, who then had a substantial garden at their now primary home in Hudson, New York, some of my Cuore di Bue Italian tomato seeds. They grew well there in Hudson.

There was a third daughter who neither Judy nor I knew about until late in our adult lives. What we then learned: she was schizophrenic and the family, unable to deal with her psychosis, packed her off to one of the "homes" for the mentally ill far out on Long Island.

To me, as a physician, it seems particularly unthoughtful for families to hide such unpleasant histories from their children. Also their failure in empathy towards the woman who the family essentially deserted troubles me. How are our children to understand the world if that presented to them is fraudulent? On the other hand, with Grandma Sara failing so early in life (she died at a young age) and the conflicts over her own care, alternatives to institutionalization may not have been possible, so judgment ought be suspended. But that doesn't justify hiding her existence from us, the next generation.

INTERLUDE: HEAR THE BEAT

I grew into my teen years listening to Beat's stream of consciousness rants on the radio in the 1950s. The guy's name was Jean Shepherd. I'm still hooked on his style. Shepherd exposed me to a world view apart.

Like the cubists—that modern art trend initiated in the early 20th century which was, to some degree, an outgrowth of French impressionism—I think he looked at the world simultaneously from various directions and recognized a fractured reality that could only be understood by seeing its fracture lines, its contradictory yet associated planes. The Britain, Berger,[28] wrote about the earlier concealment of the observer's perspective and point of view (as commoners the great artists' viewpoint of their era were usually present, yet hidden in their paintings of and for the elite) hidden within classical portraiture art in order to protect their patronage. Yet another way of thinking about how perception depends upon vantage and perspective is to imagine being in a fixed location, but viewing the same—or analogous—scenes or persons at different times in history over time, in seasons, in centuries, in different contexts, or by different cultures. We ought not forget that in this country which prides itself on its egalitarianism, Blacks were not

---

28 See John Berger's *Ways of Seeing* (1972), originally a BBC series.

only kept at slaves but they were seen as little more than property that if lost or escaped should be hounded and returned to their owners; that women were seen as so inferior in their intellect as to not be trustworthy to participate in free elections. That the indigenous people were massacred in order to pave the land. And so forth. But, not only the perspective of the viewer changes. The reality also changes. The event itself, the thing itself, the person herself/himself also change over time, and within history. More about the Beats later.

PART III

Interiors

*****BEGINNING OF THE END*****

Maybe this is about where my own story begins.

I AM NOT IMITATING
PHILIP ROTH'S PORTNOY

Déjà Vu: My first wife, Irene, left me for another man 48 years ago (1965). It wasn't that she didn't like me. We were good friends who liked each other, even loved being together most of the time. Part of Irene was too worried that my time away from home—my compulsion to fight against the war—would catch up to me and that made her lonely. I was taking her for granted. You keep protesting and acting the revolutionary and you're going to wind up in prison or dead, she once told me. You'll never become a doctor. She was right of course. Time away from home did catch up to me. She found this other guy, a fellow teacher with four kids and a wife, fell in love and ran off with him, so to speak.

I mean my life was young and my energy chaotic. From Stanford Village life in that studio apartment in a Quonset hut that was once a military barracks that first semester at Stanford, we moved into a nice rented house in Menlo Park. Maybe six or seven months later the owner decided to build condos and evicted us. I had painted the rooms in beautiful pastel colors, tended the shrubs and garden and was so furious that our "home" was being taken away that I wrote a fable, a parable or fairly tale about the house and the eviction, which I painted on the walls and ceilings of several rooms. Of course the house was being torn down, so my parable didn't matter. It did get out my rage, though maybe it wasn't the best way to spend my time.

I was still a medical student and anti-war activist. After Menlo Park we rented a cute stucco of Mexican styling on Mariposa Street in Mt. View. Our adorable scruffy-haired, medium-sized mutt—I can't remember his name so "Scruffy" will do—didn't understand cars, wandered down the block and got killed out on El Camino Real, a major thoroughfare. It was a portentous and heartbreaking event.

At this time I was the proud owner of a Honda 50 motor scooter that I rode up to campus daily. Returning home one fine spring day I rode right into and through a swarm of bees crossing the road who didn't wait for the green light and hit me like machine-gun fire. I remember instantly realizing what was happening the minute I felt the first sting. Though I was wearing a leather jacket they got inside anyway. I got stung a couple dozen times and was lucky to avoid crashing for the pain.

Sixteen months into medical school, totally preoccupied with fighting against the Vietnam War, I decided to take a leave of absence from my studies. Possibly my leaving school for an "indefinite" period (I returned a year later, but by then Irene was gone) was the event that convinced Irene I was in declination, a shooting star in a burning-up mode. We had now moved northeastward to a rented home in East Palo Alto a few blocks from where my friend, the Brown Beret and motorcycle activist Aaron Manganiello lived. The house was only two blocks from the high school where Irene taught (Ravenswood High School). We rented out our second bedroom to Steve, a "famous" political science graduate student activist and playboy. At the time I hadn't realized that a big reason Steve was famous was that he was notorious. Besides his rousing and charismatic rally speeches, he was working at seeing how many attractive undergraduate women he could bed. This didn't make the house a very cozy environment for me and my next dog, Coke, and cat, Whitey, particularly after Irene left. Once when I was outside yelling down the street for the cat, I came to the realization that a white guy yelling "Hey, Whitey" in the middle of the night in a Black neighborhood was, maybe, strange.

After Irene fled I remained clueless and more than a bit distraught by the breakup. I felt raw and very lonely. She was the only woman I had ever partnered with for more than a couple of months, ever had intercourse with; though not for wishing and sort of trying on the latter score. From the beginning of our relationship she seemed to enjoy sex as much as I did. I don't remember how we did on the Kinsey Scale Test, like simultaneous orgasms and such. I don't even remember if I understood that I had an important role to verbally explore that with her either. Did I neglect her? She'd sometimes say, "It doesn't matter." She wasn't submissive, but she was accommodatingly sweet. We had fun together. But Whitey was also too accommodating. My big German Shepherd imagined that Whitey was a toy. She'd grab him by the scruff of the neck in her teeth and shake him. Then one day when I was out she shook him till he was silly. He was unconscious when I came in. It wasn't really murder. Coke was just playing. When I rescued him Whitey wasn't actually dead yet. He was breathing and his heart was beating, but he was pretty far gone—unconscious and his muscles were flacid. I decided he was going to die, so I drove him to the marsh by the Bay several blocks away. Not knowing what else to do, I told him, apologetically, that he had to be on his own now. He remained limp, though his heart was still beating. I think he had what we now call the shaken baby syndrome and likely had permanent brain damage if not a terminal event. If it happened today, I still wouldn't know what to do—but maybe I would put him in a safer place and wait a day to see if he came around.

Irene's commodiousness was not so good a trait, being that she was married to an immature young man. At college, and even years earlier before college and certainly before I started hanging with Irene, I was fixated on the whole idea of finding at least one woman I could have sex with. I remember two very different young women I went out with in my college years who said they'd be happy to screw with me. In both cases I had been kind of set up with them—the first, a young townie from Lowell, Massachusetts I got to by my freshman year roommate who was a wolf of a guy.[29] He'd been quarterback at a well-known prep school. He invited me home one weekend. He set me up with a townie he knew and we double-dated in his folks' car. After that, the second was a friend from college at Syracuse University of my two-years-younger sister, Judy. Her friend had recently ended a relationship that was supposed to have ended in a marriage, but didn't. Her name was Susan but her nickname was Shushie. She was adorable, warm, intelligent and sexy, and lived in Coney Island. Two very different types of young women they were, in many ways, but both sexually experienced and available. When each made it clear that sex with me was fine with them, I felt so guilty about my narcissism, sullied by my own objectifying desire, that I declined their offers to fuck. Does this actually happen to other guys? A gentle way of describing my state of mind then might be: confused. I actually thought Wolf was a creep, so why did I entertain his charade in the first place and go home with him? I just did. Perceived emotional need I suppose, but I felt foolish when we returned back to Brandeis from that weekend at his folks'.

By my second year in college Wolf and I had had enough of each other. I asked for a foreign student roommate, in hopes that I wouldn't get another practical prep-jock, but someone more intellectually oriented and maybe original—perhaps someone who shared my rebellious outlook on life. My new roommate, however, was way more than different from Wolf. He was indeed a serious original. A nephew to the King of Thailand (eat your heart out Yul Brynner) and an artist, Rangrit Pramoj was super-effeminate. I had no problem

---

29 Which is to say his real family name was Wolf, but Ken Wolf was a ladies' man.

with him being gay, but given his effeminacy and his elite standing as "royalty" in a school that was oh so modern, liberal and Jewish, he stood out. At Brandeis that attracted little attention. (By the way, giving full [Larry Wein] scholarships to the kids of wealthy, powerful elites the world over was one way that Brandeis created the appearance of having a more substantial minority representation in its student body. A farce indeed.)

That second year in college I was seeing the student health's campus psychiatrist on the one hand while having a ridiculously compulsive sexual fling with a senior woman who some senior friends had sent me to to get over my sex-based neurotic guilt trip—dual therapy so to speak. The psychiatrist was a German-born-and-trained older woman (or at least she was much older compared with a 19-year-old me). She did seem very classically credible and concerned—like she was Freud's daughter, Anna, or something, but she wasn't Anna of course. I can picture her leaning back contemplatively in her large cushioned office rocking chair with a lit cigarette in her hand, speaking in soft tones with a German accent. Meanwhile, we—I mean the senior woman my friends introduced me to; her name was Esther—(she and I) had some version of neurotic sex almost every day for a few months, even practically in public—after dinner in the cafeteria when others had left, in lounges, almost anywhere. But this was nothing one could call coital…to my chagrin. I'm too embarrassed to describe the details that went on. But contrary to how Bill Clinton chose to characterize such things, it was definitely sex. I guess I was still on some kind of a narcissistic crusade, perhaps like the European conqueror-Crusaders disguised as heroic bearers of the Cross in their malevolent valedictions. But back then I did conclude, like Bill Clinton later, that I had never had sexual relations with Queen Esther —although this was 30-plus years before Monica Lewinsky hit the White House and got a foolish cheating president's semen on her dress. No, Esther didn't give me a blow job. In retrospect it does seem rather strange—i.e. that I thought we weren't actually having sex. Sex was mostly what we did together, although she was an intellectual and we had interesting conversations even during mutual arousal.

Esther had been in an emotionally and sexually abusive relationship with an older guy for some years during college—for far too long—and, with this young guy (me, that is) fawning all over her, I think she was protecting herself from being emotionally imprisoned again. I believe the prior rat abused her physically as well as sexually and emotionally. She was pretty, quite attractive. Though a bit chubby, by today's weight standards, she would likely not stand out that way. She had a warm smile, rich lips, a foxy sly look, a ponytail, wholesome breasts. My letting her say no to intercourse while sticking with her seemed to make her feel whole again. Strange thing was that she was fine with various kinds of sexual excitement except when I asked if we could fuck, which I did from time to time. I won't bore you with more prurient details.

This was 1960 and Esther had a room in the old castle (whether based on the Middle Age's European variety, fairy tales or Walt Disney I can't quite say) on campus that had apartments for upperclass women. I hung out with her there sometimes—in her room or in the empty quiet lounge. I was a sophomore, she was then a senior, I think. I brought her home to New York on Spring break and she met my parents and stayed for a while, but too long for my parents' liking. She was supposedly, she had told me, on her way to Philadelphia. That might have even been where her former abuser was situated (or maybe her parents). My parents weren't at all happy with our arrangement and begrudgingly gave her my sister's room across the hall from me. Given the nature of our relationship, that didn't matter much, so I didn't protest loudly, though there was a second bed in my room. In the middle of the night I would find her in bed with me anyway—but not fucking. My folks messed with my apparently fragile mind and successfully shattered my bond to her with their pejorative remarks. But—sex aside—she was actually quite interesting and we got along well. Esther was a math major who was politically active and had a lot to say about philosophy, history, and politics—and with her being older and intellectual, I learned a lot from her. She helped me gain my own confidence too. I don't know how she perceived our relationship, nor how badly I hurt her (if at all) when I "broke it off" back at school after the break. I worried about that, and the whole thing by then felt bad and weird. Maybe it was, but this was the Beat era, and my parents' traditionalism was going out of style. On the scale of the personal liberation that was shaking and shocking the nation, I suspect that we barely registered.

But getting back to where I left off before (which is a few years later): I don't think Irene fell in with the Cisco kid because she wasn't sexually satisfied with me. We were two youngsters, neophytes even at 23. I just wasn't paying attention enough to notice that she had other unmet needs—needed someone whose love could focus more on the relationship than I could, support her emotionally more than I was capable of—being in school, and now a sort of "dropout" doing my heroic activist thing away from the house most evenings, and with her teaching all day long with all the after-school work that teachers have to do. Looking back about 50 years it seems selfish. Ironically, I had rebelled against my own emotional selfishness when I had the chance to ball those two women back before Irene when I started dating in college; and both of them were experienced in the world of sexual pleasure; but my reaction was guilt. With Irene I didn't recognize that same self-centeredness when it was reborn because it came in a relationship I actually believed in. You know it was the time of Vietnam and civil rights and so on; and I was becoming a committed radical. I had justice on my mind, more than marital bliss. Neither of us had wanted to have kids back then.

Of course it wasn't just me that was driven into activism. We, that generation, were feeling ever more compelled, morally, emotionally, to do the right thing and Irene wasn't part of that part of my life. I had to try to end the Vietnam War whatever it took out of me; and in the end we all did make a difference, a big difference. Our ideals and much of our actions were worthy, bold, and sometimes risky and heroic. Perhaps like a death wish, we made our sacrifices and some of us did die and others did go to prison such as the members of the resistance. Muhammad Ali had his championship title taken from him. Or the Weathermen underground which I think amounted to a bunch of very smart young people acting very stupid and lacking much self-reflection of the lunacy of their behavior. I only lost my wife.

Irene didn't disagree with the activism. But she really believed that I was headed nowhere and she would be left in the lurch. She thought I'd never make it to be a doctor, let alone a butcher, a baker or a priest. It didn't quite turn out the way she suspected though. Twenty years after leaving me she died at age 50, virtually alone, forced by illness to go live back home in New England, dependent upon a hostile and judgmental Catholic mother. Irene had converted to Judaism against my wishes (though I was brought up Jewish, I gave up that kind of religion back in high school). As I said, we met in college (ironically that Jewish college) before we married; she wanted to be part of the family that way, but I wished she had consulted me first because I would have tried to stop her—maybe that's why she didn't ask my opinion. I have no idea how she dealt with that religious conversion stuff with her overbearing Italian mother later. I doubt she returned to the Catholic Church.

When I called Irene's mom's house in Somerville out of the blue one day, many years ago, I was stunned two ways to the core. Irene dead? But these supportive words from her mother? This was just a jarring surprise to me—that she hadn't cursed the day one of her three daughters married a Jew. My goodness.

I do feel that I failed Irene and particularly guilty that she hadn't wanted me there to lean on when she knew she was dying. I had leaned on her, and we spoke by phone once in a while, and yet she couldn't seek the reciprocity. Either she didn't trust me enough to even call when she knew her poor prognosis and was suffering; or else she herself felt guilty and couldn't bear the idea of pleading for support from her first ex who she had walked away from.

Irene was right to think she wasn't going to change me when I was 23; but her prediction of what would happen left, in hindsight, much to be desired. Predictions are like that. I always wonder what happened to Austin Meek. I barely knew him—a small, nondescript (to me) man. But I suspect he may have ended up an unhappy guy when, after busting up his own marriage and leaving those four kids and a wife in the lurch, his partnership with Irene lasted only a couple of years more than mine. But then my own second marriage was an even greater disaster than my first. So who am I to talk, to wonder or to judge? I shouldn't.

During our marriage kids seemed to me more than we could handle, and there was also this existential thing about how screwed up the world was (sound familiar?), so we were on the same track there, but as soon as I fell for Carrie, my second wife, the desire to procreate new creatures with her, who we would love and be bound to, hit me hard. I became more deeply and romantically inclined with Carrie and learned a negative lesson or two in that also. Emotionally, I think I saw a child as a unifying force. We did that conjugation successfully and had a daughter, but the rest of what happened— before and after—was a mess. And because there would be no successful "mediation" there, our daughter ultimately suffered serious developmental emotional losses that she surely didn't deserve.

Don't get me wrong. She's successful and has her own amazing kid, but trusting relationships are hard for her and for a long while she was looking too hard for an ideal male savior—perhaps a guy to replace that ideal (if not real) dad she never got to live with after her second birthday.

But back in Michigan in 1970, I'm sure that Carrie felt considerably less burdened by cheating on me than Irene. I vaguely remember being told one day by mutual friends—a lawyer and his wife—that she was screwing a handsome high school kid who we both knew, while I was at work at the hospital there. She was 26, doing "political organizing" with him and his high school friends. They started a "radical" newspaper for high schoolers in Dearborn, MI and she did much of the editing for them. A married woman with a child fucking a high school kid? Things went downhill between us from there. Apparently she eventually gained some sense of what damage she had done to our daughter's well-being over the years after we split, because 40 some years later—when our daughter was graduating from law school and we greeted each other after the ceremony— Carrie apologized to me "for everything". That's what I heard her say: "I'm sorry for everything." What? That was weird. Had I made her feel that guilty by remote control for 40 years? I hoped not. I think it was more her never-ending hostility toward me that eventually got to her, forcing an epiphany that maybe she should look at her own behaviors. Or maybe it was her awareness of what her daughter had lost, not only in a father but in a less-than-fulfilling mother and stepfather who did not treat her well and weren't very good parents. Somehow Carrie, after she walked away, was more angry toward me than I toward her for all that time.

I told her then, 40 years later: that it's too long ago to worry about now. Time to move on, you know. Life is too short. I wasn't just trying to be "nice". I believe it. I was a fool to have fallen for her in the first place, because she had idealized me, the activist. Once she saw through the heroic facade she conjured, she lost interest. She was a frivolous young woman who was always looking for sexual adventure or who knows what, out and about, but I guess life eventually taught her a few things. She became her new family's breadwinner, supporting her new husband throughout life. Ironically, he was considerably more emotionally domineering and male supremacist than I was.

OBLIVION: WHY ARE HUMANS STUPID? AND OTHER EXISTENTIAL THREATS (2018)

Will human civilization hit the wall before the end of the 21st century? I hope you don't believe it. I hope that you want to resist or are resisting that conjecture. But to survive, civilization must address this problem: why are humans, as a social species, always trending stupid?

Philosophically, "why" questions don't usually have good or right answers, so trying to answer them is unproductive. But, consider these thoughts: a young basketballer who worked at the YMCA (where I'm a member) cheered my Health Care for All T-shirt today. Incidentally, he's enamored of Milton Friedman, the economist who essentially founded the "Chicago School" of misbegotten capitalist deregulation that's romped destructively over and through the world's economies of less powerful nations for several decades. Z and I began talking about problems of US culture in extremis, like systemic racism, when he piped up, "Why do 'you folks' always insist on going back so far in history—it gets you mired in the past? Sure, mistakes were made. Slavery was terrible. But we've progressed, haven't we? Lincoln was better than Jefferson and we're better now than in Lincoln's day. We're solving our social problems bit by bit. Why don't we just deal with the problems of today; today is what we're up against. So let's do it."[30]

Z is a smart young lad and I'm an old coot. But smart and stupid both begin with an s and both also have a t. So, in a metaphorical comparison, they share about a third of their "genes". My point is that one can compare almost anything and make a case for that being a relevant comparison because of the power of language mobility and the imperfections of human logic. More than anything else, complex language makes us a pretty unique species. It puts our heads in the metaphorical clouds.

Now it's easy for me, or anyone, to say to Z, "He who doesn't learn from history, is bound to repeat its mistakes." But that's not what I said to Z. I won't say that to him next time either, though it's true. I won't say it because I know that such a platitude won't communicate much to him. And the purpose in communicating, after all, is to convey something meaningful—and meaning is a more complicated idea than truth. That saying about learning from history has become such a generality (or truism) that it's been drained of its actual import to the beguiled. So Z wouldn't hear its truth since he has already denied it has meaning to me. And, honestly, I sure don't think that that particular truism gets to the heart of why humans are really as stupid as we are. It's that we simply can't deal well with "conflicts in meaning" that expose our stupidity. So let me, please, tell you what I think of the how and why of stupid.

Remember Descartes? He said, "Cogito, ergo sum: I think, therefore I am." Consider this: that's a closed loop which, boiled down to its essence, doesn't actually impart anything meaningful other than

---

30 This was written back a few years ago, so with the Supreme Court just about outlawing abortion and later affirmative action in college admission, gun control, gay rights, voting rights, effort to combat the climate crisis, I can't say if Z is still locked into this viewpoint. I would hope not, but won't be surprised.

a definition: "I exist, therefore I exist." Western philosophy says it conveys the meaning of consciousness. Yes, it loosely describes consciousness, but that proves nothing, because it is true only as definitional.

On the other hand, let me say that I'm stupid partly because I actually believe that I'm so smart, sometimes thinking I'm the smartest guy around. After all, I can help people solve their problems and resolve their differences. I can pay attention and I listen to people. I know so much and have so much education and I think about so much that's big and bigger, abstract and concrete, large and subatomic and so much about logical interrelationships that I just must be really smart. Don't you think? One of my grandkids tends to (some of the time).

However, like Descarte's dictum, this too is tautological thinking that conveys nothing, yet it has no trouble claiming adherents. These statements reverb their own truth. That seems so very clever, of course, but tautological thinking is an attack on intellect, often used as a form of manipulation to gain mass adherence to almost any content. It's a trap and the source of various cult narratives and beliefs.

Millions of people believe (despite zero evidence) that Donald Trump won the 2020 presidential election and was fraudulently cheated out of the presidency. Much later all kinds of media of every political stripe were still wandering around asking those people in "Trump world" if they still believe he is the legitimate president and was cheated out of the victory. And of course his adherents say yes. And they say it with passionate belief. Most mindless fools in the media who ask this question do not probe those being interviewed on the realities—such as how then did all the court cases brought by Rudy and friends repudiate the accusations of fraud or cheating? Or, how come Trump declared the election invalid and launched plans to overthrow it BEFORE the election, not afterward, or that he demanded that his supporters employ fraud to manufacture votes or fake electors who would change the outcome? Reporters don't ask these questions because the media needs the Trumpers to not walk away. They don't want to get into a stupid argument with or be stood up by people whose entertainment value is vital to their managers.

Even when caught out about something really nasty that Trump has done, many will say, "I don't agree with that, but he's done so much for the country." Almost never does an interviewer say: "Really? Do you have a list of those things he's done that you applaud?" So, not only does the media magnify the tautological thinking of the conspiracy believers to the audience, it also affirms the belief of the beguiled that they are saying something meaningful when they aren't, strengthening their misbegotten assumptions (like, for example, in blaming Blacks or immigrants for everything that's wrong in the world). This failure of intellectual and linguistic engagement helps spread stupidity. It promotes the idea all opinions are equally based upon subjective feelings. In other words: although there is an ideological and financial basis for the particular conspiracy thinking spread by Tucker Carlson, Trump et altera, the tautological aspect of human behavior—as evidenced by Descartes' tautology—is the fundamental linguistic trap. Tautological, non-metaphorical thinking is embedded in the way that we, particularly in the "Western tradition" and more-so in the market era, now use language to shy away from exploring contradiction and the power and wisdom of dialectical analysis.

METAPHOR IS AT THE ROOT
OF LINGUISTIC INTELLIGENCE

Many living organisms communicate within their own species and even with other living forms. A good number of species have discernible and describable aural languages—birds, dolphins and whales come to mind. Others communicate in various different media—smell, touch, rhythms, visual and emotional displays (cuttlefish and octopuses most brilliantly for the latter[31]) and so forth. But it's unlikely that there is any other species on Earth that will produce dictionaries with hundreds of thousands of defined words—including words that can embody opposite definitions and meanings depending upon their usage. No other species is capable of nearly infinite possibilities in meaning through combinations and permutations of words spoken, written, sung, chanted, theatricalized. Biologic evolution brought complex language to Earth via hominids, bestowing it with incredible nuance and creating social evolution.

All evolution is experimental and empirical, not intellectual. It tries everything. Complex language is an experiment in evolution. But its use is a two-way street: meaningful or meaningless. Down in

---

31 Cephalopods' intelligence, and how their neurology better adapts them to their environment than humans to ours, will be discussed later.

one direction, as I've pointed out, is stupidity—which washes meaning, other than "social affinity", solipsism and dominance out of communication. Such stupid communication may take on the characteristic of cult thinking and social suicidality. Examples abound.

Unhappily, I think, human language came to **dominate over biologic evolution by controlling social evolution**. Through culture, human social evolution achieved independence from intrinsic genetics, and so developed its own rules going forward. And social evolution is highly manipulable. Presently, that manipulability threatens to turn humanity into a stupidly adrift species. How that works: operationalizing virtual realities that can replace intrinsic perceptions of reality is embedded in the current educational stress on math, science and technology.

Complex language (and the ideal, rule-driven theoretical language of mathematics) enables the science and technology that allowed humans to expand social existence and gain almost unbounded control over the natural world. This process empowers humans to distill "useful" meaning from that natural world. But it's also a reductionist process. For the process erodes and homogenizes meaning. It alters the myth making which originally focused on various degrees of interpenetrating creative and rational cosmology.[32] We are today replacing cosmological mythology with naive, simplistic and suicidal capitalist narrative myths and values. At this historic moment, much of the language we read, hear and see is indeed—as Trump's appointed Attorney General Bill Bar testified about the effort to create the mass belief that Biden did not win the 2020 election—no more than "pure nonsense".

Where previously "meaning" in one society and its linguistics

---

32 That over 80% of books now sold in the US are non-fiction and most people have little interest in fictional (creative, imaginative) narratives—as if they do not embody "meaning" and "understanding"—is indicative of this process.

might be undecipherable to other cultures and societies, we now have in place a universal paradigm of "pure nonsense" (meaninglessness as an explicit "market-value" in language) based in the power of money. Homogenizing cultural meaning in this way serves to enhance market penetration. It's within the rubric of "globalization"—although useful globalization actually requires an entirely new structured order sustained by a framework that expands and preserves cultural diversity.

The salient feature of "pure nonsense" in the 21st century places dominance mythology in the hands of elites who have control of the modern myth-making machinery—including religious and conspiracy sects, much of Hollywood, video games, corporate media, social media, reality TV, big tech, big pharma, the marketing industry, and the political environment.[33] Themes that provide the most effective marketing always dominate. This was already the form of the religious state (e.g. the Holy Roman Empire up through the era of the Inquisition) back in history. Unfortunately, the state under capital not only requires reverence to the older ideological sectarianism of religious fervor but it also requires stricter homogenization of cultures at the same time.

A myth promulgated by market forces screened and reverberated in my mind as I awoke this morning. It plays that a "government-run Medicare for All health insurance program" could take away from you and me the choice of doctors that we may cherish. On an intellectual level, if you've perused any actual Medicare for All bills, you'll recognize that's a flat-out lie. Privatization of Medicare (Medicare Advantage) can do that, but traditional Medicare has rules against it

---

33 Elon Musk and his Twitter gambit are just the raw tip of the iceberg. Many writers and social critics saw this coming in the mid-20th century, some even in the 19th century.

and gives individuals (and protects) the personal choices. It's written into law. But the myth is much worse than just a lie. It's a typical metastasizing social myth aimed at spreading stupidity. I'm not the only one who awoke with that mythology in my head because it's being broadcast into our brains daily, through advertising, along with all the other stupidity.

Mythology and story-telling in general may well be the human species' greatest contribution that we'll leave behind, and simultaneously the Achilles' heel that ends our branch of life's evolution. Our myths tell the tale of human experiences and wonderment and fears, but as our myths evolved and evolve, the meaning they convey diverged from the necessary evolutionary purpose they once served for earlier peoples. In the world of focused marketing manipulation, we are drawn into magical mystery tours tuned by brilliantly stupid business school grads and spectacle makers, breaking new ground, along with news purveyors and charlatans like Trump alike, rather than the rhythm of the stars or of life on this planet. Universality and harmony have been subordinated to the immediacy of marketing goals. Importantly, science and technology have been largely drained of their fundamentally social nature and value (for example, open source knowledge was turned into private intellectual property that can be owned with restricted access requiring cash on the barrel-head. Because, after all, we all need money to live in the "modern world", don't we?).

Decades ago someone came up with the news-media slogan that the news is just the filler between the ads. Demographically targeted ads, like those of insurance giants GEICO, State Farm, and Liberty are designed to capture attention, in humor, in distraction from reality, in gaining control over our feelings, our allegiance and our attention and buying habits. I myself enjoy GEICO and State Farm ads, [34] but just like ideological lies in news and editorial pieces, this

---

34 We are insured by GEICO by the way.

reorientation from cognitive to precognitive amusement induces stupidity in behavior. The declination toward absolutely non-analytical decorticated responses predicts social suicide. The process aims at re-wiring our brains to focus our attention and obedience in whatever format that marketing gurus intend. The spread of Q-Anon and other bizarre conspiracies is a product of such neural network re-structuring.

I have no idea if the march of salesmanship "progress" (replicated in political discourse) can be overcome systemically, but I am well convinced that it will not be overcome within a capitalist framework. Ironically, the Rightists and the Republican Party see that, which is why they now see socialists and communists under every rock and in every Democrat. They understand that a ruthless terrorist dictatorship is actually the only viable alternative to a necessary positive transformation of the state power into a social force existing only to achieve social purposes. That social transformation can only be achieved by ending market and money dominance in society. The Right has today almost reached their preventative autocratic goal with fascist dominance of the Supreme Court, our most powerful legal body. Thus species' survival is becoming less likely year over year under the rubric of institutions that perpetuate the decline of social intelligence.

Intelligence is fundamentally derived from metaphorical and imaginative language. That intelligence is codified in the very languages we all use through allusion and illusion and linguistic playing. Without metaphor, language—and thinking—are vacuous exercises shed of meaning.

DEATH WISH

I imagine you've heard, maybe subscribe to, the notion that risk-taking adolescents think they are invulnerable. I don't agree. Adolescents don't take risks because they think they are invulnerable. They take risks because they are aware and often afraid of their vulnerability because they don't yet understand its parameters or perimeter. They challenge their limits to understand what is possible; risk-taking is an exciting way to learn and to confront—face down—fear of the unknown. They, more than adults, are trying to cope with the terrifying existential realization that life's journey ends in death, often in pain, disability, no matter what you do or don't do in life. By 16 or 18 we've been exposed to plenty of unhappiness that wasn't fully understood by us in early years. Parents who fight or divorce; a future that remains unclear, often undefined; physical, emotional, or even sexual abuse; ambivalence about the road forward in our lives, if we have choices; rejection, failures, humiliations and successes that are measured in terms set down by society or parents. And beyond the personal, the looming social catastrophes like war, broken marriages and dreams, lack of housing, food, health care, unemployment, poverty or distressing jobs. We don't yet know who we are, how we fit in or don't, where we are going, except to a death over which we have no control. We—some? most?—recognize a conflict between values we're taught as children and the values that real adults exercise when they exploit and hurt each other.

And (now) we face larger environmental threats. What we hear of the mythic religious idea of an afterlife tends to validate that adults aren't able to cope with their own fears of death either. Unless I am an outlier, afterlife makes no more sense to a young open mind than war does. Games make sense, as long as winning and losing can be forgiven, forgotten, rejoined. But life is different and there is no "do-over". Risk-taking is a way to hurl the fear back.

My earliest experiences with death remain buried in my unconscious. My paternal grandfather died when I was about seven. My grandmother before I was born. I don't remember Grandpa. He and my father were not on good terms for many years. My father had dropped out of high school and moved away from home. When Grandpa was sick, old and alone, I believe they reconciled. One evening, perhaps I was about 11, I saw a bit of a movie on TV that I think was about World War I. A German machine-gun nest was mowing down oblivious unaware GIs as they came around the corner of some bushes or a building. Bodies were falling left and right endlessly. I went to bed but couldn't sleep. I came downstairs to my mother frightened and crying. I had believed that life must have some intrinsic value. How could people kill people so indiscriminately, negating any sense of value to a human life, just wiping out people—people like me and you? Snuffing out anonymous people who would never get another chance at life freaked me out.

Of course there is a backstory, beyond the existential, to my fear and anxiety. I was born in 1941, before the US entered WWII, but my parents were highly sensitized to what was going on in Europe before that. They were aware of Hitler's attacks on the Jews and of rampant anti-Semitism in the US. My maternal grandfather, Max Gustin, even traveled by ship to Italy to sneak two of his cousins, Ida and Dora, out before—or just as—the Jews were being rounded up to be murdered. I actually don't remember much about all this except that I did meet Ida and Dora. I'm working from and piecing together from what I heard and learned later about the Holocaust. This war, that killed as many as 50 million people (it's impossible to imagine 50 million people except as a number), didn't end until I was almost five years of age. Fear was inevitably embedded in my parents' conscious and unconscious lives, and drove many of their choices in life. I am sure I was affected by their fears and their talk—which I wouldn't have understood at three to five years of age.

Later my mom claimed that she and Dad attended the outdoor Paul Robeson concert, in Peekskill, NY on the Hudson River during the anti-communist crusades after the War. A right-wing neo-fascist gang with police backing attacked the line of buses and cars as they tried to enter the park grounds for the outdoor summer concert. The event became known as the Peekskill riots. Many people were badly injured, the concert had to be canceled and the "law" did nothing to either prevent it or to prosecute the perpetrators.

By the time I entered medical school in 1964, JFK was dead. But he had already threatened to start a nuclear war with the Soviet Union unless they withdrew their missiles from Cuba; and after the Cuban Missile Crisis he had sent 17,000 Green Beret "advisors" to prop up the US-placed dictatorship of Ngô Đình Diệm in South Vietnam (even though Hồ Chí Minh, a poet and intellectual schooled in France, had been a US ally in World War II, and Hồ admired, and sought to emulate, the democratic character of the US Declaration of Independence). In the 1964 presidential election, Lyndon Johnson who had been John Kennedy's vice president, was billed as the "peace" candidate and Barry Goldwater as the reckless Rightist who would get us into a nuclear world war. Johnson's ads showed a blooming atom bomb mushroom cloud to represent the danger of a Goldwater victory. I worked door-to-door in Palo Alto for the Johnson campaign, but Johnson's stated position as the "peace candidate" was a ruse. Upon his inauguration he initiated a massive bombing campaign against Northern Vietnam in a war that would, reportedly, claim at least two million Vietnamese lives, 58,000 Americans, leave generations—literally hundreds of thousands of young Americans—scarred for life, and Vietnam in shambles.

Vietnam's culture never fully recovered and its victory proved, to some extent, to be an illusion when Vietnam's Communist Party decided to integrate their country into the world market in typical developing capitalist neo-colonialist fashion, turning their peasants and urban workers into subservients of transnational capital. Uncle Hồ, as he was known, had died before the end of the Vietnam War. He would not have been appreciative of what became of their revolution.

Sheila and I visited Vietnam in the early 1990s just as that evolution to capitalist integration was about to go into full swing. We went with San Francisco's Global Exchange organization and met many different types of people there, including government and party figures and ordinary Vietnamese. Our tour guide was a former NVA soldier. At a meeting in Danang (once a major US airbase) I asked a communist official if Vietnam was prepared to allow or prevent money (foreign investments) from simply taking over their economy and culture. He responded that the party had plans and would never allow that. He was either deluded or lying. I will never know, but they did not put up much resistance, to my mind. They needed to develop rapidly.

As a result of the Vietnam War, and the fact that two key political science faculty at Brandeis during my student years (1959–1963) were among the key ideological designers, advisers and defenders of that war of aggression, I rapidly became a left-wing "radical" convinced that US policy was not driven by democratic ideals but by the need to dominate the world market for US economic penetration: i.e. imperialism. By the time that I took a one-year leave of absence from medical school in late 1965, I thought that dying in the resistance against aggression by my own country would be a noble way to die. Three years later, after our movement's many confrontations with Stanford University over its military involvement with the war, I joined the Revolutionary Union, and by late 1971 I was in Venceremos. In that period I assumed that many of us would die fighting against the greatest military power on Earth; after all, our romantic ideas were further fueled by the CIA hunting down and killing our heroes, like Che. This idea of dying while fighting for justice and freedom for all held no great sense of fear for me, for us, because of the power of its intentionality. Death would be merely the cost of our dedication to creating a better world for future generations. Likewise, if we had to go to prison, it was the price to pay for a brighter future for our nation and our world. Death in fighting for one's beliefs eliminates the existential sense of powerlessness in the face of forces greater than life itself. The thought of simply growing old and dying without that moral intentionality was considerably more frightening to me, and yet here I am, on this treadmill, still trying to fight the good fight, and as confused and puzzled as ever about what is to be done.

I'll admit this: fighting for a just world can sometimes reflect a way that people hide their own fears and insecurities about challenging the exigencies of a more ordinary personal life. That Brandeis psychiatrist was right about that. But there is also a different truth involved in this kind of almost "death wish". The truth is that death is what gives life meaning. A willingness to die fighting for a firmly held belief brings death into one's life as a twin partner to life itself, establishes the value of life, brings meaning to our choices, to who we are and what we do (or don't) leave behind us for posterity. Of course, approached in the grandiose way that my mind often did, death was also a way to look my fears in the mirror and to refuse to give in to their depressing impact. I was also talking to myself. Thus my Quixotic title.

Earlier, I wrote that adolescents take risks in order to explore the limits of life and the boundary between life and death. That then is the sense in which death gives meaning to life. It's only through a kind of denial that Western culture trains people to remove death from its central role in our being. Human consciousness of past, present, future—of time itself—requires that death be ever-present and thought-provoking.

Earlier I also alluded to our friend, BG, who was chronically depressed and suicidal. She was an active person—socially active, politically active—and she worked hard enough to get a PhD and become a sociology professor back East. B married a doctor I know, a public health physician who has also done good things for workers related to investigating and exposing causation and remediation of industrial and environmental catastrophes/exposures. So on its face they were both contributing valuable social benefits to our nation and culture. But even before they married, J knew that BG had attempted suicide in the past; and that her own mother had killed herself. So death lurked within B's breast in a different way from how it resides in most people's.

B's suicide occurred at the pinnacle of her personal success after she had achieved a professorship and taught successfully for a while in that position at a prominent university. She was well received both by students and colleagues. Her life had reached its greatest social meaning, and perhaps within that reality her success wasn't enough to annul the helplessness and desperation she felt to her core, as bequest from her mother. Unlike adolescents, B's exploration was not about learning the limitations of, the parameters and perimeters of life. She had done all that. What she was exploring—undoubtedly with the unrequited memory of her mother and the meaning of that suicide—was death as a conscious act, as a reflection of a sense of her own life's unmeaning.[35] For us, who wish to live and be happy and ful-filled for as long as possible, the act of suicide is not translatable into meaning. But for someone like B, death (as opposed to its partner) was itself the embedded meaning of her life. Most suicides are intentional. By definition, then, they have some meaning to the suicidist, even if it is that life was too painful to be allowed to dominate the dialectical dance of finity.

---

35 F. Dostoyevsky explores this process through a suicidist in his novel, *Demons*.

THE RUN AWAY DISEASE

Running from the Devil

Drapetomania was a supposed mental illness described by American physician Samuel A. Cartwright in 1851 that caused Black slaves to flee captivity.[1]:41 Today, drapetomania is exposed as an example of pseudoscience,[2]:2 and part of the edifice of scientific racism.[3] (Wikipedia).

(below "Billie"—a song I wrote about running away, circa 1965: in C maj/A min)

Once I ran, till the earth met the deep blue sky,
And there I swam, like a fish in deep water.
And as I roamed, afraid to know where I belonged,
These thoughts called out to me, Billie where can you be free,
And I heard her muffled cries, she knows I have not died.

Run says me, and drown yourself in the cool swell sea,
Fly says the sky, to a world that is built on high,
But lying awake at night, far beneath the stars so bright,
I heard her muffled cries, she knows I have not died.

I remember the morn we first knew, that a child would be born
    to you,
And the glorious look in your eyes, when I said that we would flee
    and hide,
From this land of fire, with its deacons beneath the sacrificial pyre
To some far-off shore, where fear would be no more.

'Nigger' they said to me, we're gonna hang you from the nearest tree,
Right there I closed my eyes, hoping for a while that I would die;
But she called out to me, Billie you can run away and still be free,
And some day I will come, and bring to you your son.

Then I ran, till the earth met the deep blue sky,
And there I swam, like a fish in deep water,
And as I roamed, afraid to know where I belonged,
These thoughts called out to me, Billie where can you be free,
And I can see her dark brown eyes, she knows I have not died.

Being neither Black nor having a slave ancestry, I had no reason to run away, but that didn't stop me. Moreover, my father had run away from home at the age of 16 and started a new life. I don't think that worked out for the best (though he might disagree because he worked, got married, had two kids, moved to the burbs, held his family together and provided me with all the opportunities that he had not had growing up). My dad had solid traditionalist values. Nevertheless, he had his first heart attack at age 52 and was dead ten years later. Stress played a big role. I don't think his life was one of great joy or fulfillment, although he was starting to get there when he was cut down; in the 1960s I carved a woodcut that I titled "rainman". (it's of a sad man's face, suspended in air, somewhat reminiscent of Dad, with rain falling all about him).[36] For me, growing up in that family, I often heard my parents arguing, and by adolescence I often thought that they would have been better off getting a divorce. Mom's family—her parents and four sibs—had its internal problems too, but they all hung together. Dad fit in there, but stoically in my view.

There was much sadness in my dad's life. He had opened a large machine and tool company, a storefront on Bruckner Blvd in the Bronx that went bankrupt in 1948 when I was seven, just as my parents were buying us a suburban home in Yonkers. To assure a regular income he threw in with my mother's parents and brother and brothers-in-law in the Gustinettes shoe-manufacturing business.

Like a lot of first generation-born Americans of that era my father saw me—his first and only son—as his own personal redemption. This is never a good idea. Our kids have to seek and find their own paths. They may love us and honor us, they may learn values and a lot more from us, but they need to also follow their own "chi" as the saying goes. I did run from my father once, though I can't remember exactly what triggered my behavior. I was about 14 (maybe even 16) at the time and he told me to do something or he criticized me. Why that irritated me a lot then I don't know, but I refused; indeed I both rebuffed and then disrespected him with some epithet. He got up and started for me, and I ran out the front door and up the block. It was an idyllic spring afternoon. My dad hadn't had his first heart attack yet and, despite being overweight at around 230 or so pounds on his six foot, not-well -conditioned frame, he still had the sprinter in him. He had run track and speed skated in high school. I got about 200 yards up the block before he ran me down, grabbed me by the collar and took me home;

---

36 I learned the art of woodcutting and printing at summer camp one year. Three of my woodcuts are hung on the walls of my study. Two are semi-abstract; the third is titled *Vietnam Conscience* as was printed in an arts newsletter when I was in medical school.

there he hit me a few times across the butt with his belt—which was a first for both of us. I was so terrified by his anger (something he had rarely shown) that I didn't even feel the belt.

That was the first time I ran from the man to whom my life was tethered, but it was not the first time that I had run away from an upsetting situation. I've mentioned elsewhere that around the age of ten, on the first day of summer camp I ran away from my counselors and hid for what seemed like a long while in the woods under a black birch (the wintergreen tree, which was my favorite Connecticut tree—I had learned to chew on small branches for their remarkable flavor) until I was coaxed to come out of hiding by calls from a search group. This was not my first summer at Camp Ella Fohs—a place I loved. Who upset me? What was said? Why did I flee? I can't say. But I calmed down and surely I was well treated and understood because I enjoyed that summer experience as I had the previous year, became an excellent swimmer, socialized well, loved the sports, learned to harmonize folk music, to canoe, gunnelling, and caught my fill of frogs and turtles with open hands. Yet, I was still trying to learn how to survive the slings and arrows of perceived insults in the human world.

Two years later, at PS 15 down below the hill we lived on (Colonial Heights), we began to have different teachers and classrooms for different subjects in 7th grade. We were now junior high schoolers. I enjoyed the move back to PS 15 from PS 28 (which was nearer to home where my teachers—Ms. Shafer, 5th grade, and Mrs. Fee, 6th grade—had been wonderful during the first two years that new elementary school had been opened). But now it felt like we were finally growing up and being treated more like adults. I was a good and generally obedient student, but one day the male social studies teacher—whose face, and thick black-rimmed glasses, but not name, I now see before me—used ridicule against one of the other students. I stood up and yelled at the teacher, called him a jerk or something, and ran out of class, and all the way home. I think my mother and I had to meet with the principal the next day, but I don't think there was collateral fallout from either my behavior or the teacher's. It was a declarative sign that I was planning to have a problem with the blind and crass exercise of authority, which made me feel very fragile. I think I was 12 years old.

That next summer I went away to Camp Ella Fohs again, to the camp just north of New Milford, Connecticut run by the YMHA of the greater Bronx. The camp director, Barney Lambert, was a friend of my parents from when we lived in the Bronx. His family lived not far from us in Eastchester. This was the third year I had attended the camp. I think Barney, like a lot of my parents' friends, was part of the Left movement.

Barney Lambert, whose kids also attended the camp, did a great job making it a nurturing and culturally exciting environment for children. There were scholarships for some and so a very diverse— ethnically, culturally, and economically—camper population. Performers like Pete Seeger would occasionally show up to play and sing with us. I would later serve as a counselor at Ella Fohs. That year, however, was the year I migrated from the wooden cabins the younger kids stayed in to the tents of the proud and pubescent teen-agers. Though attracted to "sexy" girls, I wasn't even close to puberty at that age and the mixture of kids who were and weren't proved not so friendly. Like most boys I knew plenty about sex by that age, even if it wasn't from first-hand experience with girls. But insecurity, or whatever kinds of needs he had, caused one of the boys to go around telling the bigger boys that I thought women got pregnant through their belly button or some such nonsense. Compared to what we hear of bullying these days in schools, this wasn't much in the way of hurtful. Nobody beat me up; I was just being embarrassed. How-ever, the intimidation factor was real and calling the fellow out and denying his myth (which I did) doesn't really get one much currency in that type of situation. I may or may not have given him a shove or two, but, as I say, I was still a small kid just around five feet tall and that might not have been a reasoned response. In any case, though I didn't run into the woods that time, I did make a decision not to go back to camp the next year and I stuck to it firmly.

And I wasn't yet finished with the running away. For it often struck me that the world was not a very welcoming place for people. And that hostility that I sensed in various environments never seemed just personal to me. In other words, when I came up against things that upset me I rarely thought that it was only against me, even when it was me that felt the hurt. I wasn't paranoid, yet my sensitivity to insult and assault was keen and left me highly tuned to perceived injustices. I think I absorbed a lot of this from my early childhood environment rather than my genes—a young child during World War II, the Holocaust, anti-Semitism in the US at the time, and then the McCarthy era with many of my parents' friends accused or taken off to jail. None of this was in my consciousness. Even though I knew that Frankie Emspak's (a classmate of my sister I believe) father (a United Electrical Workers' Union leader and a well-known communist) was in prison, we weren't close with that family and a lot of these things were around the edges, the periphery of my life. But the gestalt of that world created a scary undertow. I was preparing to fight back, but I didn't yet know against what or whom.

ON BECOMING A FARM WORKER DOC—MY TIME WITH CESAR CHAVEZ AND THE UFW (1973–1978)

(An older version of this essay, written in 2005, is posted with hundreds of others by former UFW staff on the website: https://libraries.ucsd.edu/ farmworkermovement.

In April 1973, a year and a half after the heroin-addled Vietnam vet held a gun pointed at my head, I began working with the United Farm Workers union one afternoon a week as a volunteer doc in their new Salinas clinic, actually a two-bedroom house at 1047 East Alisal. Two years later, in April 1975, facing yet another type of personal crisis in my life, I joined the National Farm Workers' Health Group (NFWHG, run by the UFW Union) full time, remaining on staff with La Union for almost four years. At the end I was the only practicing physician left on staff from a remarkably dedicated group that had staffed five NFWHG clinics up through 1978. Among clinic volunteers many went on to become nurse practitioners, physicians assistants, physicians, and health para-professionals. The UFW paid for the medical training of one dedicated UFW volunteer (Marion Moses) but by the time she finished her training the five clinics had been closed and Marion's chosen area of expertise and interest (farm workers' pesticide exposure and other work-related problems) could not be incorporated within our clinical program because the clinics were gone.

All memory is selective. Some parts of this essay are based upon available documents, but others are just my best recollections. Like most of the volunteers with the UFW, I have both enriching and troubled memories of those times. In preparing this essay I read through the excellent pieces by Gilbert Padilla, Dan Murphy, Margaret Murphy, and Kathy Murguia on the https://libraries.ucsd.edu/farmworkermovement website before I started. When I wrote LeRoy Chatfield to ask if I might still post a piece he asked if I would include my thoughts on why the clinics closed. I will. Anyone who reads the posted essays will gain a good background on the UFW movement, thanks to LeRoy's hard work that went into creating the project.

In early 1973 Margaret Murphy heard of me and called at home. I agreed to work an afternoon a week at the new Salinas clinic. Having resigned my Obstetrics and Gynecology residency in New York in late 1971, I was now a general practitioner working only part time for Santa Clara County Health Department in their teen clinics. Sheila and I had recently moved to East San Jose, in fact to the Latino barrio, "sal si puede"—get out if you can—not to be confused with "si se puede"—yes we can—where the CSO (the Community Service Organization) had its office. Cesar Chavez cut his "eye teeth" with the CSO. Sheila and I had been to UFW support events and boycott lines and so were generally known among people Margaret would have asked for medical contacts.

In July 1973, a few months after I began volunteering in the Salinas clinic, a 55-mile drive south of San Jose, Sheila and I drove to Southern California to support the grape strike around Arvin and Lamont. The growers were feeling the workers' pressure and had signed sweetheart contracts with the Teamsters Union who suddenly claimed to represent the workers on the ranches. The Teamsters brought goons to the UFW picket lines to intimidate the workers and physically attack organizers and strikers.

At a tree-shaded park where the strikers and their supporters were rallying and organizing, we heard Cesar speak. We witnessed his charisma, the sincerity and humility in the way he listened to small groups of farm workers here and there trying to hear directly from them their concerns about the ranches they worked on, how the strike should be organized. We could see what an effective and coherent leader Cesar was.

The next day, while we were on the strike lines, my family back in New York sent word through the union that my father had died unexpectedly while on a trip to Europe with my mother. I left Sheila in Arvin and flew back to New York for the funeral. When I returned to Northern California, I learned that Sheila was in jail in Bakersfield with a group of farm worker women, some badly mistreated by goons and police. After Sheila was released—unharmed—and returned to San Jose, we formed a small farm worker support committee with friends, did some picketing and leafleting and got Gallo Wines removed from the Pink Elephant liquor store on King Road (a block from our home) and from several other stores in East San Jose. Later we launched a successful effort to get scab grapes removed from the Alum Rock School District's lunch menu. We thought the district's ignoring the grape boycott to be of particular importance because the vast majority of students in the Alum Rock District—in which our children were students—were Mexican-Americans.

In April of 1975, as detailed elsewhere, I decided to leave San Jose and offered to join the NFWHG medical staff full-time. Dr. Dan Murphy was then working alone at the Rodrigo Terronez clinic at Forty Acres in Delano, after three other docs left suddenly. I was assigned to the Delano clinic and I moved down with my German Shepherd. In this era I had a 1959 baby blue Ford Galaxie 500 convertible purchased for a few hundred dollars. When the Galaxie died on the road just outside UFW Headquarters in La Paz on my first visit there, I sold my Honda 450 motorcycle and bought a used Chevy Nova (the "white box"), with a 327 cu. inch engine and a stiff racing clutch. It was a menace—very difficult to prevent stallings.

After agreeing to work for the union I was offered an apartment in the Agbayani village at Forty Acres, about 50 yards walk from the clinic. There I lived alongside the retired, mostly Filipino, single male farm workers, who were wonderful company for this suddenly bachelored 34-year-old Anglo-with-large-dog. I heard their stories and learned how the "village" was designed and built from Chris Braga. Chris was a young LA activist who had spearheaded the retirement village effort for the UFW. I also became friends with Filipino-American Philip Vera Cruz, one of the UFW founders, and a vice president of the UFW board of directors.

Dr. Dan Murphy was a few years older than me. He became my mentor in medicine, and a good friend; Dan far outstripped me in basketball skills as well. He had a great outside jumpshot and was ferocious under the boards (even at six-foot three). Dan was the main man in the clinic in the best sense of the word. I can add little to his essay's description of the clinic function. But I'll relate a few vignettes from my own experiences.

I remember the oppressive heat of the Central Valley that summer. Someone raised in cooler climes could seriously begin to appreciate what farm worker life in the fields might be like in the heat of summer. On a given day it might be freezing cold or broiling hot in the early pre-dawn hours, but always over 100 degrees in mid-afternoon. One night the lowest temperature overnight outdoors was 99 degrees (God knows what it was inside). Sleepless, around midnight I dragged a mat or sleeping bag to use as a cushion onto the grass in front of the clinic and lay down next to a small row of artichoke plants in bloom. There was a full moon and I could see everything at

Forty Acres clearly. I slept only fitfully in the heat, knowing a hard day's work lay ahead in clinic. The next day I called Sheila in San Jose and asked if I could bring down our only window air conditioner to put in my room. By then, only three months since I had moved, we were visiting each other back and forth (and we would soon be back together for good—a reunion that has lasted these many years). I told her I could pick up the cooler on my weekend visit (Dan and I rotated weekends on-call). Sheila agreed.

My seven months with Murphy were like a three-year Family Practice residency in quick time. I learned Spanish on the job. When I asked Dan for a translator my first day he said, "We can't afford staff for that. You'll learn faster without it." (In truth I did have some rudimentary Spanish from working in the Salinas clinic, and I was able to learn fast enough.) Dan's essay is accurate in that there was no medical challenge that he/we would not accept. If he thought he was in over his head and the extensive clinic library could not clear the muddy water for a diagnosis and treatment plan, Dan had a marvelous stable of academic experts all over the state to call on the phone or to ask to see our sickest and most complicated patients. I remember a young recent immigrant farm worker about 19 who came in with a sore throat. But just looking I could see it wasn't merely a sore throat. He had a white necrotic mass back there by one tonsil. We got him to the right people at UCLA or USC within a day. He was rapidly diagnosed with a malignant lymphoma and begun on a radiation and chemotherapy regimen. Although this unfortunate young man died within a month, I knew that he had gotten the best care that the US could offer for his aggressive disease in 1975.

It was from Dan that I learned to take up such challenges and stay in the middle of the total health care process. That is the best way to assure good, comprehensive care with continuity and support for the patient. You learn, you teach, you motivate and are motivated to be exceptional. Those experiences served me well later in my career when I became the medical director of the Center for Elders' Independence in Oakland, a position I retired from in 2001 after nine-plus years. CEI is part of the Program of All-inclusive Care for the Elderly (PACE) keeping frail elders in the community to the end of life. It is based upon the same "si se puede" (yes we can) ethic as the UFW and the philosophy of integrating a collective professional culture of caring and curing into the culture of the community being served; breaking down barriers.

By that first summer Dan Murphy and his wife had decided to take their first vacation in many years. They left the clinic to me and Dan's Murphy-trained staff of barefoot doctors and nurses. All went well except for that week's baby production. I think there were eight or so, but every one of those kids decided to come in the middle of the night. Maybe these ninos knew I was alone and were trying to make sure they didn't take away clinic hours for farm workers, but by the time Dan returned I had spent several sleepless nights delivering babies and was pretty frazzled.

By then we had moved the deliveries out of the clinic and into the Delano Community Hospital, something I had advocated for. Before Dan went on vacation we had had a situation regarding the deliveries in the clinic that worried me. There were two lying in beds for 24-hour care at the clinic. If we had people who needed overnight intravenous fluids or other care that could be achieved without hospitalization we would do it there. But those beds were also the beds where women, postpartum, stayed with their babies until they were stable enough to go home.

One day we ended up with a woman and her infant in one bed and a patient with a rather florid gastroenteritis (a bacterial diarrhea) in the other bed. I thought this was a serious problem, and that it would be best if we categorically reserved the beds for sick people and moved the deliveries to the community hospital. Dan's response was that we needed to avoid the pitfalls of hospital admission and the serious problems within the US health care system that farm workers faced—from language barriers to racism to financial issues to immigration status. Although this argument had traction with me also, I thought safety was of greater concern at that moment. But I wasn't the one making the decisions.

Despite my great respect for Dan, I decided to go over his head. I talked with Esther the clinic manager first, but Cesar came to talk with me. I told him my concerns, and suggested that we move the deliveries to hospital. Cesar heard me out, took my concerns very seriously and he asked Dan to change the clinic policy. I was, of course, impressed that Cesar was willing to hear me and pleased that he took what I said seriously. I knew how much Dan respected Cesar and I was sure there would be no bitterness on Dan's part if Cesar thought that there was a danger to the UFW, the clinic, and farm workers should an infection spread to a newborn or mother. Thankfully that never occurred.

There were a couple of other obstetrical dramas that stand out in my mind. Among other things, they showed how Dan stayed focused and undaunted in a crisis. Before we stopped doing deliveries at Forty Acres, one day we had a delivery during clinic hours where a baby was born in terrible condition. Dan attended the delivery and I was there assisting him. I think Murphy made some limited attempt at resuscitation but I could see he wasn't seriously into it, which wasn't like him. In a short while it was clear the baby was not going to breathe with or without help and he allowed it to die peacefully. After consoling the mother Dan and I sat down across the hall and he pulled out a book from the expansive library. "That's what I thought it was," he said to me. "Potter's syndrome. This baby has no functioning kidneys and underdeveloped lungs. He was doomed. He wasn't going to breathe and there was no chance of survival."

"How did you know he had that?" I asked. "It was the chin and face," he responded. "Go back and look at the face and you'll see he has no chin, a beaked nose. I noticed it when I tried to intubate him. The features are a telltale sign." "Were you sure?" I asked him. "Hell no," he responded. "I was anxious and sweating bullets that we might have an unexplained neonatal death on our hands, but at the same time I was **almost** positive I had it right." It was this balance between self-examination and honesty on the one hand and a determination to learn and to go all out to assure the best for the patients, the farm workers, and the UFW that I admired most in Murphy.

Another time I was on call at the clinic and a woman came in around midnight, in labor. She had had many children before which can sometimes cause postpartum problems. The delivery was quick and routine around 2:30 or 3 a.m., but afterward as I waited and waited and waited—well over 15 minutes—the placenta did not separate and the woman began to bleed. She wasn't bleeding heavily but I was a bit anxious and tried to coax the process by pulling on the cord. Though I was experienced in deliveries and knew not to pull hard, but gradually and gently, I obviously pulled a bit too hard for along with the placenta the uterus turned inside out (inverted). Though the woman had not lost a lot of blood, the inversion caused her blood pressure to fall dramatically. I put in a second IV line, turned both lines wide open, broke into a sweat, and rushed across the hall to a phone and woke up Murphy. "What do I do?" "I think you just push it right back with your gloved hand," he said. "But I'm sure it's there in the book. Look it up in the OB book."

Oh my God I thought, *is there time for this?* But as I was hanging up the phone there was a loud pounding on the back door to the clinic, no more than 20 feet from where I was. I ran to open the door and in walked a traveling obstetrician-gynecologist friend of Dan's and the union's who had serendipitously showed up in town and had been out jogging in the middle of the night (I know it's hard to believe). It took only a minute to tell him the situation and he confirmed Dan's advice. "Nothing to it," he said. "It's happened to me and others. I'll watch over your shoulder for moral support while you do it. Just put on a sterile glove, make a fist and you'll push it back into place." I did and the woman did well.

The parents of one of the babies I delivered while Dan was away bestowed the greatest of honors on me, asking if I would be the baby's godfather in a church ceremony. I couldn't say no, but I asked them if it mattered to the church that I was Jewish. No it didn't. I worried whether I deserved this honor, knowing that I could easily disappear from their lives even before the child would have any relationship with me. But I accepted nonetheless. At times I dwell on the thought that I betrayed their trust in losing track of them when I left Delano only a few months later. And I wonder what happened to that child, who now would be 30 years old. But I also believed they just wanted to give thanks and were proud to be able to offer this honor to a union doctor.

By the end of summer it was quite clear both that Sheila and I were back together and since she was committed to continuing her work as a union organizer (UE) in National Semi-conductor's computer chip fabrication factory in Silicon Valley, I would be moving back to San Jose. I told the union and Dan that I wanted to stay with the UFW full time but to remain a UFW doc I would need to transfer to the Salinas clinic. I'm sure the leaders, from Dan and Esther Uranday at the clinic to Margaret Murphy and others at Delano and La Paz, were disappointed with this decision. They needed support for Murphy in Delano. But somehow they would find someone else and, deciding that half a loaf is better than none, they convinced leadership to allow the move.

But soon there was a trade-off. Dr. John Radebaugh, a board certified pediatrician, who manned the UFW clinic in Sanger (near Fresno) had become demoralized by the siphoning off of clinic staff for other union roles, causing functional problems in keeping the clinic going. John took (to my mind) the inappropriate action of publishing a broad critique of UFW leadership dysfunction in *The New England Journal of Medicine (NEJM)*. I didn't understand John's action. Although I knew that many of his criticisms deserved consideration, why he thought publishing internal union problems in a prestigious national medical journal could help the UFW or farm workers was beyond me. If he wasn't going to bring his issues to some forum within the UFW, John could have just resigned. Dr. Joe Goldenson and I submitted a response to John to the *(NEJM)*. The UFW was having so much trouble recruiting physicians that we needed to let young doctors know that the positives of providing health care within the farm workers' movement clearly outweighed the difficulties. And that their help was needed and would be welcomed with heartfelt gratitude.

Years later, back in San Jose, John and I became colleagues when he was faculty with the San Jose Hospital Family Practice residency. He worked occasionally as a fill-in for our pediatrician at the Gardner Community Health Center in the Sacred Heart Church in the Latino community when I was medical director there. One day John saved the life of a baby at Sacred Heart whose heart stopped right in the clinic.

Though the union had no way to replace John, leadership decided to fire him immediately. I was asked by Kathy Murguia to keep the Sanger clinic open. I agreed to drive down from San Jose and work two days a week there (with the other three days a week in Salinas) but for a limited time only (two to three months). The Sanger clinic was not doing hospital care like Delano. I knew I couldn't sustain that clinic for very long with a four-hour drive each way (in comparison my daily drive from San Jose to Salinas was only one hour). But at least I could give the union time to recruit a replacement for John and, if not that, to decide on an alternative plan (closing was not the only option because, for one example, Fresno General Hospital had physician residency training programs and might be induced to take over the clinic; for another there were non-profit clinics in the area that might have agreed to take over the patient load if enough patients were insured by the UFW's RFK insurance plan; for a third, recruiting a graduating resident from somewhere to begin in July 1976 was always a possibility).

Working in Sanger I gained a farm worker family of lifelong friends (the Santos family) in Reedley. They offered that I could stay overnight weekly in their camper. Aurelio Santos and his wife, Rosa Marta, originated and co-lead the Reedley Social Services Center providing legal assistance to many farm workers. Aurelio was a volunteer in the Sanger clinic. But faced with its many other problems and priorities, the UFW did not find a way to keep the clinic open during that time and the Sanger clinic closed later in 1976 after I left.

When I decided to work full time with the UFW I had no financial reserves. Sheila's job at National Semiconductor was paying barely more than minimum wage (though she had additional income from a family trust). If I were to make farm worker union health care my life's work—which was my intent by the time I left Delano—I thought we needed some minimum income from the work. The vast nationwide boycott movement and the UFW volunteer staff had been recruited around the same moral imperatives as the civil rights movement. People acted/participated because of their belief in "la causa". There were few material benefits, just the joy of working together for what we believed in, and the cultural sustenance of joining the farm worker community. To change that, to create material incentives as the basis for employment with the UFW, could have weakened the movement and, besides, the UFW had essentially no money to spare. I knew these things, but I also knew that there was a big difference between recruiting idealistic youths to join the farm workers' movement for two years—or Catholic liberation theologists seeking to re-dedicate their lives to their calling through the UFW— and lawyers and doctors, often with big debts, who were being asked to forgo the incomes available to them as career professionals. The union agreed to pay me $600 a month, plus $50 per child (by now there were three) for a total of $750 per month, the same as they were paying legal staff.

I know that some others also received such stipends. However, the idea of getting paid some basic wage never became part of physician/ nurse recruitment efforts. I recall having discussions with union staff people (like Kathy Murguia) in which I argued that some basic stipend was necessary if we were going to recruit enough medical professionals to make the NFWHG clinics a permanent institution that could grow and prosper for the farm workers. Although I don't remember if I had any opinion on the legal staff asking to raise their monthly income to 900 or 1,000 dollars, I do remember that I thought all permanent staff of the union could only be retained if there was some salary. For me personally, even the small sum of $750 a month made it easier to be able to stay with the UFW indefinitely, barring unforeseen events.

However, unforeseen events did indeed occur. On Sanger: the closing of the Sanger clinic revealed that the UFW was having trouble recruiting new physicians. However, this recruitment problem was not the ultimate cause of the closing of any of the clinics. The maelstrom that ended the NFWHG swirled around larger events.

In Kathy Murguia's essay she reveals she lost her twins, born premature at 28 weeks while living under stressful conditions in the auditorium of Father Boyle's Sacred Heart Church in San Francisco. Years after losing her twins, now with a flock of healthy children, Kathy and her husband Lupe were assigned to the Cleveland boycott, only to be relocated to Detroit that same year. This, she writes, took a toll on her children and she realized that she had to protect herself and her family's needs because no one else would do it for her. She didn't quit, but did place certain conditions on her continuing— as I had myself.

I doubt that there has ever been a political movement with great ideals and goals that did not demand everything from its adherents and in the process unintentionally damaged many of those adherents. Belief is the mother of motivators and can easily override our attention to personal needs and details. But beyond the altruism there is also much left unspoken in this paradigm. There is also the asceticism of monks meditating and hibernating in catacombs until death, the self-flagellation of extreme believers. The damage we can do ourselves to prove our worthiness is not always unintentional; sometimes it seems like a purification.

I think Kathy was in charge of the NFWHG during much of my UFW service and she was open-minded, supportive and did a great job. She went through this battle within herself, remaining in the heart and heat of the struggle for many years. I can imagine the tendency of people close to the center of the movement believing that to put personal needs on a par with those of la causa was a betrayal. Kathy was there in La Paz when I joined up and she was there when I left in 1978. Sometime in the late 1990s I received a call from Kathy's son who had learned about the inner union turmoil of the earlier period when he was a child. He wanted to know my views and experiences regarding things that happened.

I know that depersonalizing events can lead to a sterile reportage, yet the personal perspective presented alone can dull the intellectual assessment each of us might want to bring to the process of recollection and evaluation. Larger mistakes of the past that we pass over without notation and discussion are likely to be repeated over and over again.

Was the reluctance of many UFW staff to discuss UFW controversies a result of loyalty to Cesar's memory and courage? Or something more troubling? In any event, it seems to me that union leaders of that period are still holding back from a productive analysis of the general crisis within the union that began somewhere around 1974–1976. That crisis culminated in the purging of a significant proportion of the staff's volunteers, the closing of all the clinics and the firing of the legal department. I believe it also coincided with a declination in contracts and the weakening of much of the national support movement (by the 1980s). Some have suggested the crisis around the loss of Proposition 14 was the root problem (in 1975, I was working so hard in the Delano clinic that I really had almost nothing to do with that monumental event in UFW history). Some have raised the specter of COINTELPRO as the gorilla hidden in this closet. Perhaps. Others write of the coming of reactionary times as Ronald Reagan became president and as the Agricultural Labor Relations Board (ALRB) faltered and fewer elections were protected and upheld. But truth be told, it will take the frank and open assessments of many people from within the UFW's center to ever usefully understand these problems and processes. I was too far out on the periphery to contribute much.

However, Margaret Murphy's essay reveals in a subtle and sensitive fashion a number of the little things that would later summate into crises. She mentions Cesar's firmly held opposition to the clinics giving out birth control. She points out that pressed by the needs of farm worker women, the clinics handled the issue on an individual basis, taking their lead from the workers. That is both true and a gentle way of saying that we tried to do what was right for the workers without getting into a policy debate with Cesar, an argument we, as volunteers, and non-farm workers, could not win. However, Margaret's remark is only four-fifths true. Somewhere in 1976 Cesar got very inflamed when he heard that various types of birth control were still being given out at clinics and he issued a written edict from the president. I recall a confrontation with the Coachella clinic staff which sent a letter to Cesar openly defying his order.

As in the case of John Radebaugh, I thought this a reckless move. All the clinics were following the non-policy (non-defiance) approach in the way that Margaret discusses in her essay; trying to be for the farm workers, without going against Cesar. What we had to do was avoid a challenge to Cesar's leadership. That could come to no good end. In Salinas we never stopped giving out birth-control which farm workers wanted and needed, but we also never had a confrontation with Cesar over this. In the end I believe that the birth-control conflict was the proximate cause of the second clinic shutdown, at Coachella. But I doubt that it was the fundamental cause.

Margaret, almost in passing, mentions the names of two people who were brought in to La Paz around 1976 to implement a process of transforming the UFW to "business" trade unionism. This was one of the stories of a coming disaster foretold. Cesar himself had forged the idea in the 60s of merging the Filipino Union and the National Farm Workers Union under the banner of a political and cultural "movement" of and for farm workers, rights. La Causa, La Raza, these were social, cultural calls that drew into the fight hundreds of thousands of farm workers and their supporters. The AFL-CIO could never have achieved the successes of the UFW by using old-fashioned economic trade unionism, ignoring problems beyond wages and working conditions. The UFW was addressing housing, poverty, health care, ethnic and national discrimination, and the culture of the Mexicanos, Filipinos, Arabs and other groups ground into the rich earth of California by indifferent millionaire farmers, agribusiness and the larger political system. It was clearly a political movement for farm worker rights, not just a trade union. Yet by the late 70s the AFL had much influence within the core (not only with Cesar).

The ideology of the "movement" Cesar had spawned could not withstand a contradiction with the AFL's conception of how to solve poor union management techniques. After all, poor management was a problem. Someone might write an entire book about how George Meany and the AFL (and the California Democratic Party) gained such a high level of influence within the UFW. Perhaps such a book would start from the moment Meany provided vast AFL-CIO financial resources for the strikes and boycotts and then demanded that Cesar shut down articles critical of US foreign policy in *El Malcriado*, the union paper, as an absolute precondition for continuing to receive the strike funding. He had Cesar and the UFW cornered. I'm not the person to write that book, but I do remember a disheartened and highly reliable *El Malcriado* editor[37] telling me, when I visited La Paz early in my service, that the paper, a great rallying cry for both the farm workers and the support movement, would be closed and why.[38]

In her essay Margaret also relates hearing of the Synanon Game (a method of extreme group confrontation and psychological pressure, including berating, designed to get drug addicts to become and stay clean and sober) being brought into the union. "The game" was instituted at La Paz by Cesar in 1976 and Margaret heard (I think from Tasha Donner) that it was becoming required of union staff as a fixed institution. She pondered this and realized that sooner or later clinic staff would be required to play the "game". This absurdity confirmed the rationale of her already made decision to leave the UFW.

There was, by chance, good timing in my moving from Salinas to Delano and then back to Salinas (three days a week with two days a week in Sanger). I could not go back to Salinas full time immediately

---

37 Maria Rifo.

38 Just before final editing I noted a comment in the May 2004 internet dialogue insinuating that *El Malcriado* was a nest of anti-union activity—that some on the *Malcriado* staff had destroyed many rolls of Cesar's film. I think that such accusations, offered without any evidence, should not be tolerated by those who care about the UFW for they may be used to mask the misdeeds of others. If films did disappear, those entrusted with them need to be asked to explain what happened rather than stand accused, unnamed and in absentia, of nefarious motives.

because they then had more staff than examination rooms (two) in their small clinic. But a doctor was leaving and it would only be a few months before I would be needed to fill that gap. Perfect. However, somewhere in that period another doctor arrived in Salinas from Detroit. Isadore ("Iz") Kolman had retired from Urology practice with the United Auto Workers union hospital in Detroit and wanted to contribute to the UFW efforts. Iz had a hand tremor that made writing difficult and so he would type his notes on an ancient portable typewriter he kept on a small desk in one exam room. It was a great luxury for me to have an experienced urologist in the next room to consult with. When I first drafted this essay Iz was still alive (at about 90 years of age) living here in Berkeley where Sheila and I settled in the mid-80s.

In a short while, as Margaret noted, the Salinas clinic had an influx of energetic new staff (Randy, Jane, Wren and others—volunteers, medical students, PA and NP students, etc.), some with enough experience to take on practitioner roles under guidance. But we were living in a sardine can. The small house with two bedrooms could not accommodate the need to serve more farm workers nor the luxury of having a growing staff. The union decided to embark upon a renovation that would add exam rooms and extend the kitchen to make a "real" laboratory. This project was accomplished on a shoestring budget with volunteers coming down from the Bay Area and around Monterey County. My older stepson, Shep, then 17 years old, came down several days to help the construction crew. He also spent time working at La Paz. The energy and enthusiasm of the crew on the renovation project was typical of the "si se puede" culture around the movement in those days, but the renovation also led to an unfortunate conflict.

As important as the renovation was, it was stopgap. The longer-range plan was to build a complete union clinic on recently purchased land where a new field office and service center would be located. Also in the short run, the renovation could not be allowed to interrupt our continuing care for the farm worker patients. There was just no way to shut down the clinic for several weeks since and we had no way to move to another location. We were not consulted by the union leaders on how to solve this conundrum, but I accepted the decision when Margaret told us that we would work on seeing patients through the construction period. This created potential risks to both the staff and patients. At times the dust inside the building was so heavy that we were walking around in a potentially lung-toxic fog. We could barely see each other. The noise and commotion created an ambiance of absurdity, seeing farm workers sitting there in the waiting room in the dust and noise as if there was "no problem".

For Iz Kolman and several others on the staff it <u>was</u> a serious problem, a matter of health and safety. They demanded that the clinic be closed during the period of major construction and when they were ignored they actually set up a picket line outside and refused to work. I, and some others, didn't join the picket line, but kept working. I can't say what might have happened if we had all united and refused to work (I suspect nothing good), but I just wasn't prepared to picket the union. What did happen was that Iz left the UFW (voluntarily). I don't fault him or those who picketed (some of whom stayed on). I just thought we could survive this if farm workers could survive the conditions they had to endure in the fields every working day of their lives; and that we had to keep the clinic open for the workers. But the failure of leadership to consult the staff about how to effect the renovation in a way that would minimize problems and assure the best coverage for patient care was a harbinger of the events that would permanently close the Salinas clinic in October 1978.

Unlike Delano, the Salinas clinic, beginning back in 1973, was an operation manned by part-timers. It had never provided the full range of coverage and services that Dan Murphy and his staff did.

Margaret relates how Wren and Jane would follow pregnant women right into the hospital and postpartum, but it wasn't that way in the beginning before Jane and Wren and others were doing it. When I returned from my exhilarating experience in Delano I set my sights on (and worked with Margaret) trying to expand our commitment to enhanced continuity and comprehensive care in Salinas so that it might match Delano. I joined the staff at Natividad (County) Hospital and became known in the private and public sector medical communities so that we would have more contacts with specialists when we needed them. In my files I have a letter I wrote to Cesar detailing a challenge we made to racist practices at Natividad Hospital by a physician who behaved inappropriately, I thought negligently, in the care of one of our patients. I wrote letters in the local paper regarding important health-related issues such as adequate funding of the hospital, access to care, and pesticide exposure. More than just a service center, the Salinas clinic was becoming an element in the farm workers' movement for justice. Everyone on staff was conscious of us trying to play that role, and this made the experience all the more exhilarating and validating for us all.

Even though I saw other cracks in the UFW foundation as early as Delano in 1975, for a while I could believe that the closing of the Sanger clinic was only an unfortunate perturbation in the upward growth of the NFWHG, not a sign of crises to come. Well after the Sanger and Coachella clinics closed and Margaret left, a young, inflexible, non-medical bureaucrat, Rick, arrived at the Salinas clinic, placed as administrator to dictate to staff. Now our fate was sealed.

The problem with a culture that adulates leaders is not just in the danger of uncritical obedience. That danger is real and serious enough. But the process which begins with the adherence of true believers—and this has been true of so many idealistic political movements, from the Russian Revolution to the Chinese Cultural Revolution to Jonestown—can easily transform into a culture of social climbers whose obedience is little more than a form of self-aggrandizement. This second wave can creep right into bed with the first or even arise in the minds of true believers. As I write these words, the neo-con social climbers around George W. Bush, who are just beginning to fall to earth, present an outstanding example of that blurring of the border between idealistic enthusiasm and miasmic selfishness and self-delusion.

Although I did speak with Dan Murphy about what was happening, I had no first hand knowledge of events surrounding the closing of the Calexico and Delano clinics. But by 1977 Cesar had the Synanon Game going full bore and was of the belief that there were cabals of conspirators, mainly communists, within the union and volunteer staff who were dedicated to wrecking the union and bringing him down. The Synanon Game, he thought, was a way to expose troublemakers who were challenging the unity he sought and either bring them into line or get rid of them. Of course there were all kinds of Leftists and idealists within the movement. That wasn't any secret. And probably some of us shared our opinions more than was thought helpful (I did). But I imagine someone was feeding Cesar specific false information to heighten the claim that much dissension to his policies and leadership could be traced to specific conspiracies to weaken the UFW.

It is not difficult to create such an illusionary web from facts mixed with fantasies. For example, the RCP (Revolutionary Communist Party) had a campaign attacking the political fund of the union because it was used consistently to support Democratic Party candidates even those not involved in support of farm worker efforts. I thought the RCP attack on the Fund was poorly conceived, similar to Governor Arnold Schwarzenegger's attack on unions in proposition 75 in the 2005 California special election. In my view RCP's approach was an attack on the union rather than a specific criticism of how the Fund was being used indiscriminately on behalf of the

Democratic Party. The political fund is an important part of progressive political unionism, and so, I believe, should be supported enthusiastically. I think that most union members understood this distinction. I don't think the RCP made many friends with their ploy. And their influence was not of particular significance. But they and other small groups became foci of rumors of conspiracies.

By 1977, Cesar seemed to me less interested in the differing opinions that he had earlier sought out from workers, staff and volunteers, and was more worried by such minor irritants. Perhaps the union's path forward was unclear because significant voices of discontent had also arisen among farm workers themselves. This was not the same man I had heard interacting informally with farm workers in Lamont only four years previous. As a result, a broad purge began and anyone who criticized the surprising practices then being implemented would inevitably fall, in Nixonian-McCarthy-like fashion, onto the enemies list. The stigma of having been labeled, reminding me of the Chinese Cultural Revolution, may still contribute to the reluctance of many former volunteers, even today, to write and speak frankly about that period.

My last day as a UFW staff member, October 5, 1978, I was called, without advance notice, before a meeting of union members at the Union Hall in Salinas. I had patients/friends on various ranch committees who would later confirm that word of this meeting did not go through the ranch committees, many of which were not informed. I was publicly accused of being a member of the RCP (which was untrue) as well as charged with trying to wreck the UFW. By then the union leadership had already shut down all the other clinics.

Why? As medical director of the Salinas clinic I was a member of a clinic staff majority (I think there were one or two who disagreed) that had decided to draw a definite line we would not cross. That line divided our consciences, values, medical ethics and support for the UFW and La Causa from destructive practices we were told we had to carry out. The issue was not something as limited as the birth control issue. We had told Cesar we would not agree to cast out from the clinic roles hundreds or thousands of patients, loyal to the UFW and Cesar, just because they were not currently working under union contracts, no matter the reason. The UFW supporters at ranches without contracts were, in fact, the most in need of our care, and the most vulnerable to medical problems and most unable to obtain healthcare. They were many of our most long-standing and loyal patients. For when the clinic opened there were no contracts. And these workers had put their trust in us as representatives of the union for over five years.

To prevent a public discussion of the dangers to the union of shutting out many of our regular patients, union leadership created a different discussion, inviting me alone from the clinic staff and populating the hall with their most loyal people, without notifying all the ranch committees. The preface to closing of the Salinas clinic was the closing of the Rodrigo Terronez clinic in Delano in 1977. I have earlier written of my experience that Dan Murphy was one of the most loyal people to Cesar of those I had met. But in 1977, bureaucratic control over and interference with the Delano clinic was now wreaking havoc with that wonderful experiment. Dan, usually going along with whatever he was ordered to do, had worked too hard not to raise his voice against these practices. I am sure he did it in a sensitive way, but that wouldn't have mattered by then. He was now a "dissenter" in a "dissent-free" environment. What is clear is that without Dan Murphy there would be no Delano clinic (past or future) and if Dan was being forced to resign it meant that Cesar had decided that the entire NFWHG was dispensable. Delano was the flagship. I didn't believe it when I heard that Delano and Calexico clinics had been closed in 1977. Salinas was now the last clinic left; an irony because I had by then written many critical letters to Cesar himself and the board about a number of very broad political issues such as the decision to attack Tony Orendain when he refused to go back to the boycott and instead went back to organizing farm workers in Texas for the UFW, and the turning in of undocumented workers that Cesar had ordered.

Even with Dan's resignation, my oath to myself was that I would not quit. I was going to stay with the union as long as I could without compromising my own beliefs in the practice of medicine. I did stay, as long as I could, until Cesar—I presume with the approval of the board of directors majority—decided to throw out the patients not under contract. We refused and Cesar had me fired, providing a reason, transparent though it was, to close the last clinic.

At the Fresno Convention of 1977, Cesar had already inflamed some tensions with Philip Vera Cruz and the Filipino community by visiting the dictator Marcos in Manila and then placing one of Marcos' representatives as an honored guest on the Dais. (Who advised Cesar in these decisions?) I think it was at the next convention, which I did not attend, that a group of about 50 elected ranch committee representatives tried to present a nominating petition from the floor for an alternate slate of candidate to Cesar's slate for the board. This was precedent-setting. Some say they had little support in this effort, but we'll never know. The union leadership clearly overreacted to this challenge. The 50 elected representatives from various ranches were simply expelled from the union. To compound matters, union staff ultimately colluded with the growers, letting the growers know that the UFW would not challenge the firings of these key leading workers if they weren't let back into field work.[39] This led to a lawsuit from fired workers against the union and in the coup de grace the UFW countersued (in SLAP suit fashion) for millions of

---

39 In the list serve dialogue the defense of the leadership behavior in firing these workers omits the fact that the union initiated this collaboration with the ranchers. If my recollection serves me it was this vindictive collusion, not only the firings from union positions, that precipitated the lawsuit.

dollars against these now-unemployed farm workers. This series of events seems unimaginable. Perhaps that is why we hear so little analysis of how this could have happened, even today.

To understand such terrible events probably requires looking further back in time to other mistakes and problems. Already at the moment I decided to join the ful-time staff, and unbeknownst to me and many UFW members and supporters, union leadership was directing field office staff to collaborate with the Migra (the INS) in the deportation of undocumented farm workers. The rationale was that these workers could be intimidated by ranchers to vote against the union under threat of being turned in to immigration. I don't know how long this terrible practice went on, and I don't know if it was ever written down, but Dolores Huerta, Marshall Ganz and other board members still living should be challenged on why they allowed it to go on.[40]

Gilbert Padilla, in his essay, writes fondly of his work with Tony Orendain, one of the founders of the UFW, of Pancho Botello, a great organizer, and others. Gilbert hints at some of the tensions that arose here and there in developing and effecting UFW policy. Looking at the UFW in the context of other important movements—the civil rights movement, for example—I realized that such movements must function like armies at war. Voluntary discipline, but discipline of the highest order, is required when you are fighting powerful forces and all you have is your numbers, your organization and your will. For example, it took Cesar's incredibly strong will and leadership to impose the strict practice of non-violence on the members and staff. This in turn made it possible to keep the focus on the growers and to neutralize the threat of police violence and state intervention in many of the communities where strikes and boycotts nevertheless became

---

40 Deborah Vollmer relates in the web dialogue that Philip Vera Cruz was adamantly opposed to this practice. But where was the rest of the leadership?

very militant. That unity worked.

Within the leadership circles of such movements, like the UFW, there are inevitable battles in planning the best course of action to advance the cause. How a leadership core learns to collectivize its decision-making process for key decisions and in response to crises is determinant in the future successes and failures of that movement as a whole.

In the UFW there were a number of brilliant and decisive farm worker leaders. Tony Orendain was one of them. Often leaders divide into those who decide to simply ratify the views of the central leader unconditionally and those who assert their own personal values, knowledge and experience. But here is the conundrum: if a general's decisions are misguided they may lead to great losses, even to losing a battle; but if the general's orders are not obeyed this may damage the unity of the movement which may lead to great losses, even to losing a battle.

What is the solution to this riddle? The viable course is to encourage everyone to vigorously put forth their views until the final decision is made. If the outcome goes badly a good team of independent strong leaders will re-evaluate and recognize which views and proposals were at fault and which might have carried the day. If the discussion of different views is not carried out vigorously, the reevaluation cannot be rigorous. Obviously there is no formula for correct decisions, but only a conceptual framework for learning from positive and negative experiences. That is, sober, dogged, informed evaluation, a refusal to engage in hero worship or blind obedience, yet a willingness to submit to collective will and discipline.

Gilbert Padilla was a close comrade of Tony Orendain. Tony was a valuable and key UFW leader from the beginning. But Tony's words on the Texas farm workers situation, the importance of strike support and permanent organizing in Texas did not carry weight with Cesar. Cesar had decided that the UFW should not spend major resources in Texas with the battles raging in California. Tony's viewpoint and his direct experience in Texas was that the Texas workers were becoming every bit as active and militant and intent upon joining the UFW as those in California, and so had to be supported. When Tony refused to return to the urban boycott, insisting that the Texas work was reaching a critical juncture, Cesar became angry and dictatorial. Instead of looking for some middle path to support Tony but not spend much UFW resources, he used his power as UFW president arbitrarily and capriciously, expelling Tony from the union totally.

Gilbert was soon assigned to go to Texas and seize the office that Tony had established for his UFW work and return it to a couple of UFW volunteer functionaries who were sent to Texas to counter (i.e. undermine) Tony's independent efforts. When Tony opened a new office and began the Texas Farm Workers' Union he did so only because he was no longer allowed to represent La Union. Why did UFW continue to disrupt his efforts which were in no way intended to be against the UFW, even then? Tony Orendain, a key organizer and leader from the UFW core and Gilbert Padilla with a similar mantle were forced to confront each other in this way, though both later said they could see no rational purpose in this confrontation.

What was going on inside the board of directors during this tussle? Did some people dissent? Did they stand up to be counted? Was conformity in such decisions a problem with roots going back into the 60s? The board of directors were the people with the leadership responsibilities, abilities and the sophistication to realize that only collective leadership can keep each individual leader honest and humble. If a group constantly asserts the infallibility of a supreme leader just because he has made many outstanding decisions, what leader will not come to believe in the mantle of infallibility and act accordingly? Cesar's charisma and successes were awesome. But did an awestruck board of directors contribute to his believing too much in the mystique of his own perfection?

I have conflicted feelings about my history with the UFW. I always tried to be honest with leadership, writing my own assessment about things that were going on, then as well as now. I did write to the board of directors criticizing their attack on the ongoing Texas work, begun and continued by Orendain. I did write to the Board criticizing the union's collusion with the Migra. I am thankful that leadership allowed me to continue to work for la causa. As medical director in Salinas I also did offer detailed organizational suggestions and support for the development of a permanent NFWHG. I believe I played a role in some reforms that made our Salinas efforts more effective and coherent. I believed then that I could do much more and asked to be allowed to make things happen in the NFWHG clinical/health realm.

Like Kathy and others, I put my life on the line for a cause and movement I believed in dearly. But because of the way I separated from the union, I tended to suppress a lot of my wonderful personal memories and experiences, dwelling more on the sad final political events. How could I not remember the final confrontation with Cesar's hand, Frank Ortiz, in Salinas (which occurred after Cesar himself failed to achieve a confrontation with our clinic staff at a meeting when he called us to La Paz, closing the clinic for three days during the summer of '78).

I always remember that I had brought on the final conflict—even though there seemed no way around it. Not only had we refused to expel thousands of non-contract patients but I had told many patients about the controversy and (with their approval) accumulated the names and phone numbers of many ranch committee members in the valley from our patients. I was hoping that when a confrontation occurred over this decision, we might be able to bring out more farm workers against this plan than the field office could bring in support of it; and even change the decision. The field office or Rick, the clinic bureaucrat, may have gotten wind of this plan, or not. But Cesar was a brilliant tactician in any case, and my thought that we could prevail was unrealistic in that context. The way the final event was scripted by him preempted any possible open discussion of whether it made sense to expel large numbers of union-supporting patients from the clinic.

When I heard that LeRoy Chatfield was going to post this website with staff/volunteer essays, initially I decided not to participate; why stir up things that no one wants to know or hear. I didn't want to participate because I felt that my critical eye didn't belong amidst the forever-uplifting mystique of a Disneyland UFW and the heroic Cesar Chavez mythology. But when LeRoy announced that all the essays were posted online I went to see what people had written. I saw the essays of people I had toiled with and highly respected, people who had treated me kindly and fairly, despite my own failings; saw them still trying (appropriately) to validate the incredibly great efforts and accomplishments that took place under the UFW banner. I felt a renewed kinship and, yes, as well I also detected a common, if cautious, effort at self-reflection; an attempt to surface some understanding of the problems and underlying fault lines that weakened our movement, the farm workers movement, the movement of La Raza and of the Filipino farm workers in the heyday of the UFW. This cautious honesty I sensed in the essays of Gilbert, Margaret, Kathy and Dan was, for me, inspiring. It motivated me to contribute my own story—less cautiously, but hopefully just as honestly. Writing it has helped me grapple with some of my buried feelings. I hope it serves the reader as well. We all share the burdens of the past and the responsibility to learn how to do better in the future.

A TRAVESTY

I've mentioned that back in 1965–1966 I had taken a one-year leave of absence in a quixotic effort to expand my efforts against the US government's war on Vietnam—alone. I say quixotic because by then I was already a member of a core group of graduate and undergraduate students (and several faculty) active on the Stanford "Farm", and I now was choosing to go it alone in the wider world. We had held a hugely celebrated and highly attended teach-in on campus, for which I had drafted the "call", the very night in 1965 after LBJ began the massive B-52 bombing of Vietnam. Stanford ROTC was on the ropes (and would be dropped). We sat in against CIA recruiters, disrupting and exposing them. Students were being prosecuted left and right by the university's kangaroo faculty court. The undergraduate campus was roiling, transformed from a sleepy haven of the sunbathing, fraternity-sorority life for the kids of the white super rich to a hotbed of radical activism, electing two radical Left student body presidents (one the famous draft resister David Harris). Yet, I hoped I could do more outside the rich humus of this hothouse and felt compelled to act upon moral compulsion; how wrong I was. After a year on the "outside" I realized that the big wide world was a much lonelier place within which to try to bolster a new culture, so I returned to med school—only to have the dean, Robert Glaser, call me in the very day I returned to proclaim, "You know, we really don't want you here."

I wasn't offended, but I was surprised at his boldness, revealing his frustration and ultimate powerlessness—he surely knew that our cause was just and the university's role was corrupt. I was a student in good standing and he was just being nasty. But I soon found out that the broader "WE" he referred to was taking us quite seriously.

Two years later, in my final year of med school, I learned that Dean Glaser's vindictiveness had not ended with his unfriendly remark. When I applied for post-medical training via the national "Match" program, I was to learn that I had not matched anywhere. And why. Stanford had by then abandoned the practice of students seeking faculty recommendations to send to the residencies of their choice. Instead the dean of students (not Bob Glaser), working with the advice and comments of faculty would write a generic recommendation for each student. That single recommendation would be sent out, in the name of the school, everywhere we applied. In principle this would appear to be fairer and more objective than students asking their favorite profs to do the recommending. But human subjectivity being what it is, politics couldn't be kept out of the equation in that new model. Vaguely alluding to my political activism without being explicit, the dean's letter for me said that, "had he not engaged in so much outside other activities, Sapir might have been one of our top students". The hook was out there for any residency director who might consider appointing me to give a friendly call to the dean of students to ask: "What is that all about?" The response of course would be "off the record" so who knows what might have been said about arrests, sit-ins, disruptive and outrageous anti-war behavior.

Although my grades were middle-of-the-class and I had done well enough on nationwide exams (the Medical Boards),[41] I did not match

---

41 Part III of the Boards, taken after my year of internship were, significantly, much higher than in Part II, so I had learned most of my medicine in that one year. Perhaps Stanford's recommendation put-down was right on the facts, or maybe Stanford Med wasn't all that it was cracked up to be, but in any case, it was inappropriate nonetheless to so prejudice the applications of a graduating medical student.

to any hospital at all. At that point the dean of students called me into his office. "I'm sorry," he said, "that you haven't matched. But," he then added in a friendly tone, "we (myself acting for Stanford Med) are prepared to get you right into any residency position, anywhere in the US that is still not filled." He handed me the national list of spots that were left open. I found a perfect fit for myself at Wayne County General Hospital, it being a public county hospital serving mostly poor and people of color and a hospital affiliated with the University of Michigan's excellent medical school. Only four of us would be first year county hospital residents not assigned to any specialty residency at University of Michigan while all residents above us and all faculty by whom we would be taught, would be U of Michigan-based. Stanford had made its point about power and influence. I had had no interest in a medical or surgical specialty residency to begin with, so their repair of their slap down led to an excellent outcome for me.

This was not my first experience with Stanford's abuse of power in trying to slap down or impede activists. As a student, when I took the required surgical rotation I was really into it—that is to say I enjoyed the art of the surgeon. I was never late for scheduled surgeries or didactic lectures and I did whatever was asked of me efficiently and thankfully as a (usually) second assistant in the operating room. Surgery is like a form of highly skilled manual labor combined with the deep knowledge of the sometimes inconstant anatomy and physiology. Thus a need for attention to detail and wariness for atypical situations and sudden crises, as well as a potential relationship with patients. It all attracted me. At the end of the rotation we took a written exam and my grade was in the 80s, which was one of the high grades for that exam at that time in our rotation group. Yet in evaluating my performance for the rotation the faculty evaluator had actually given me a **fail**. Of course, I protested to the dean of students. I had done well on an objective exam and there were no disciplinary or other marks against my performance in other areas. The dean agreed to look into this. He returned with a passing grade (at that time Stanford Med had transitioned to a pass, fail, or exceptional grading protocol). I might have even rated an exceptional rating, but that was of no importance to me then.

Other incidents also revealed the game of the university's tit-for-tat wrath that was going down. By sheer coincidence, when I took my year leave in 1966, those of us who sat in against and blocked the CIA recruiters were about to be tried by a faculty judicial board. Some were suspended for a semester or two. Not currently a student, I wasn't tried, and when I came back after my leave it would have put the university in a bad light to try to suspend me more than a year later. Then, in 1969, back in school, I participated in a militant demonstration against the military research at the Stanford Research Institute's facility on Hanover Street in the Stanford Industrial Park. SRI was a wholly owned subsidiary of Stanford and was deeply involved in designing both military and advanced police weaponry, like the new CS tear gas—actually a form of nerve gas. They had perfected the helicopter-mounted spraying machinery that was used against protests in Berkeley. Almost 600 of us marched off campus into the Stanford Industrial Park with the explicit intention of shutting down the entire industrial park by blocking the main intersection where one of the SRI buildings sat. We were demanding that Stanford stop all military research for the war going on at SRI (and for domestic use as well—we had evidence of both).[42] Lady luck shined on us all day that day for the action coincided with the massive June 5 protest in Berkeley that has been dubbed the "People's Park Riot". Under the mutual aid pact between cities and counties, hundreds of police from all over the Bay Area and all their tactical

---

42 A vote of students, faculty and staff would overwhelmingly make the same demand with over 10,000 people voting.

squads were sent to Berkeley. Ultimately, then-Governor Ronald Reagan called out the National Guard. James Rector, who was just observing the protest from the roof or window of a building across the way, was murdered by a police shotgun blast. They also injured and arrested many other essentially non-violent protesters trying to protect People's Park's decimation by the university a struggle that has never ended.

Meanwhile, down in Palo Alto, we had marched into the industrial park early in the morning, but it wasn't until late in the afternoon that the police could mount a sufficient force that was bussed in to attack us. During that time we totally shut down the crossroads into the industrial park. We were well prepared for an eventual confrontation, organized in small affinity groups each with its own leaders and plan of action. As a street medic I was dressed in a white jacket, wore an armband and had a red cross on my bicycle helmet. I was carrying medical supplies. Another group was outfitted with heavy gloves and gas masks. But (before police arrived) all we did that morning was block the intersection with people and dumpsters and wait, effectively closing down the industrial park. Around 3 p.m. we watched as a cordon of well over 100 tactical police in riot gear, gas masks, batons, and shields descended from buses a block away. Setting up an attack formation they then marched down Hanover Street toward us and—on approaching—they lobbed tear gas canisters into the mostly student crowd on the street as they advanced. Unfortunately for Stanford and SRI those canisters were picked up by the designated affinity group and thrown through the entire front of large plate glass windows of SRI, along Hanover—along with rocks as well—essentially gutting the building in the span of just a few moments. What then ensued was imagery out of a Keystone Cops silent movie of the past with the cops attacking and people running in every direction up, through and around the hilly and dry tall grasslands that stretched toward the foothills about half a mile to the west behind the SRI building. Small affinity groups of youths would be chased by one or two cops in heavy, indubitably sweltering gear and then these clutches would break into ever smaller groups leaving each cop only the option of chasing one or two people—generally catching no one to club or arrest. If any of the protesters were caught and arrested that day it could only have been a few.

In video footage I was easily identifiable in my white coat and other attire, and so arrest after the fact seemed likely. But the police didn't move quickly to arrest those they identified. Instead they waited, and waited. A month later I was doing an internal medicine rotation (I had chosen to do it at PA Veterans Hospital where Stanford faculty were also engaged). It was on my actual birthday that the police came for me at the VA Hospital and handcuffed me in front of my patients and marched me off to jail. As a side bar to this attempt to humiliate me, the Stanford professor who was in charge of my medical rotation, then proceeded to fail me, requiring me to re-do a second medicine rotation. I chose, at that point, to get out of the line of fire, applied for and completed that internal medicine rotation requirement at UC Berkeley in the Cowell Student Hospital. There my mentor/teacher was a brilliant and supportive internist, Mort Meyer. Mort, now long dead, would, in the 1980s, after we moved from San Jose to Berkeley, become my own primary care doc. And in the 1990s, as medical director of the Center for Elders' Independence, I would join the staff of Alta Bates Hospital where Mort Meyer's private practice was based. But at Cowell Mort Meyer taught me well, providing more good clinical medicine than I had learned at Stanford.

An earlier episode parrying with the University demons involved another arrest warrant. The town and gown coalition of anti-war groups had a number of demonstrations against the war in downtown Palo Alto. Within those demonstrations was a small organized group that called itself the Red Guard[43] that was interested in mixing it up with the Palo Alto police, which had a very nasty "Red Squad" that did beat up people, especially people of color and people who had the chutzpah to call themselves communists. The police were then, and often still are, fond of declaring peaceful and law-abiding demonstrations to be illegal assemblies and issuing dispersal orders via bull horns—sometimes audible and sometimes not. If people didn't leave, the cops attacked. If they attacked all hell might break loose. Despite my involvement in many protests I was never into fighting with police just to fight the police. I witnessed times when people had little option other than to defend themselves from police assaults, but there were young people—and cops—who just wanted a good fight. On the other hand, I obviously knew that if they were going to declare demonstrations illegal, the agents of "law and order" were required to have some legitimate reason to do so—and they often didn't.

At one of the Lytton Plaza demonstrations downtown, the police declared an unlawful assembly and the shit hit the fan. Eventually the cops captured the little plaza where the rally was being held and they detained and arrested a number of people. I wasn't arrested or detained, because, having dispersed, I went home. Time passed and then to my surprise the police issued a warrant for my arrest and intimated that I was in hiding and refusing to submit to the warrant. First of all, I hadn't done anything wrong. Had I not left or fought police they probably would have arrested me at the Lytton Plaza rally. Secondly, I hadn't known they were looking for me. They knew where I lived, so they knew I wasn't avoiding arrest. We decided to make their lies look bad by holding a public event right at the medical school in an outdoor courtyard to expose the absurdity of their

---

43 I was not affiliated with this group.

claims. I would invite them to arrest me there. I'm sure that must have irked Dean Glaser and other Stanford officials, who did not like the look and feel of Stanford having outside police on campus.

The event was fairly well attended by med students and faculty opposed to the war. One fellow med student, Bill Gray, a somewhat older though youthful-looking fellow, who already had been a commercial pilot and was strongly opposed to the war, was on a surgical rotation (I believe OB/Gyn) at that time. When he notified the surgeon he would be taking lunch time to attend the press conference where I would speak, that faculty member took Bill totally by surprise, slapping him across the face. I believe the surgeon was mildly disciplined. We had over 60 Stanford med students at that time (including BG and myself) who signed a pledge to refuse to serve as physicians in the war effort. Around 200 med students at UC San Francisco, Harvard, Johns Hopkins and Stanford signed that pledge. I believe they all honored that pledge and none served in Vietnam, though years later I learned that two of my then friends had, to my surprise, become Republicans.

SERENDIPITY AT WORK:
HOW I BECAME A GERIATRICIAN

Over 20 years later, in 1992 I became a geriatrician providing care to disabled and frail old people as the first medical director of CEI. I was recruited to this position with the Center for Elders' Independence in Oakland. That is to say, I didn't look for it or apply for it. This job, which I resigned nine years and three months later on my 60th birthday (July 3, 2001), came looking for me 22 years after 1970 and the shotgun incident that culminated in my being charged with assault on a police officer with a deadly weapon. CEI was my most intensive, extended and important work as a doc.

In 1984, only 43 years old, I felt burned out. I had been working 13 years in community-based, non-profit clinics. I had spent several years—1975–1978—working for Cesar Chavez and the United Farm Workers union and been through their internal wars. After that I'd then been two years with the clinics of the Alviso Foundation and then three years as medical director of the Gardner Health Center in the old downtown Latino Gardner District of San Jose. By 1984 I had yet to find a non-profit agency or governing board that wasn't dysfunctional or rife with internal divisions. This reminded me of the RU breakup, the CLP disasters and the UFW civil wars and I needed a break.

After leaving Gardner Health Center I set up my own private medical practice and got bored. After ten months, though I had accumulated a few hundred patients, I knew this was not the life for me. Coincidentally, the two gynecologists I was renting my office space from had suddenly gotten into a bad argument and broken up their lifelong friendship and closed their joint practice; so I had to make some decision about my own future. Serendipitously, John Radebaugh stopped by that week and told me Stanford community medicine needed opportunties in 'real' community medicine for students and I should take one of the open community clinic medical director positions in the South Bay.

Meanwhile, I had noticed that there was a lot of talk and writing going on about Alzheimer's dementia. It then seemed to be a new disease that was hitting the news and I didn't know much about it, though dementia in aging had been known for thousands of years. The couple of articles that I had read seemed to suggest that no one else knew much about it either. I became intrigued by the incongruity of major news reports on this "new disease" that did not seem backed up by much knowledge or understanding and the fact that it wasn't "new" at all.

The way science and medicine begin to appreciate a disease that is becoming more prevalent is through the research field called epidemiology (the study of the behavior of diseases in whole populations of people). Although I had learned little about Alzheimer's (and similarly knew little of epidemiologic methods), I was very interested in factors that cause and spread disease in our communities. Therefore, I determined to go back to school in public health and become versed in epidemiology—and to probably become an epidemiologist.

I visited the University of California at Berkeley and met some of the leading epidemiology faculty—Warren Winkelstein and Bill Reeves (later my mentors, both now deceased). They seemed enthusiastic that I wanted to become one of their students and assured me that, even though their program was popular and had limited admissions, I would be accepted to gain a master's degree in epidemiology from UCB School of Public Health. To my surprise, I was not accepted. When I spoke with the epi faculty, reminding them that they had agreed to admit me, they apologized and told me to reapply.

I did, but also responding to John Radebaugh's request I signed a one-year contract with Tiburcio Vasquez Health Center (TVHC) in Union City. I had been forewarned, however, that the newly hired TVHC administrator was a grandiose self-promoter whose honesty was questionable. I took the job anyway—after all, hadn't I been through this before, and this would be an interim job—on a one-year basis while I awaited admission to the epidemiology program.

As an undergraduate student, back before the US destruction and invasion of Vietnam dragged me headlong into Left politics, I had romanticized becoming a cancer researcher. Six months after becoming medical director at Tiburcio Vasquez Health Center, I visited Stanford, met a young immunologist newly appointed to the faculty, and he agreed that I work in his research lab a half day a week in immunology research at the medical school (we were then still living in East San Jose) so he could evaluate whether I would integrate well into his lab. As I waited for a response from UC Public Health, my part time research work at Stanford moved forward and my faculty sponsor, Alan Krensky, pleased with my work, enthusiasm, and insights submitted my name to be his post-doc fellow. We began to work on writing research grants for an HIV/AIDS project. The AIDS epidemic was in full swing and I was going to try to genetically transform different types of human T lymphocytes—the helper and killer cells—into each other because we knew that the HIV virus was wiping out the helper (CD-4) cells.

Yet another unexpected turn of events occurred. Alan, as a new faculty member, had his department chair (in the Department of Pediatrics) reject my appointment. The chair had been on the Stanford faculty during the time of the Vietnam War. Alan and other research faculty said they had never known of a case where a faculty member's choice of a fellow to work in their lab was blocked by an administrative action of this type. The Department Chair told Alan that Stanford wanted their post-doc positions to go to their own doctoral students. Perhaps it was partly true—but probably not the whole story. Interestingly, my brilliant stepson Joel, many years later, was unable to achieve a faculty position in his field at the University of Wyoming because, he was told, he had attained his PhD at that university, and they had a policy of not keeping PhDs they had trained. That university wanted to keep open their positions for new blood from outside and did not accept former students. (Joel went on to became a tenured prof at university of Montana and a prominent glacier researcher.) I have my own thoughts about what was going on at Stanford, recalling the tales of my days as a Stanford medical student activist. Institutional memory can sometimes be like an elephant's.

Thus, Stanford squashed my post-doctoral appointment. But, as life is unpredictable, this didn't turn out poorly for my future. Shortly, I was accepted to the UC Berkeley epidemiology program. Entering in August 1986, I was a highly motivated, enthusiastic and diligent student, took substantially more credits than required and had a 3.88 GPA. In addition to doing well academically, I served as student rep on the school's faculty academic senate and worked three different part time clinical jobs in addition to my schoolwork. At the age of 45 I was still able to stay up doing homework till 3 a.m. without too much loss of cognitive capacity during the 8 a.m. classes the next day. I particularly loved the challenge of statistical analysis.

So what does this have to do with my becoming a geriatrician—a doctor of aging and the aged? Well, recall that I became intrigued about epidemiology because it seemed to me that there wasn't much clarity on the cause, incidence, and behavior of this disease. Alzheimer's disease, some people kept insisting, was going to be the disease of the future as populations aged. My epidemiology student days repeatedly lead me back to my questions about dementia and aging.

To complete the epi program, each student had to choose a topic for a thorough review of the epidemiology literature. The reviews were presented in a seminar format, as a sort of masters thesis paper. Each student would give an oral presentation and/or slide presentation, and answer questions and critiques on their topic before the year's epidemiology students and faculty. There was no other topic competing in my mind with dementia—particularly because popular topics like coronary heart disease and the AIDS epidemic were bound to be selected by one or more fellow students. I preferred having my own subject and I still didn't think I knew much about dementia. Here was a chance to find out what was known and what wasn't. Despite 15 years of medical practice, I hadn't been caring for people with dementia or memory loss, so far as I knew. I chose Alzheimer's dementia and, in addition to my literature research on this topic, I signed up to take a course called "The Epidemiology of Aging". Some of the leading figures in this field were guest lecturers in this excellent course. I was headed toward some degree of proficiency, at least on the academic side of it—in aging and dementia. In my 15 years in medical practice I had never found the subject of aging or care of the aged any more interesting to me than other topics and yet here I was pointing myself in the direction of aging—as I was heading toward aging myself. When I finished the epidemiology program I think I knew quite a bit about dementia though so much was still unknown. Yet this academic exercise had no bearing on where I thought I was headed with the rest of my professional life.

When I left school with the MPH in epidemiology I wanted to do epi research, hopefully in HIV/AIDs in particular. But that isn't what happened. The wife of Larry Platt, a pediatrician, fellow classmate and friend, was an RN working in the public health sector in HIV. One day when I visited at their home up the hill from ours she pointed out: "The city of Berkeley has a health department (one of only three cities in the state, since most health departments are countywide) and they have been without a health officer for some years. They are now looking for one—realizing they have to either have one or close the department. You'd be a perfect fit with your political advocacy for justice and fairness, your health policy reform advocacy and your past medical and management experience."

I followed her advice and became Berkeley's public health officer (acting)—for all of seven months, at which time I chose to leave in what was another of my life's miscalculations. The administrator who hired me (Glen Lynch, the acting head of Health and Human Services) had promised to assure that the city council would fund a permanent health officer position. But seven months later Glen suddenly announced his retirement. The city had not yet voted to make the position permanent (though they later did). I left for another job. I walked away from work I was enjoying and where I was making good contributions because of Glen's broken promise. Four years later I found myself running a geriatric program. In the interim I had been San Mateo County public health officer for five months, then organized the effort for the High School Health Center in Berkeley, then worked outpatient clinics for the Alameda County Medical Center and ultimately accepted the position I hadn't looked for as first medical director of the Center for Elders' Independence.

PART IV

The Center for Elders' Independence and the Program of All Inclusive Care for the Elderly (PACE) (April 1992—July 3, 2001)

A CEI fishing excursion to Lake Chabot in the East Hills above Oakland. To my right in the photo is Paul Johnson, then lead driver of our transportation system.

I retired (though Sheila says, "You resigned," because CEI did not provide a retirement benefit for its employees) from my position as medical director when I reached the age of 60, having put in nine-plus of my best years of medical caring. Then later in 2002 I was commissioned by CEI's director, Peter Szutu to write the "history of the program". Kindly, Peter accepted my counter-proposal to write it as a series of essays mainly focusing on our participants and their evolution in the program (with one section dedicated to an administrative history and overview). The book has not been published but CEI has a copy on file. Some of the essays follow.

From the introduction:

Memory

When I ran into my friend Barbara Gregory in early 1992, I had just finished setting up the Berkeley High School Health Center. I was working in the clinics of the Alameda County Medical Center and doing intake exams in the psych ward in an 80-year-old, many-fingered building behind Oakland's Highland Hospital. The Community Adult Day Health Center, an independent program for elders, occupied an adjacent wing of the same squat 1906 SF Earthquake-era building as psychiatry. It was by chance that Barbara and I were walking up the driveway at the same time. Perhaps her then telling me I was a perfect fit for medical director of the new comprehensive care (PACE) program was an act of desperation on her part. They would open just a month later and had no doctor. But, beyond any flattery, what moved me to accept this role was the obvious collective power of a team-based and community-based model of caring which I experienced after she and her co-director persuaded me to visit On Lok in San Francisco.

At the beginning, the thought of making tough medical decisions in very frail elders in complex medical situations where sudden crises require quick judgment—and errors might contribute to death or suffering—worried me. Although I had spent two decades doing family medicine, that was mostly in outpatient settings. I was pretty good at that kind of medicine but hadn't done hospital care in years.

When I thought about working at the Center for Elders' Independence, the idea of caring for dementia patients struck me as particularly unfriendly. In 1986, when I entered the epidemiology program at Cal and chose Alzheimer's dementia as the subject of my major literature research review paper for the year, that was based solely on inquisitiveness. While at Berkeley I also wrote a separate paper on the classification of dementias for another course, "The Epidemiology of Aging" led by George Kaplan, then director of the Alameda County Population Study. Looking back it seems as though I had unconsciously steered myself toward eldercare, but that was actually the farthest thing from my mind.

By the time that I went to work for CEI in 1992 I knew quite a lot of what was then known about dementia. I was unconvinced that most dementias fit neatly into two simple categories as popular and professional pedagogy portrayed it (Alzheimer's and Multi Infarct Dementia). I won't digress here into an academic discourse on my views on dementia classification. I present this background only to say that knowing more about dementia did not make me more interested in working with people who suffer from it. To the contrary, except for a need to master some of the cognitive testing necessary for mental status assessment in patients, I believed, without good evidence, that working with dementia patients would be tedious and boring.

I enjoy social interactions in working with people. And as a physician I enjoyed the privilege of being allowed to be nosy about people's lives, including their inner lives. I believe doctors need to be inquisitive. My own inquisitiveness about people's lives often served an important role for patients. But that's also how I accumulate fascinating life vignettes and tales. Unfortunately, people with advanced dementia can't tell you much about themselves. And they can't get to know you because they won't remember you. They may notice only that you are someone they have seen before. "What is it you do around here?" I have been often asked by dements. "You look familiar but I can't quite place who you are." And when they are ill they usually can't give you a useful history.

One can only imagine how such a blank response feels to the loving daughter or son who one day finds their parent's dementia has reached the threshold of loss of personal recognition. Though my own mother died with late-stage dementia two months before her 98th birthday in 2014, the one mental faculty she somehow managed to retain was recognition of my sister and myself to the last day of her life.

No, I thought, *dementia is not my cup of tea; it doesn't fit my personality or abilities.* Yet, about 40% of participants in the CEI program then had some degree of cognitive impairment with short-term memory loss (though severe dements were only about 15–25% of the population). The Reading and Reminiscences group which I founded early in my tenure and led, inspired by Ms. Kingsby (see below), was how I tried to cope with these feelings and concerns. But that was before I learned how to engage effectively with dements.

INITIATION:
THE RITES OF SPRING
—ARA BELLE KINGSBY[44]

In the early afternoon of Easter Sunday, April 1994, a deeply religious and dearly loved 87-year-old African American woman I knew and cared for died of pneumonia, dehydration and cancer. Beyond her children and grandchildren, the silky-voiced poet Ara Belle Kingsby left 35 great-grandchildren, and five great-great-grandchildren to celebrate her "homegoing". I've edited down the epitaph written by her family:

> *Born Ara Belle Dalphinia George, the eldest of five children,*
> *in Mornings Port Louisiana, Mother Belle as she was to be later*
> *called, graduated a valedictorian from the first high school for*
> *African Americans in Shreveport, Louisiana. She devoted her*
> *life to family and community, married twice, and had herself*
> *five wonderful children. She served as an elementary grade*

---

44 It is customary, in presenting medical cases, to conceal the names of patients to protect their privacy rights. This essay was submitted to Mother Kingsby's family for approval because I felt that her particular historical individuality was a part of this story. As I suspected they would, the family photocopied the essay and distributed it to all of her children, who approved its contents and agreed that names not be changed. That was in July 1995.

*teacher, a local church and community missionary, a community
activist, and a health nutritionist. In the 1940s she moved to
Oakland, California. In later years she dedicated herself to her
church and community work.*

I first met Ara Belle Kingsby when I became the medical director
and first physician at the Center for Elders' Independence (CEI),
Oakland, Ca, in April 1992. She had a gentleness and peacefulness
about her demeanor. I had not taken particular note of her, nor her
past life, until a center picnic outing to Crab Cove, that same year.
Crab Cove is an idyllic small park on the San Francisco Bay, with
green grass, groves of trees and picnic tables set back from a sandy
semicircular beach facing Southwest on the Bay's eastern island city,
Alameda. I had brought my guitar at the request of our young South
African-born activities director and was just preparing to sing and
lead the elders in a few songs including Negro Spirituals and folk
songs. I began with Huddie Ledbetter's "Goodnight Irene". Lead
Belly became world-renowned, practically the godfather of American folk music, after he was discovered by Alan Lomax and Pete
Seeger in a Texas prison serving time for murder. Due in part to their
intervention he was released and joined the growing number of traveling folk singers in the 1930s and 40s.

Climbing up on a picnic table so I could be seen by all the elders,
I introduced the song by asking how many had heard of Lead Belly.
Most of the 35 or so folks there raised a hand or cried out in affirma-
tion. Then I heard that wispy voice of Ara Belle from one of the
farther-out tables call out, "I knew Ledbetter."

Despite her ethereal voice, Ara Belle Kingsby was a strongly
framed and far-from-frail-appearing woman. She was hefty, though
not obese—still attractive in her mid-80s. She had a lilting Southern
accent. "Tell us about that," I asked of her, and she continued, "His
sister married my brother. After he got out of prison he would come

by our house in Shreveport and talk and sit out on the front porch and play guitar and sing of an evening. All the people from around would come over when he started to sing and play. I remember him real well." It was as if living history from back over 50 years before had blossomed totally unexpected.

Listening to the stories of other patients' lives, I realized that these folks in our program (PACE model[45])—most of whom, though living in Oakland, were Blacks raised in the South—held within themselves a treasure of living history. And so from that realization I decided to organize a reading and reminiscences group for mentally high-functioning members. The group met in the day center weekly for several years.

---

45 A rudimentary description of the PACE model may serve the reader. 70–80 PACE programs across the country effect a very specific model of care for frail and disabled elders. To gain entrance elders must be certified as disabled and at risk of nursing home placement, then join the program and get all their medical care from that program although they live wherever they choose out in the community— often with family and support in the home. Program goals include keeping people out of nursing homes and other institutions through the end of life and maximizing quality of life. Although PACE may use hospice methods sometimes, PACE differs from hospice care because many participants are not terminally ill and some members have survived ten to 15 years in the program and lived to over 100 years. Each PACE site has several adult day health centers with daily programs providing social activities, a medical clinic with doctors and nurse practitioners and physical therapy. The care and care planning of members (participants) is coordinated through broad interdisciplinary teams. Teams of a dozen or more professionals and semi-professional staff (including drivers, social workers, day center staff, occupational and physical therapists and medical staff, and homecare workers) meet daily to discuss care plans and problems—chronic or new—of participants in that program—including non-medical, social, family, housing and other problems as well as medical issues. Participants may be seen in the clinic or the therapy center daily (as needed) and care plans can be changed according to changing conditions, at any time. The social activities of the day center are central to the program. Other details are suffused within these essays and more info about PACE can be found at www.npaonline.org.

But at Crab Cove, hearing Ara Belle's brief talk took me by surprise. I had sung and listened to Lead Belly's songs then for over 35 years. "Goodnight Irene", a sorrowful prison lament, had a particular significance to me because I had been married to a young woman named Irene. We divorced after only two and a half of marriage and I later learned from her mother that Irene had died of liver cancer at the age of 50. In any case, this introduction to Ara Belle Kingsby as relation to Lead Belly began for me a new and different type of relationship between us and, for me, a greater insight into how fortunate I was to be so engaged with this community of elders at CEI.

PACE program members live out their lives in their own homes. At entrance to any PACE program new participants are asked how they want to be treated or not treated in crises and end-of-life situations. Ara Belle Kingsby had, from the time she entered the program, stated that she did not want to be hospitalized or placed on machine ventilation in the event that her heart stopped. She based this on religious convictions. She had lived, she said, a long, satisfying, and prosperous life with her large extended family. She was prepared to pass on when called by her God. She believed she would be going home to a better world. Doctors were only going to add unnecessary burdens.

A few short months after I arrived at CEI, Ara Belle had an abnormal PAP smear (a test no longer recommended for women this old). She acceded to a biopsy by a gynecologist and this showed moderate cervical dysplasia—possible early signs of cancer. As a result our nurse practitioner then scheduled her for a recommended curative biopsy procedure called a LEEP that is done in the doctor's office. On October 14, 1992, a day before the procedure, Mrs. Kingsby declared that she would not go. She spoke carefully and calmly, without any touch of hostility in asserting that it would be best if she were left alone. About this same time she also refused to go for a recommended eye exam to check for glaucoma. She clearly said she did not want to be bothered with all of these doctors. I had then been medical director of CEI for only five months.

Just two months later Ara Belle developed a rapid irregular heart rhythm and was briefly admitted to the hospital. A short time later in January of 1993, she developed a blood clot in a leg vein and again required a brief admission to start on anti-coagulation. In the tension of these episodes of acute illness, she did not resist the care strenuously but when her general condition was more stable she again asserted during her next complete exam (this time to a woman physician on our staff) that she wanted no treatment for her cervical dysplasia.

Nevertheless, on June 30, at her next quarterly examination, at my persistent urging, she again acceded to see the gynecologist anyway. Ominously, I also noted she had an enlarged liver and an easily felt abdominal mass. A C/T scan was done with her agreement and revealed two different masses in her colon—presumably cancerous—with one probably expanding into the gallbladder.

Meanwhile, Ara Belle had been again scheduled for the cervix (LEEP) procedure. A tug of war was going on, and in retrospect, Ara Belle was wiser than we were given that her abdominal mass was menacing her life, not her cervical dysplasia. On August 9, after being taken to the gynecologist's office by our transportation staff, Ara Belle emphatically refused to transfer onto the table and then insisted that no further evaluation be done.

Once back at our day center's clinic she again patiently told me that her life was in God's hands and she would like me to let her live and die as God wished it. Apparently, I then realized, we had been ignoring her wishes. I had simply not wanted to "just let her die". Somehow it had seemed to me too early in her medical evaluation—despite her age—to give up. However, in consultation with Ara Belle and her daughter Ruth I agreed to better carry out her wishes. A gastrointestinal procedure to diagnose the abdominal masses was canceled. Ara Belle well understood all the time that she might have an abdominal cancer and that she was risking its further spread without treatment.

At the same time, though understanding that I should carry out her wishes, I was still failing to see that I had to give up the typical medical role for Ara Belle. I felt that, as a doctor, I now had very little to offer her. And, moreover, that the clash between our two value systems and personal judgments about her situation lent itself to personal failure for me. I liked this proud woman, but unlike more feisty (sometimes obnoxious) people I had to deal with, yet could easily laugh with, she was unnerving me. In her priestly, gentle way she had an untiring resolve; she was unbelievably forceful in her gentility. She challenged my self-defined role as physician. The situation was complicated. I was new to geriatrics, to dying and palliative care.

Certainly I had had patients to whom I could minister mostly emotional support, companionship, guidance, and a soothing influence even when I had little to offer as a curing physician. And I have always felt that the doctor role was as much caring as curing. *But what if Ara Belle had a curable cancer?* I thought to myself. *And besides that, what could I offer someone so accepting of death in her righteousness?* Thus, when a second doctor joined our team and I had to divide the patients between us, Ara Belle was one of those who I passed on to him, with her agreement. She expressed no concern. We still saw and spoke to each other frequently at the center. She greeted me cheerily each time nonetheless and lived on.

In September 1993, Ara Belle Kingsby suffered a second deep vein clot in her leg and was hospitalized for five days. Two weeks later, at a family conference with her new doctor, her daughter and her social worker, she again made herself clear, declaring that she wanted "no further work-ups" of her medical problems. Three weeks later she came to the center with visible blood in her stool.

By December 21, she had developed right-sided abdominal pain in the area of the mass; but she did not want any evaluation. She was treated with pain medications and her condition stabilized for a while; then, on March 7, 1994, she was hospitalized for two days with a urine infection. A day after leaving the hospital she came into the center seeking to be seen in clinic. I examined her for complaints of vaginal and anal pain and found she had become incontinent of both urine and stool. Her stool was brick red and tested heavy for blood. Her blood level had fallen progressively over a one-month period; she was anemic, anxious and in pain, and under these circumstances she agreed to my insistence that we do colonoscopy to finally identify what was happening and whether we could do anything to help. I wanted this done because even assuming her cancer was incurable, surgically preventing a bowel obstruction—a terribly painful way to die—or stopping the internal bleeding might still be possible and a useful palliative measure to make her end less difficult. She agreed. We treated her for abdominal pain.

At colonoscopy the gastroenterologist found that the higher up mass was, as expected, a bleeding and invasive cancer, too advanced to be removed via colonoscopy. With these findings, her answer, firm as it had been so many times before and now communicated through her daughter, was, "She doesn't want any surgery," not even to prevent an obstruction of the bowel. Nevertheless, the following week Ara Belle came in to CEI in even worse pain and now she was jaundiced. Under these stresses she acceded temporarily to seeing the surgeon. Two days later, before evaluation by the surgeon, her jaundice was worse; she was bright yellow and the mass was very tender. Our usual surgeon was in surgery all day, so I scheduled her to see him the next morning, but that wasn't to be.

At 5 a.m. that morning I was awakened by a phone call from Ruth that Ara Belle was unable to breathe and Ruth had called 911. I met them, and many other family members at the hospital emergency room. Ara Belle's blood pressure had fallen to 60/40; with a pulse of

130 and her hemoglobin was six, reflecting now potentially life-threatening blood loss; but she was conscious, alert, breathing well and, as usual, calm and reflective. We had talked about palliative care. I had discussed with Ruth the issue of Ara Belle dying at home in her own environment. But now they both preferred that if she were dying she spend her last days or hours in the hospital with nursing attention and family by her side, and so she was admitted.

At that moment—knowing that Ara Belle Kingsby would die from this malignant condition (later if not tonight)—I tried to think and act as if Ara Belle. We worked on the palliative principle that Ara Belle, who reiterated again very clearly and even blissfully that she was now ready to leave, was in the hospital only to make her dying easier, with less pain and suffering.

Although this palliative approach is followed every day by practitioners and nurses in hospices and hospital settings for terminal cancer patients, my relationship with Ara Belle had unfolded in a most unusual way. As I have mentioned, when I was appointed medical director of CEI I had already been practicing family medicine for 20 years, but I had little geriatric experience and no end-of-life care expertise. I was now the student of Ara Belle as well as her guide.

Ara Belle was admitted to the oncology ward for cancer patients who were under palliative care. The first day I did nothing but prescribe small morphine injections for pain; her condition did not change; she was alert; she ate dinner, shared time with dozens of family and friends, spoke about her passing as a blessing. At night, she began to have more pain. With the advice of staff nurses, her treatment passed on to an intravenous morphine drip which would, I hoped, control her pain, but also the desire to eat or drink; Ara Belle became more lethargic, but also pain-free. Yet on the third day she showed no signs of weakening. Her body was strong. We did not give transfusions for her severe anemia. Then I realized that the IV, which had been placed only to allow access for medications, was providing her some sustenance. The IV fluid rate was decreased to almost nothing, though she was provided any oral liquids she desired.

At the hospital, I visited with her daughters and other family daily and I told them she would likely die within two or three days from dehydration, a painless, almost dream-like death. But Ara Belle was not yet ready to die. In making such a prediction I learned an important lesson about the unpredictability of the trajectory of life and death even under such conditions. Ara Belle wandered in and out of consciousness and mental clarity and did not die.

As the days went by, misgivings about my decision to not do anything besides pain medication haunted me. I doubted myself, worried that somehow I had failed her. The family, on the other hand, remained close by and calm. Each daughter and her son fondly provided me, as well as Ara Belle, their support; told me I was such a wonderful person to be there daily going through this with them. I re-examined my ambivalence accepting that, even if "brought back to life", Ara Belle would only live to suffer a more tortured death from metastatic cancer—soon, very soon. To force her in this, the gravest moment of her life's vulnerability and hypersensitivity to noxious stimuli, to have palliative (not curative) surgery she never wanted, to suffer that pain and indignity as she was dying, would have been a terrible assault.

As firmly as the family stood by Ara Belle, they stood by me standing by Ara Belle. That helped me develop confidence in this almost shamanic role, which was as much a symbol of caring as anything else. As her state worsened we progressively raised the level of the morphine drip to treat her restlessness and any apparent pain. She became semi-comatose and more relaxed. The hospital nurses on this ward had been through this dying process with cancer patients hundreds of times before and they offered suggestions and parameters for the morphine drip. I was using morphine levels that were common for terminal cancer pain, they assured me; we were not doing anything unusual under the circumstances.

Two nights before Easter, Ara Belle had an increase in muscular spasms and tension. Back in my doctor mind I imagined uremia from her kidneys shutting down; electrolyte abnormalities; hypocalcemia, hypercalcemia or other causes of nerve-muscle membrane instability; hypoxia and acidosis, the pneumonia she had now acquired. I could guess but not know; *I must not become the "distant" investigator,* I thought. Clinical diagnosis and treatment was not my role. I ordered the morphine to be upped to the "usual" maximum dose and I imagined inside Ara Belle's mind: Ara Belle wondering if she might have the privilege of dying, of being "resurrected"—for she surely believed she was "going home" on Easter Sunday.

On Easter Sunday morning I visited Ara Belle and three of her daughters, and found her comatose and relaxed. The neuromuscular instability had been broken by the morphine. Her breathing had now become agonal. She was dying. I suctioned her briefly myself, talked with three of her daughters—Georgia, Ann and Pam—and stayed around a while believing she would die then. It was now the tenth day since her admission. I had given up thinking that I could predict the procession of this process. The family was calm and resigned to her death. I went on home. Ninety minutes later, around noon on Easter Sunday, 1994, the nurse called to tell me that Ara Belle Kingsby had died.

Two days later, four of Ara Belle's five children attended a prayer circle for her at CEI and presented me with a scrapbook of photos of dozens of family members taken during the prior ten days in and around Ara Belle's hospital room. Seeing them taking flash photos I had—on the second day—asked if I might have some family pictures. And despite their family crisis they had gone a step beyond and assembled this scrapbook. At the prayer circle they spoke of poems that Ara Belle had composed for each of them when they were children and they read some of her religious poetry.

I also spoke—though not of Ara Belle's enduring faith—but of the wonderful support that she and her family had given me as we had moved through her dying process together. "I cannot imagine," I said, "a family (including my own) giving me better or more deeply felt support than I have received from this family. It is an honor to have served and known them."

From Ara Belle Kingsby I learned more about myself than I would have thought could happen. Because I am Jewish, I have never believed in euthanasia. I identified assisting death with eugenics; with the reality that governments do try to decide who is to live and who to die, who is too old, too frail, too dangerous, inferior, and expendable. I am also uncomfortable with the idea of someone assisting the death or suicide of a person with whom they are not deeply familiar, because what a person says they believe or want at any particular crisis moment may or may not reflect the totality of their lives, their values, their being, themselves. But I learned from Ara Belle Kingsby and her family that, if only we try, people can allow each other to get close enough to understand and do the right thing.

What I also learned from Ara Belle is that some of the gifts of life can come to us in the most unimaginable ways and from the most unexpected others, such as in the form of death and dying friends (and patients) who simply reach out and ask to be understood and accepted, still, as equals. (First draft written 1994.)

A 1968 photo of Mrs. Kingsby with grandchildren,
taken about 25 years before I knew her.

The author with Georgia, one of Ms. Kingsby's daughters
(herself a grandmother), taken by another family member 3/27/94,
at Alta Bates Hospital in Berkeley, six days before Ara Belle's passing.

HOW DEATH SAVED
BARBARA'S LIFE

Barbara was looking for a real home. She came to us almost lacking an identity, almost a non-person. She did have an apartment, unkempt, reflective of her disorganized, withdrawn and depressed self. It was in an unsafe neighborhood in Oakland. It was all she had; that and a distant, dismal past, and no sense of a future. Her married name sounded Italian; but her own background never came into focus.

Barbara had been long estranged from her two living daughters (children by different alcoholic husbands). One daughter refused to ever visit or talk with her. Barbara herself had a lifelong history as an alcoholic and as a mother who had neglected her children and had had them taken from her. She carried a diagnosis of chronic schizophrenia and was being maintained in the community by the public mental health clinic on a dose of Haldol (25 milligrams) that would probably put you or me to sleep for days. Despite the diagnosis she carried, however, Barbara had for many years manifested only social isolation and withdrawal with no psychotic behaviors, hallucinations or delusions. But she did almost nothing, except chain smoke. And she was just a sad sack.

Five-foot three, with an indifferent look, coarse reddish-brown/graying hair, an average build, a wardrobe neither striking nor particularly shabby and a weight of 122 pounds, Barbara didn't stand out in a crowd, except for a tendency to protrude her lower jaw in an underbite, and her anxious pacing which suggested a restlessness that lived just beneath her stoical surface (perhaps a side-effect of her medications).

Everything about Barbara suggested an inner world of resignation. She rarely initiated conversations with anyone. Her moderately lined face, though not unpleasant, had the appearance of a hardened mask. She sometime seemed to float above the ground like a specter; at other times she paced like a zombie. She responded only when probed, though she was intelligent and observant. Her memory and her thoughts were often clear, even sharp and perceptive, yet fleeting; and she seemed so indifferent. Like many elders with schizophrenia, the disease—and perhaps the years of medication—seemed to have burned out her life force.

When Barbara was referred to the Center for Elders' Independence (CEI) she was, at 67, nine years younger than the average participant. She had been recently hospitalized for shortness of breath, the cause of which was not determined. No pelvic exam had been performed, but she was referred to a community gynecologist for a vaginal exam due to an odor. The gynecologist had found that she probably had a cancer with many symptoms that she had been ignoring and not telling anyone about, but the doctor was unable to perform the exam adequately for diagnosis.

The day of her initial visit to CEI, I consulted a different gynecologist and then referred Barbara to a radiation implant specialist for full diagnosis and his treatment recommendations. Not only did we hope to help her get rapid treatment, but our multidisciplinary team needed to know if she was likely to survive long enough to benefit from our day center and comprehensive support program; we needed to decide if she was a candidate for team evaluation and admission.

The specialist's answer came back in a matter of days: it was an invading cervical cancer that had expanded into the bladder and out to the walls of the pelvis, forming a tract between bladder and vagina that drained urine. But the tumor had not yet spread to lymph nodes or distant organs. Once radiation treatment had shrunk down the size of the tumor there might be a small possibility of cure of the cancer. She would also need to have tubes put in her kidneys through her back to drain her urine because either the tumor or the radiation would probably block the ureters. And since she was also having a lot of local infection and irritation, these could get more serious if we allowed urine and debris to drain constantly.

But Dr. Demanes thought that even without cure Barbara could maintain a stable quality of life for a year or so with treatment. He offered to stay closely involved in her care for the duration, not just during her treatment phase. As Barbara then agreed to be treated, we decided that she could benefit from CEI and enrolled her.

Stoic and depressed as she was, Barbara went through the heavy radiation treatments as though it were like getting dressed and brushing her teeth in the morning. She had her kidney tubes placed; they blocked or fell out periodically and she would have to return to the hospital to have them replaced. The radiation procedures involved repeatedly placing a large insert with many radiation probes inside the vagina and pushing it high into the pelvis. There must have been pain, but she never complained or admitted to much. "It was kind of uncomfortable," Barbara said. And then, "It did hurt a little when it was in there," she would casually monotone. We had sent her to live in a nursing home for supportive care during, between and after treatment as a temporary measure. Barbara lived at that convalescent hospital for three and a half months.

Meanwhile she became a regular attendee at the day care center, finding places to lie down, rest, or sleep frequently, but nevertheless getting to know staff and participants and slowly making a new home. She still had the attention span of a hyperactive child. She would come into an activity, sit for three to five minutes, then get up and wander restlessly about the center or find somewhere to lie down; or rush outdoors to chain smoke compulsively.

So our team tried to develop an interactive strategy to engage her, calm her, and slow down her restlessness. This included bingo on Wednesdays, small tasks, a try at the reading and discussion group, symptom management with her social worker, Rachel, drama therapy on Thursdays, art and mural work and talking with Rachel on Mondays, working with children when they visited, and so on. I steadily reduced her Haldol dose and decided to treat her depression if it didn't respond to the social stimulation. We waited to see if she would become more agitated on less Haldol.

Often now I came upon Barbara sitting in the hall, smiled at her, took her hand, and talked with her briefly. As time passed staff members, especially Rachel, were also developing a more interactive relationship with her. But Barbara's responsiveness was marginal. She seemed disinterested in life's nuances. Still, she offered that she liked the center, and felt supported.

When she started at CEI Barbara was told, and she acknowledged, that she had a serious cervical cancer that had spread, but amidst the talk of treatment, and "possible" cure, and the support she received— as she later expressed herself—"I thought I was getting better." In a sense she was right. On the other hand, denial ran—had been running—rampant through Barbara's conscious life for a very long time before this. It wasn't just death or the cancer. I hoped that, if perhaps briefly, denial might serve her positively. Besides that, one kind August day with treatment completed, the team returned Barbara to the community to live in a small residential home.

Improved independence, improved health. Barbara heard her doctors say that the tumor was shrinking. And in the first six months or so her weight had returned from 100 back to 120 pounds and her strength improved even during radiation treatment.

Despite new stable surroundings, however, Barbara soon became progressively weaker, with reoccurring weight loss, and increasingly difficult ambulation. She began to faint frequently after compulsively smoking cigarettes, finishing each one in about 30 seconds; she fell and had several minor injuries, once requiring five or six stitches to her scalp. She was obviously anxious and worried. Asked if she thought her cancer was getting worse or the fear of that possibility was bothering her, she flatly denied it. I started her on an antidepressant.

The CEI team noticed the changes and intensified the effort to involve Barbara with a painting project, for she had wanted to paint again. She got partway through, putting in five to ten minutes each day at the center during two different weeks; she sat in a reading and discussion group for only a few minutes. Though she anxiously sought cigarettes and, if not provided, smoked butts she scrounged or scavenged in the street and ashtrays, on some intangible level she seemed to be feeling more secure. I wondered how, paradoxically, Barbara could be feeling better and worse at the same time; I could not understand this contradiction then.

Throughout those months, Rachel and I maintained close contact with the daughter who had become, the past year, very involved in her mother's support. Sheila, 40ish, a woman who seemed to share

Barbara's serious and unreadable facial expression, worked successfully in a professional capacity with a local county health department. She had helped Barbara to accept us and the various housing changes we pressed on her. Barbara had initially resisted leaving her own apartment; and though Barbara had successfully moved in August, a while after returning to the community she initiated—through slovenly fecal incontinence—a confrontation with the residential homeowner and was expelled. But now, by early 1994, despite the fainting, the weight loss, and weakness, things had calmed on the home front. She was happy with her second new home of three months—as she was with CEI—important areas of calmness and achievement.

In early February, at her new board and care home (the Nest) which she shared with four or five other residents, Barbara became increasingly withdrawn; she started to stay in bed all the time at home and to resist coming to the day center; she began to have more frequent stool incontinence. Her Haldol was increased from five to ten milligrams. Now she became dramatically weaker, confused and increasingly more withdrawn.

This was not a psychiatric flare-up. Blood tests showed that Barbara had hypercalcemia (known as the para-neoplastic syndrome—it was due to regrowth and spread of her cancer) and she had become dehydrated, explaining her increased weakness, confusion, and withdrawn behavior. She was hospitalized, treated with intravenous fluids and pamidronate, which lowered her calcium, and this rejuvenated her. Just two days after admission she was lucid and alert; and so, with Barbara's agreement, I called Sheila and asked her to come to the hospital for a much-needed conference.

Barbara was able to walk from her room to a big, well-decorated lounge at the end of the corridor with comfy sofas and chairs spread about. She came without support, wheeling her own IV stand. She sat down; she sat quietly, peacefully smiling at times. "I'm sorry to tell you that you are dying of the cancer," I said. Whether weeks or months remained to her life, I could not know, but the process was inevitable and the calcium problem would probably keep returning. "Did you know that this was coming?" I asked Barbara. "No, not really," she responded. "It seemed I was getting better."

Then Barbara and Sheila warmly shared their feelings and fears with each other for an hour on that Saturday morning in the empty hospital ward lounge that was way too big for three people seated alone in a tight group. I sat witness to a sadness and a harmony blended into a common acknowledgment of each other and of themselves. For Sheila, particularly, it was an epiphany, because she and her mother had never, to her recollection, shared so much.

But what did Barbara feel; Barbara, who was dying? Finally I asked her if she was frightened, for she had often said that she was afraid of dying and wanted to live. "I'm not afraid anymore," she replied directly. I heard a lightness and relief in her voice. Did I imagine this? Was I projecting? Read on.

Barbara stayed in the hospital a few more days and then went home to her nest. We agreed upon a plan of support and palliation. Her center days were cut back to three a week and I told her she could be in control of whether or not she came in and whether to continue her medicines. On any particular day she could stay home if she wanted to.

Immediately, she showed a new outward assertiveness. At the center she began openly discussing her impending death with people she related well to. She no longer was interested in smoking. She did decide to stay home more often, but she was not withdrawing. On March 17, with her wanting to stay home more, I negotiated two days a week at the center with her, telling her I needed two days to monitor her medical state. She agreed.

Later in the day, back home, she refused all medications, including her Haldol. By phone I could not convince her to reverse the decision. My goal had always been to get her off psychiatric drugs and she knew it. Barbara was not hostile; to the contrary she was friendly, peaceful and determined. Now she spoke more frequently, and assertively. She smiled more spontaneously. She was relaxed and she initiated topics and conversations. At one point, out of character and somewhat out of context, she said to me, "Dr. Sapir, I just want to tell you how thankful I am for your kindness."

On March 18, now two weeks after Barbara's hospital discharge, the staff at the Nest went into rebellion over their fears of someone dying at the home. They had been instructed that Barbara was terminal and that both she and CEI hoped to keep her calm and happy until death at home (residential care staffs are not licensed nurses). Placing Barbara, who was not demented, in a nursing home at this time would be taking away her home and security for no reason. She was finally achieving some sense of self, some real autonomy, and with this an ability to direct her own life positively, with dignity.

Our program's home nursing director visited the nest home staff and gave them an in-service on terminal care and dying patients and assured them that we would manage any medical issues 24 hours a day. She helped the staff express their personal fears. Though no permanent agreement was reached, peace was restored. At least for the moment, Barbara could stay, and our team assigned a health worker to spend several hours a day supporting her at home to supplement the staff of the nest.

Now over the next week Barbara's hypercalcemia began to return, and she became weaker and unable to come to the center. She stayed in bed much of the time. Nevertheless she responded to encouragement and continued to keep up her intake of liquid and calories by mouth so that she did not suffer the disorientation that had caused her earlier hospitalization. In the midst of an overwhelming cancer burden, she remained in focus, in harmony and intact. And she was not becoming depressed. She received intensive support from Denise, her home health worker who had strongly bonded with her.

On March 23, with Barbara no longer able to attend the center, I also began home visits. The next day, she was calm and resting. I sat beside her. We conversed about her contentment with the room and bed location that she had. From her room, sometimes even from her bed, she could watch the squirrels in the back yard playing in the trees. "I love to watch the squirrels," she said, smiling. "I'm not afraid of dying," she told me, at her own initiation. "And I'm ready to die."

Four days later, Barbara did die, peacefully, in bed at home. That very same day she had still been able to get up with a little assistance and walk to the bathroom. Her incontinence had improved dramatically and there was no indication that her life was at its ending. A few minutes before death she had actually been up talking. I thought: *Barbara's death had become one of the most vital and developed works of her difficult life; it was a work of art as well as of her humanity. For her death was serene. Or it at least appeared so. What evidence?*

Time passed after Barbara's passing, after her wishes to be cremated had been carried out, after a remembrance and prayer ceremony had been held with the participants at CEI's Day Center. One day Sheila stopped in briefly. Thanking me for helping her regain a meaningful relationship with her mother, Sheila agreed that Barbara had found both inner peace and some kind of meaning in the last weeks of her life.

Then she hands me a sealed envelope that Barbara has asked her to deliver to me. The envelope is simply addressed "Dr. Sapir". I have no idea what to expect. I hesitate briefly then open it. Inside is a card. On its front two cherubim gaze upward toward heaven from a famous painting by Raphael, faces posed in idyllic wonderment. I open the card. Inside is written "Dr. Marc Sapir" then the imprinted words "Seasons Greetings". It is signed simply "Barbara".

Though briefly stunned I began to chuckle and could almost feel Barbara's presence. This card hung on my bulletin board beside my desk at CEI for years. As I looked up, or still think of it, I could never, can never, help from smiling, warmed by the black and wry humor of Barbara's post hoc greeting—and remembering the harmonies of her passing. My glimpse of Barbara's humanity, poignantly revealed—as well as the wonders of PACE—evoked this essay.

Barbara F.'s after-death greeting card (from Raphael's Sistine Chapel painting).

FAMILIES AND KIN FOLK

Doctors save lives, cure diseases, comfort people; but we also
make mistakes that can cause pain, suffering and death

Christine and Helen

Christine was already a member of the freestanding Community Adult Day Health Center (CADHS) in Oakland, CA when it transitioned into a PACE project as the Center for Elders' Independence (CEI) and I was appointed medical director of CEI. She was a friendly and pleasant "young woman" of 58 (average age of our elders was close to 80) who had suffered a stroke and had a hemiparesis (paralysis of one side of her body). She had a mild dementia (perhaps stroke-related) with some loss of short-term memory but no significant progression and her speech was not affected. She was obese—though not rotund—wheelchair-bound, and showed little motivation to work to regain any physical independence. Christine always complained that she wanted to walk but then she resisted the work in physical/occupational therapy necessary to achieve that, though staff thought she had the potential to walk independently. Immobile, she developed a gigantic pressure ulcer on the outer surface of the dependent leg which lay heavy and useless against her wheelchair's leg support and against her bed at home. The ulcer was open for most of a year and a half, breaking down even after skin grafting because the pressure that caused it continued. Ultimately, however, Christine did heal her leg wound.

Additionally, she had that most common of heart arrhythmias in the elderly (atrial fibrillation). For several years she received Coumadin (warfarin) to prevent future strokes which atrial fibrillation can cause. Then she got fed up with blood being drawn to regulate the Coumadin, refused to be tested and said she preferred to be taken off Coumadin. Before stopping the medicine we told Christine several times she would be at risk of another stroke before stopping the medicine; but she was stubborn and she took that risk, either not believing us or not caring. Staff and other participants were fond of Christine despite her stubbornness, irrespective of her failure to take any actions to improve her condition. She was direct, very friendly and personable, and in other respects she had positive life energy—a seemingly strange contradiction. But as I said, she wasn't an "old" 58, but a young "58".

A few years later, we enrolled her mother, Helen, in the program too. The mother and daughter lived apart. Christine was cared for by her own adult daughter (Eu), and Helen was cared for by a sister of Christine's. African American, Christine was unsurprisingly Protestant by religious upbringing, but her mother had converted to Catholicism. The two were quite close emotionally; they had no friction over religion.

Both women separately declared their end-of-life health care wishes to be DNR (do not attempt resuscitation when the heart stops). Christine in particular was adamant from the day she entered CEI. "Don't put me on those machines, no matter what," was her mantra. Her mother was a bit more vague than Chris. She often seemed to be in denial about her own situation as a disabled elder. Upon first meeting her, one might easily imagine that Helen had memory loss from the vague way she interacted. Yet despite this, she did not show any dementia on testing with the mini mental status exam, scoring near perfect. Her vagueness was like this: after successful surgery for colon cancer, Helen flat-out denied knowledge that she had had cancer in the first place. Nevertheless, when it came to end-of-life discussion, Helen was very consistent over time, if not as demonstrative as Chris. The discussion was repeated as part of quarterly examinations and as part of hospital care, and she always asked for no resuscitation.

When Christine first declared her DNR status at intake, CEI was a new PACE program and I was a new PACE physician. Our CEI procedures and protocols, which I was to write myself, were not yet fully codified. Though I obtained Chris' wishes, I did not suggest to her, as one always should, that we discuss her advance directive with her own daughter, who was her main caregiver. Nor was it brought up at the sign-in family conference when her daughter was present. These omissions were not without major consequence. Some months later we realized that we did not have a filled-out DNR form on the chart or in the home, as required by the Emergency Medical Services in order to prevent resuscitation efforts in an emergency. And so I had Chris sign one, made a copy and sent it home with Chris to be kept by her bed in case of emergency. Unfortunately, this simple (and necessary) act initiated all manner of disasters which continued until Chris' death in August of 1995 over a year later.

In large part because our team had failed to discuss end-of-life care wishes at the family conference with Chris' daughter present, Eu viewed the appearance of the DNR form as reflective of a desire by CEI to euthanize her mother, rather than our failure to engage her in a conversation and dialogue about her mother's wishes. In response to her phone call of protest and anger, we scheduled a meeting to help clarify our processes and goals and the rights of our participants.

But we had put ourselves, as they say, behind the eight ball by then. Despite our desire to start over and reestablish a trusting relationship, Eu could not be calmed and would not accept the idea that her mother could make such a decision for herself. General medical ethics and principles of autonomy be damned. She insisted that we had manipulated her mother who "just doesn't want to offend you". She also insisted that her mother was not competent to make such a decision; and that since she was the primary caregiver she had as much right to determine these matters as her mother did. (During my future years with CEI I had similar experiences with several other family caregivers who felt their opinion on such serious matters was more important than the patient's. As a result, I eventually understood that even though the law and medical ethics are clear that it's the rights and autonomy of the individual patient that are protected in this situation, that doesn't necessarily hold sway with someone who is sacrificing their own life and autonomy—whether out of love or obligation or both—to care for a disabled parent or other family member.) There was no consoling Eu. Discussing death was for her as if to bring her mother's demise nearer. And then, of course, the similar wishes of her grandmother came to light which only made matters worse. Eu saw the center as conspiring against her mother's and grandmother's welfare. The discussion took on racial overtones.

She then enlisted the support of Christine's two sisters in decrying the conspiracy we had visited upon them. She thought the entire program was designed to euthanize the African American population (since most participants of CEI were then African American). Attempts to apologize for not having involved them at the earliest (and more appropriate time) were rejected, as were explanations of individual rights under the Patient Protection Act and customary medical ethical canon. So we asked that they all come to a CEI ethics committee meeting where they would meet community as well as staff members willing to hear them out and help mediate this crisis.

This began a crash course for me. Moreover, many "crashes" of a different type were yet to come.

Ethical dilemmas generally arise from mismatches in perception, understanding, philosophy, values or perceived need. Thus an ethical crisis or dilemma at the end of life is not usually a new problem but the culmination of an unresolved cultural divide made acute by an impending death. Back in the early 1990s doctors and other health care providers in the US were rarely involved in values assessment discussions with the people whose lives they were entrusted with. Often a medical crisis resulted in a social crisis; sometimes in legal actions against doctors and hospitals. As a result of such conflicts and inappropriate end-of-life care, there are now laws requiring that hospitals and doctors carry out end-of-life discussions to ascertain patients' views and wishes, to document them, and to follow the patients' wishes. The design of PACE integrated these discussions and methods into the care of disabled elders way back in 1979 when the model was first designed by On Lok Senior Health Services in San Francisco. I learned "on the job" how sensible the design of the PACE model was in assuring that our health care teams actively engage with families' and participants' views, values and desires long before medical crises are apparent. We need to understand and to try to resolve any potential mismatches, and to develop mutual trust and understanding over time and not wait for a life-threatening crisis.

The word mismatch implies a social and cultural context: two or more sets of values and experiences. Chris and Helen's story is far from over, but even to this point it illustrates how the PACE model, though dealing with disabled elders near the end of life, looks at people's lives through a fundamentally preventative, cultural and socially integrating lens. As I unfold what happened to Chris and Helen you'll see how their story reveals the dangers and poor quality of care that result when a health care system doesn't honor that effort.

Eventually CEI required that any participant and their family who is to be discussed by our ethics committee be invited to ethics discussions of their case. However, this was the first time that we had asked a participant or family members to attend an ethics committee meeting. I had high hopes that, because we had some very good community representatives on the committee—including African American members—there would be a congenial atmosphere, a meeting of the minds, and a good outcome. My hopes were dashed when the family, led by Eu the youngest member present, did not come willing to listen or to discuss, but only to accuse. Indeed, the three women—two of Christine's sisters and her daughter—focused their accusations on the African American social worker on the case and the other African American community members on the committee who had, to their thinking, betrayed their people and Christine and Helen. The family stormed out of the meeting in mid discussion and threatened to take Helen and Christine out of the program although neither participant was willing to leave or to change their health wishes. Our attempts at an open, safe, and fair ethics discussion had failed and we were at loggerheads. Not only that, after the meeting some personal threats were made against staff members and that worried us and added to the challenge.

On my own initiative, I notified Eu that we would transfer Christine's care to our other physician, an African American, and he and I agreed that he would not press the health wishes issue with the family, yet try to carry out the participants' wishes in any crisis, if at all possible. We knew full well that this dilemma could not now be easily resolved, and this plan was intended to temporarily defuse the tensions. Further negotiations would have to wait. Our hope was that when death came, like most deaths, it would not be under circumstances that required consideration of resuscitation or other life prolonging actions.

However, six months later the other physician left CEI and I was back on both cases as the primary physician. Then, a few months later, Christine suffered an unusual slowly evolving stroke. We tried to monitor her out of hospital hoping that the damage was small and would stabilize, but on the third day she became almost totally unresponsive while sitting upright in the center. Hospitalized, she continued to deteriorate, falling into a coma. Eu demanded that I get off the case. We weighed the options of disenrolling Chris from the program because of an irresolvable dispute with the primary physician, but decided that our obligation to <u>both</u> Chris and Helen precluded such action. Violating Chris' wishes and acceding to Eu's demands regarding resuscitation seemed better than leaving her and her mother without our comprehensive care and support under these circumstances. Christine had entrusted herself to us. Our consulting neurologist agreed to temporarily become the primary physician in the hospital.

After about ten days in the hospital, with Christine showing no improvement, the neurologist felt the prognosis for recovery was terrible. Despite her assessment, however, Eu insisted that Chris receive a long-term stomach feeding tube placed through the abdominal wall in a simple surgical procedure, something Chris had said we should not do to her. Chris also developed pneumonia, but, despite staying in a coma, she did not require ventilation and was breathing on her own. The neurologist felt uneasy about the primary care management at this point and asked to retire from that responsibility. She knew that Chris' right to refuse the G-tube had been ignored. With nothing more that we could do, Christine was placed in a nursing home to live out the rest of her unconscious life. Because of Eu's hostility, after discussion with CEI's executive director, I found a physician who had many patients at that nursing home and was willing to take responsibility for her care, to coordinate with us and communicate regularly with me. CEI remained responsible for Chris' care and her mother Helen remained in the program.

Christine remained in a vegetative state for two months and died at the nursing home. No efforts at resuscitation were made. She was found dead by nursing staff. Though her wish to not have a feeding tube had not been honored, at least she had not been put on a ventilator. The case was sent to our Professional Medical Advisory Committee for review and discussion. I recognized how the omission I made early on contributed to this outcome, although we have no way of knowing if a better relationship might have been achieved had we told Eu of Chris' wishes at the initial family meeting. At the least, we would have had some years for Eu to get to know myself and our team members on a personal level; Eu would have had time to discuss this situation repeatedly with Christine and come to some agreement between them. Or perhaps not. But if not, we would have at least been in a better position to honor those wishes in the care we provided.

Helen

Death usually signals the end of CEI's relationship with participants' families, but in this case it did not because Helen was still a member. Two months after Christine died, Helen fell at home and suffered a hip fracture. Despite her age (79), she was in good enough physical condition that surgery could be considered. She and her family wanted her to have surgery and our orthopedic surgery consultant agreed. He thought he could perform it successfully. Surgery was performed. However, Helen developed cardiac complications under anesthesia, though the cause remained undetermined. I never received any evidence of an intraoperative error, but the anesthesiologist was later censured by a hospital committee for negligent behavior, which I should explain.

On the day of surgery, I was leading a meeting at the center when I was called away to answer an important call from a physician. The anesthesiologist on Helen's case, who I did not know, told me that Helen was in recovery but had not yet awoken. She asked me if she could go to a dentist appointment that she had scheduled for that afternoon. I was confused. I didn't understand why I was being asked this. "How long has she been in recovery?" I asked her. "About 15 minutes," she responded. "Is this situation within a range of normal? Might she still wake up? What can you do for her?" She responded that there was nothing else she could do and I told her that she should do whatever she thought right. Only later did I fully understand that this anesthesiologist was actually seeking my permission to leave an unstable patient who needed her attention. Caught unawares of what was going on, with neither adequate knowledge nor a good enough understanding of what had transpired to respond, I did not act assertively enough to tell the anesthesiologist she had a responsibility to her patient (our joint patient). And I had, without understanding this, unintentionally collaborated with her desire to leave an unconscious patient in the recovery room to go to an appointment. Shortly after the anesthesiologist left her, Helen suffered a cardiac arrest in recovery and was resuscitated by the orthopedic surgeon, who then notified me of what had occurred. She never regained consciousness, and ended up in a coma on full life support in the ICU.[46] Helen had been in good general health and had survived that colon cancer resection (mentioned above) only a year earlier. She was only 79, average age for our program. No one had anticipated a bad surgical outcome, although the family was, of

---

46 Typically, DNR orders are suspended during and just after surgery on the grounds that ventilation is required under anesthesia and even a cardiac arrest during or just after surgery would not be a "natural" event, but could easily be related to the surgical and anesthesia intervention.

course, briefed by the surgeon and anesthesiologist in the usual way about risks of surgery and anesthesia, particularly in the elderly.

The orthopedist later explained to me that there had been a short period of time when he applied the glue to the bone when fastening the new hip ball, that Helen's blood pressure had fallen dramatically. He said he was aware of a few reports of isolated cases of this glue causing a sudden drop in blood pressure. He had no way of determining if it was the glue that caused Helen's blood pressure to drop, or if the drop in her blood pressure was so severe that it caused her brain to become oxygen-starved for too long, or if the anesthesiologist made some other mistake or was negligent during the surgery. That mystery remains. But my own feeling of collaboration with the post-operative irresponsible behavior of the anesthesiologist leaving her patient in trouble to go to the dentist, remains with me.

Because specialists are higher in the power pecking order than primary care physicians, few primary care physicians would be assertive with a consultant specialist. But even though they have important expertise, even though they earn as much as ten times the earning of primary care docs, the primary care physician has to play the role as the patient's chief advocate within our too impersonal health care system. Although I was then being manipulated by the anesthesiologist, I nevertheless did fail to carry out my full responsibility to Helen. Likely the outcome would have been no different, but regardless I should have called out the anesthesiologist.

We would all like to live in a just world, but sometimes bad behavior is rewarded and good behavior punished—that's hardly fair. The peri-surgical brain damage to Helen was terrifying. There was a thorough case investigation at the hospital. The anesthesiologist was censured for leaving and for calling me. If there was negligence during surgery she should have suffered a worse fate. But I can only surmise that there was no evidence, only her word.

In the end I was patted on the back by the committee that reviewed the case and told that I had done nothing wrong at all. Perhaps my behavior was not egregious, but I did do something wrong. I failed to advocate sufficiently.

Nonetheless, despite earlier tensions around Christine and Helen's health care wishes, the family, to my amazement, responded very differently, supportively and positively in this disaster. The sister of Chris, who was the caregiver of Helen, took me aside in the ICU and said that the family understood how emotionally involved Eu (her niece) was with these crises (of both her mother and now her grandmother), and that they would manage her grieving and help her work through the need to allow her grandma to die. She asked me to discuss changes in Helen's status with her or the third sister first and that they would then include Eu in family discussions after they had prepared and calmed her. I breathed a sigh of relief and thanked her.

Based upon the earlier events around Chris, they had learned how to respond to Eu's fragility and supported her differently. And despite much emotion and some commotion, Eu was, indeed, able to allow the process of withdrawing Helen from life support to proceed as the daughters (her aunts) wished.

Helen died in the hospital, in an irreversible coma probably resulting from low blood pressure during surgery for a hip fracture. She never awoke. After she was resuscitated and sent to the ICU on a ventilator, her EEG the next day was consistent with much brain damage, but was not a flatline. On the fourth hospital day with no change in condition, the family agreed to stop support of her blood pressure and then to remove ventilation and to not attempt to feed her through tubes. Off the ventilator she was transferred to the ward and lived several hours and died peacefully. In the aftermath the family was remarkably supportive of CEI and the care provided, wrote us letters (which I kept) and thanked myself and other staff for all that we had done for Chris and Helen. I had tried so hard to get things right for Christine and failed, with much resulting tension and hostility; I did little for Helen in her crisis and the one thing that stands out in my mind was that I made an error (in my own judgment) when that anesthesiologist tried to use me to cover her unethical behavior. This surprising turn of events ended one of the most complex and difficult ethical crises I experienced.

So we learn. And I learned. First, to always include major players in decisions and let them know your expectations unless the participant forbids it. If a family member cannot allow the participant any autonomy at the outset, be prepared, if that patient is admitted to a hospital later, for ethical dilemmas. And never assume that some written rules of medical ethics supercede real life. In real life family members have more than just some rights. They are who they are and that's important in a crisis with an unconscious participant; their collaboration is inevitably necessary. Thus, when one assumes responsibility for the full healthcare of a frail patient, understanding the family and support system dynamics needs to start at the very beginning of the relationship, in part to learn who you can rely on to support your work over time and in part to begin to build relationships that will endure through these travails. Signing people into PACE or any other comprehensive program without their families' presence is not a good idea, as many cases and problems have repeatedly demonstrated.

Families learn from experience just as we professional staff do. I spent the next six years explaining to new staff what happens when families are not involved with the team process, care planning and health wishes from the beginning. I won't say that we achieved 100% performance and no similar problems ever again occurred, but we learned to highlight these issues. This family saw the disaster that resulted from a younger generation member (Eu) whose emotions complicated their relationship to the health care team they depended upon. They were not willing to confront their niece at the early stages when it was her own mother who lived in her home, and who was at center stage. At that point their familial loyalty forced them to do things they might not have wanted to do or say. However, by the second instance they did realize the need to surround Eu with support and love and to be able to blunt her initially inconsolable emotions.

I spent the best years of my medical life learning about the lives, families and histories of disabled elders in our communities. Even if I should get dementia before I pass out of this world myself I won't forget Christine and Helen. Nor will I forget that phone call from the anesthesiologist asking me if she can leave her unconscious patient (and mine) to go to a dental appointment. And the non assertive answer I gave that compromised my own values.

Race Man

I remember the term "race man" from a description by Langston Hughes—in the satirical Simple stories[47]— whose "race man" (Jess B Simple) was—in the disguise of a simple-minded silly person—the very conscious Black man aware of his bond with his people, their culture, their suffering, their exploitation and their need to stand together. I also heard Malcolm X, and later Nelson Peery, an African American communist, use the term race man on occasion. To think of it, probably the last time I heard that phrase it was spoken by Gus,

---

47 In analogous fashion to some of Shakespeare's brilliant fools, Jess B Simple is a satirical character who is both foolish and silly-wise. He's a screen for Langston Hughes telling it like it is. If I were smarter, I'd be able to use more narrators, like Jess B Simple, but in the end I'm not Simple enough.

a participant/patient at Center for Elders' Independence in 1992 or 1993. I was appointed medical director at CEI when it became a PACE site in 1992. Gus was there before me, when it was just an elders' day center. He was one of the sweetest men you'd want to meet and he had an exquisite, mellow but strong tenor voice. He was slender and tall and would sing "How Sweet Thou Art" sometimes for those in attendance at CEI's first Day Center. And I can hear him hitting the high note on "come sing my soul" as I type this. Gus was getting along in years (probably in his mid-to-late 80s) lonely, had few, or no, remaining relatives, and he was beginning to show some dementia and tendency to wander, but he was still clear minded enough to tell you about himself and his life. Gus said he was a "race man" but the most difficult part of his life was that he had been rejected by many Black people as not being black enough. His light skin tone was not quite as lacking in pigment as mine, but he was quite fair, and did not, on first glance, look African American. He was out front about how painful the rejection was for him. His attitude toward "race" may have been intensified by this pain, but one had the sense that the depth of his identification with the discrimination and hatred his people had suffered for so many years right into the present was more profound than just his personal stake. He understood the world in the way that Langston Hughes portrayed the race man.[48]

---

48 The inter-disciplinary team at the Center for Elders' Independence struggled mightily with the problem of individual autonomy vs security and collective responsibility regarding Gus. Below is another essay from my (unpublished) book *I'll Fly Away* about Gus and that dilemma.

Gus' long trip home

Gus was slender attractive, youthful, with a fine upright posture, a small chin and fine lips, about six feet tall and quite shy. He stuttered a little when anxious—though never while singing—and had to be drawn out in conversation. He had a high smooth forehead, mostly bald pate with short hair and an engaging smile. Gus was fair complected and his features did not suggest his ethnicity. With quite a good number of participants having varying levels of dementia with memory loss, you can imagine the frustration to tell people what and who you are and have them forget a few minutes later. Part of the issue here was that Gus too had a little dementia; not bad, but enough to confuse things a bit. But I'm getting ahead of myself for a minute. Anyone paying attention knew that Gus had one beautiful gospel singing voice and that could clue them in that he might be African American. Gus' favorite song was "Ne'er by God to Thee" and he loved to solo on that piece, straining his tenor for the high notes. His voice was strong enough that someone decided to capture it for posterity on CEI's professionally made video, "Still Singing" and you can still here him singing today many years gone if you please. As an aside, I found that even severely demented participants retain their musical talents and particularly received great enjoyment from singing. Several were in Lillian Stoval's "heavenly choir" which won a state award.

I don't recollect Gus having family and he was living at a Board and Care home. Gus had a great love of the city of Oakland, his hometown. He was like a wandering minstrel. Many dementia patients take to wandering in their confusion, but Gus was a wanderer going way back. We had other great travelers in the program, such as William B., but William was a purposeful traveler, always on his way somewhere in particular, often by bus, sometimes on foot, but always out there. Gus on the other hand just liked to wander the highways and byways. Maybe he missed the independence of living alone, or the friends who had passed or moved away, or family, or just loved to walk. But we all knew he could be seen almost anywhere around town and that became a concern for the team. Reports began to be fielded from the Board and Care of Gus missing in action at night, of his being picked up and brought home by the police at odd hours. Naturally we tried to talk with Gus about this situation. He didn't see the problem, just shrugged his shoulders and gave his shy friendly grin. Then one night he was rolled and wound up at the ER with, luckily, minor injuries–cuts and bruises to his face.

The team had been working with the Board and Care to try and have them not let him go out at night. They tried to monitor his coming and going but were not successful. He kept disappearing. He often made his way home, but the risks and dangers seemed to grow. As Gus' memory slowly worsened the team discussed whether to put him into a nursing home to protect him. After a lengthy debate it was agreed that wandering was so integral to Gus' quality of life that institutionalizing him beyond a Board and Care would be an attack on his personhood, his identity, his joys. Instead a new Board and Care, thought to be more protective of its residents was found. The new home had few doors and a staff member always at the main exit/ entrance. Gus would be allowed out at reasonable hours of the day and otherwise talked into staying home.

For a while that worked. We had protected Gus' quality of life and found a solution to a difficult problem. Until we learned that he was getting out again. Gus had been able to subvert the system in a fairly short time but it took longer for us to learn this. Whether it was his cleverness or our misjudgment of the level of monitoring and con- cern at the new home we will never know.

Perhaps a few weeks or a month went by after we knew of the

problem again. One night Gus was reported missing. The next day he was found dead face down in a creek. He had apparently tumbled down a small embankment and hit his head on a rock. There was no evidence of foul play. Gus was not ill at the time. He didn't really have any serious life-threatening illnesses. The Team was shocked, heartbroken, guilty. We all felt great loss.

The next day we carried out a "debriefing" review of the case. We gnashed our teeth and wondered and worried. In the final analysis the logic of who Gus was pulled us back to reality. We had done well for Gus. We listened to him. He knew what he wanted. He was clear on the importance of being able to roam (as he always had done). We had agreed to take a risk that was necessary to keep his life worthwhile. Gus' death did not mean that the risk was inappropriate or inordinate because we affirmed Gus. The team decided that our commitment to who Gus really was reflected the humanity of the interdisciplinary team/PACE approach to supporting frail elders. Gus died doing the thing he loved most, walking the city's streets.[49]

In the 20th century, science propounded that "race" as it relates to humans is a social construct created by racists to justify the dehumanizing of ethnicities, nationalities and so on. . . . There are no meaningful biological subdivisions of race within the "human race" unless you are looking to segregate and oppress for profit or other gain in power and dominance.

---

49 Later I've drawn a contrast between the quality of life approach and American technical medicine in the sad tale about the life and death of my good friend, Hal Carlstad.

Most of CEI's department managers, circa 1999 (photographer unknown).

WRITING: MENDEL

In 2004 I published a small satirical surreal parable—a novel about the second Bush's years leading up to the Iraq invasion and occupation. My publisher, iUniverse.com, is an on line organization which is, Sheila tells me looking down her nose, in the genre of the vanity press—i.e. self-publishing. iUniverse doesn't charge a whole lot to publish your book because they do "on demand" publishing. Instead of typesetting and printing out some thousands of copies that have to be stored in a warehouse until (if ever) ordered, they print books only to meet orders.

They use photo-copying methods instead of printing presses. Their books are available through Amazon and Barnes and Nobles; copyrighted and registered in the usual way. The assembled books are every bit the aesthetic equal of books typeset in the older way. The name of my novel is *The Last Tale of Mendel Abbe—Sonny Bush and the Wise Men of New Chelm.*

For just a few hundred dollars extra iUniverse promises to have your book evaluated by literary academics and if it meets muster the book can be listed on their editor's choice list of recommended books. I foolishly thought that getting on the editor's list would help get the book distributed to booksellers. I paid the money, then had my book copy-edited on my own. It got a great review and was put on the list. I thought iUniverse would care about the distribution of the books they publish, particularly those they list as editor's choice, because they do make money off of sales. I now believe they make most of their money from the authors even though their charge is not exorbitant. My book looks great, but iUniverse did little to promote it. I suspect their book PR and distribution efforts are budgeted in the region of zero dollars per year (perhaps that's an exaggeration). So I had a "good-for-nothing" published book. I put it in a few bookstores in the Bay Area and did a reading at our local independent bookshop down the block where, over a year and a half period about 50 or 60 copies were purchased by local folks, some of whom know me. All told approximately 100 copies were sold and a similar number given away. In the year 2012 my royalties from iUniverse book sales amounted to $1.32 of which $.34 was take out as income tax withholding.

Since 2012 I've been called repeatedly by different folks supposedly "representing" the publisher who offered to help get the book distributed and would come up with a "business plan" if I was agreeable. I feigned interest, but by now I knew that a major line item in their business plan would be for me to pay for their efforts up front—again. I also knew that a book about the Bush years, even if funny, amusing, damning, insightful and historically accurate, was dated. Had W been tried for his crimes in recent years—as he ought to have been—at least that might have stimulated a market for my satire. But President Obama dropped that ball, although the evidence of the crime of torture by Bush-Chaney was not hard to find. In this, Barack Obama himself became an enabler of presidential crimes. The "business plan" people (I wonder if maybe they are freelancers who work for iU on commission only or wholly independent) seem to have become discouraged by my failure to return their calls.

Whatever, but in 2004, having been "retired" since 2001 and then also written my first play, *Zara's Faith,* and then my book of essays about Center for Elders' Independence, I decided to attend the Squaw Valley Writer's Project workshop on Writing the Medical

Experience. A very wonderful week for me, it was. I got to know the amusing and amazing writer-doctor and surgeon Richard Selzer as he led our small sub-group; then a married young woman from Iowa pursued me—right into the next year and to a San Francisco conference as well. She was a Midwesterner, perhaps looking for a way out of her marriage, but I surely wasn't going to be that path. Unsurprisingly, she was really pissed when I told her I wasn't available.

Though I received good criticism on the one CEI essay I took to Squaw Valley, the lazy me didn't try to edit the book into publishable form for about a decade. When I did, I thought I had agreement with a small all-women publisher in Georgia, but at the last minute they told me they wanted the entire book re-written to their framing—yes, at the last minute. I couldn't believe they asked me to change the entire focus of my work.

One day at Squaw (now Palisades) during a break a young fellow—friend or relative of one of the other doctor/writer participants—was having lunch with us on an outdoor patio. I mentioned my little novel and he wanted to know more about this Mendel Abbe. "He's really you isn't he," this fellow quipped. Well, writers often share aspects of themselves with their characters, but no, he isn't really me, I responded. He wouldn't take that for an answer and kept teasing me on his point.

I invented Mendel Abbe, so he is me, but then again he isn't. I needed him and he needed me and that was our marriage (his wife Sophie, the narrator of the second half of his story might be offended by my language here). In fact, the little secret I did not divulge is that Mendel Abbe is my actual Hebrew name. And Mendel's disappearance by the American Jewish Nazis and the Bushites, did come from within my long dwelling fear of one day being renditioned (as opposed to auditioned) by forces beyond our democratic control. And yet I was not dissembling when I insisted that Mendel Abbe, as narrator and protagonist, was not me, but another "real" person.

However, as I've pointed out elsewhere, how much do we really know about ourselves. I think it wise to confirm that Mendel is one of my manifold beings—a personality that I sometimes adopt and adapt to. And even if personality and multiple personality may be the wrong words (for personality and personality disorders do have a distinct meaning in the Classification of Mental Disorders (DSM series) I remain convinced that the human mind is chimeric and not so fixed as we want to believe it to be.

HOW DID I BECOME A DOCTOR?

I became a doctor by accident. Or so it seemed to me. Maybe I had blinders on. To my parents, living after WWII in an American environment of bitter anti-Semitism which characterized the United States (read Arthur Miller's only novel, *Focus*, which takes place in Brooklyn where my dad grew up) what they wanted for their children was security, the "middle-class" life and happiness. How do you achieve such things? You spin flax into gold. What Jewish mother didn't hope to be able to introduce, "my son, the doctor" to her friends some day.

Epidemiologists, particularly those who evaluate human events such as falls and fractures, the back pain of bus drivers, work related injuries, auto accidents, insist that "nothing involving human behavior is accidental". Most "accidents" have knowable causes that can be ameliorted. Many bad outcomes (accidents) are preventable. Thus we now require seat belts while riding in cars.

As a child of nine or ten I imagined myself a composer or orchestra conductor. I was by then playing clarinet and had prominent singing roles in the school choir. I loved music so much—as did my father who sang in the shower and in the temple choir. "Doctor" wasn't appealing. But there were telltale signs that I wasn't sufficiently driven for a career in music. I studied piano for less than a year with a friend of my parents, Mauri Brown—mother of my friend Walter. I quit, lacking dedication to practicing, though my sister, younger then I continued beyond me at her lessons and became proficient. Walter would be the first chair clarinetist in high school. I was fourth chair in the first clarinet section, but I knew I would never match Walter's sweet tone since he took his lessons and practicing seriously. I was happy enough just to be in the first (of three) clarinet sections. When our concert band conductor one day asked if there was anyone interested in playing the bassoon (the school had one, unplayed) I volunteered. I did quite well from the start. I took lessons and then performed in a section of the All State High School Orchestra as well as in school. I played in a Westchester County Youth Symphony for two years; later I played for a year or two with the Brandeis Orchestra taking lessons with a Boston Symphony bassoonist. After college I studied about a year with the principal bassoonist with the New York Philharmonic. In the 70s–80s I put in some time on bassoon with the West Valley Community Symphony in San Jose and in 1987–1988 with the University of California Berkeley Symphony as well and was invited to play with an undergraduate honors group of music majors working up Mozart's "Quintet for Piano and Winds". But I was nothing special.

In my teen years I learned folk guitar and Travis picking at camps and in college. I then wrote my first song, Miss Liberty, about the Cuban Missile Crisis, in 1962–1963. Over the ensuing years I have written more than 20 songs, including one for each child and our grandchildren. More recently, in 2008, I got a renewed hunger for what I had missed by quitting piano, so I took a one semester class in piano at the Berkeley Jazz School here in town. But my wish to compose classical music had died an early death.

I was quite content to remain a child as long as possible, living in the present, unconstrained by the future and its exigencies. Even in high school when it was clear that I had talent and tone as a bassoonist, I had no more than the remotest ambition to become a professional. As a youth, my passions were not yet fully formed and not churning with any idea of a future me. This worried my mother who thought (I distinctly recall this) that I played "too much" with younger children (like Gilbert Colby and Danny Friedman, who Michael Vogel and I taught to play baseball).

Although I loved music, however, I was fascinated by science. My parents promoted it, but I was on board too. I remember reading the book, Microbe Hunters, by DeVries in awe. It's about great discoveries in the history of medicine and the men who made them (a few women, like Madame Curie, were included). Then one high school summer, my folks lined me up a fantastic summer experience working with the lead pathologist, Frank Kaldi, at a Manhattan hospital. The hospital's director was Dr. Schwartz, who happened to be the president of our temple in Eastchester (where Dad was vice-president—and they were friends). Such social relationships undergird what some Americans disingenuously claim as the American "meritocracy". Having connections as a path to advancement surely isn't a definition of meritocracy, unless you're using a strange dictionary. Nevertheless, I'm glad I got this opportunity. Frank Kaldi, a Hungarian refugee was kind, helpful and gave me grand opportunities. He took me into autopsies and into surgical operations where he was performing microscopic frozen biopsy evaluations for cancer right next to the surgeons with patient's bodies opened and waiting under anesthesia for a diagnosis of cancer or no cancer. I also investigated and wrote up a paper on the intrinsic blood coagulation biochemical cascade. I loved that summer. Though I didn't decide to become a doctor then, I began thinking about a career in cancer research and hoping, maybe, to cure some forms of cancer.

So I went off to Brandeis in 1959 thinking abut cancer research and since I wasn't at all sure where I was headed I chose the "general science" major that allowed me to fulfill all the course requirements for medical school while taking whatever biochemistry and microbiology courses that interested me, as electives. But my determination level still couldn't have been too high. I just got by with C's in math and science where I had excelled in these fields in high school, and had particular difficulty with the calculus course for science majors. The concepts behind the area under a curve and differential equations stymied me as reading had done in 2nd grade. Meanwhile I was getting A's in english composition, humanities, and world history and I was particularly infatuated with writing papers that analyzed literature.

In my third year, however, I lined up a job on campus working in one of the important biochem labs.[50] I think the professor's name was Maurice Sussman. I admired his research and he was a nice boss, but the only thing I really remember about the experiments I performed was that my work involved radioactive phosphorous and at some point I spilled a lot of P_{32} on the lab floor. I guess the radiation level wasn't very high because my radiation badge never got me off work and I didn't contract leukemia like atomic bomb survivors from Hiroshima and Nagasaki, Nevada and other Western states.

Also in my third year I took the famous Brandeis course in organic chemistry. I say famous because the professor's methods were widely known. If you attended class every day, wrote down every formula and studied the mechanistics he put on the board and could handle those equations deftly you'd always do well. If you didn't you'd never survive his rigorous exams. Kindly, he stated this himself. At that point, though I enjoyed the subject, moving around electron dots and bonds and such, I was deeply into an existential crisis. I was cutting classes all over the place, sitting in the library in a daze, watching co-eds bodies and not doing my school work, although I wasn't on any particular substance I could blame this on. My interest in music

---

50 I was also assistant to the university photographer, developing and printing his photos.

led me to take the Bach and Handel course that semester. I went to class, but then when I was in the library supposedly diagramming and dissecting the music, that exercise seemed meaningless to me. I just listened to the music and didn't think about it at all, just listened. By the end of the Fall semester I had a D going in Bach and Handel and my outlook didn't look better in organic chemistry either. At that point, dean of students, I Milton Sacks, called my parents and told them I was in danger of being suspended. Sacks was also a political science professor and a nemesis to those of us who wanted to stop the growing US intervention in Vietnam. He was an advisor to JFK, a staunch anti-communist and advocate for American aggression there.

But Sacks calling my parents ended up being a pivotal turning point in my life. Mom and Dad got in the car right quick and drove up to Waltham from New York to have a talk with me. "Look," I said, "I want to take time off from school and figure out what I want to do." I was thinking of possibly going into psychology at that point. "I am unhappy right now," I told them, "and I just need to find myself." They didn't buy this one bit. I suppose they had thought they'd steered me onto a path where self-motivation would take over. Mom pleaded desperately, that I was going to ruin my life. That I'd never come back to school and so on. I think she may have been thinking about how quitting high school had had such a negative impact on Dad's future life; and how I had almost got myself not graduating from high school too by never opening a book in senior English. "But if you do stay, you've got to make up your mind to do the work," they said. "We know you are capable." This was a full court press and I caved. *Maybe they are right*, I thought. But as important as that, I hated seeing them so upset. I didn't want them to be so distraught. On the spot I not only gave in, but I accepted that to stay in school I would have to actually overcome my lassitude and get serious about the work.

I'd had two and a half years trying to find myself and "grow up absurd". [51] Now, it seemed, I had to actually "face the music".

I decided to work hard, study hard and apply to medical school right then. I still hadn't thought about actually becoming a doctor. My mind was still on medical research. From that point on I think I got straight A's through graduation (perhaps one B). I ace'd the organic chemistry final. I actually loved that stuff even more when I got it down.

---

51 *Growing up Absurd* is the title of a book by sociologist Paul Goodman about the Beats and the impact of the cultural release and existential crises young people faced from America overcoming the straitjacket of the 1950s—the conformism, the McCarthyism, and the Korean War.

Maturation, Pedagogy and Social Evolution

THE BERKELEY HIGH SCHOOL–BASED HEALTH CENTER (1988-1991)

Introduction

It struck me that we cannot have a just society if our young people are not inspired by the public education system; if they don't find it user friendly, supportive and resourceful, teaching analytical tools that amaze them with their own intellectual power. It struck me in 1988 that this was a political problem we could probably do something about in Berkeley. I had been acting health officer for the city in 1987 and our daughter had just entered Berkeley High School in '88. I realized that Berkeley High had all of the problems of any large inner city high school, particularly high dropout rates, racial divisions, and a tracking system wherein most of the wealthier kids are steered toward classes, teachers and training that help them get to top colleges while the poor kids often struggled just to survive.

In 1988, as private citizen, I got appointed to the mayor's task force on youth and drugs. Around that time I was already developing the idea that we should form a model school health center for Berkeley; a center that would be a resource to help young people deal with all of the issues and problems they face. I worked on the high school project from late 1988 until early 1991 when the center opened under its first permanent coordinator, Kris Maltrud. In 2000, I was invited to write the history of the early phases of the health center by Glenda Pawsey of the advisory board, so that anyone interested might understand not only why but most importantly how we went about achieving this health center. Who made up the "we" that did the "doing" is as much part of the story as what we did.

Jump Start

From my work at the City Health Department in 1987, I knew some key people to contact for support of this project. First, I sat down and talked with Laura Anderson, coordinator of the city's clinic at 6th and University Avenue. We agreed to work together to form a committee that would have the coherence and the drive to achieve success, starting with the City Health Department. In looking back at the notes of the planning committee, I am amazed to see that only two years passed from the time of our first meeting on December 13, 1988 until we opened the center at Berkeley High in early 1991. Here is how we went about the task.

At the very beginning the health center was designed as a collaborative project—between the Berkeley Health Department and the Berkeley Unified School District (BUSD) with strong community leadership involvement. The community involvement later took the form of a vital community advisory board made up of a diverse group of parents, student and school representatives who provided strong public advocacy. We understood that all three elements needed to be well represented as a precondition for success. One reason we succeeded, in my opinion, is that the City government and the school board were each dominated by competing political groups that did not trust each other and were not working together effectively. They needed help. Once both groups endorsed the project in concept, both would surely want credit for this innovative, successful in-school program, and would want to be seen as a major contributor. This competition was good for the project so long as there was a dedicated core committee that would keep the project moving ahead, on track.

It seemed to me that the way to keep the City and school district convinced that the project would succeed was to involve committed activist parents and students as well as administrators from the city and BUSD. The activist core's determination to overcome all obstacles was apparent. As we moved from a planning process to an implementation process, the particular make up of a community advisory board, and exactly who they were advisory to, was going to be a big factor in whether we achieved our goal. And even before that stage, it was very important that some known community people like myself, Steve Lustig, Claire Brindis, Stewart Coulter and local activists take a strong role in design and leadership. Indeed, if I were asked what my main contributions to the project were, I would have to say, first, getting it started; and second, making sure that community people were a strong force, particularly in the implementation phase when things always tend to get diluted, watered down as it were.

There were many reasons why we reached our goals. But one important reason was that we had a strong ally in then Health and Human Services director, Emmett Jones, who backed the project, advocated for it, placed it within his domain and assured we conformed with city requirements. Another is that we had dedicated community leaders who were not going to quit until we succeeded.

Details of the Planning Committee's Inception and Growth

After a number of informal discussions, the following key individuals met on December 3, 1988 and agreed to join together in an ad hoc committee: Vera Labat, RN, PHN, school district consultant, Stewart Coulter, State regional coordinator for AIDS prevention and a high school parent, Marc Sapir MD, high school parent, Fred Medrano, PhD, city director of mental health, Laura Anderson, MPH, health educator and city clinic coordinator, Julie Williamson, MPH, health educator and expert in community-oriented primary care, and Clair Brindis, DrPH, specialist in development and evaluation of school based clinics.

At that meeting we agree that:

1. Psycho-social issues would be a major focus.
2. We would conduct a needs assessment survey of students at the high school.
3. We should consider including younger ages than high school in the target population.
4. We would try to focus on youths having the most difficulty, including youths not attending school.
5. The project should be based on-campus at BHS and open to students from off-campus (e.g. the East Campus alternative school).
6. The clinic, besides providing direct services, should help young people gain access to other needed services (not just health-related) from other providers. We envisioned including Young Adult Project counselors and other service providers at our high school site.

7. We would like to include other interested individuals and groups in the planning committee such as parents, youths, school staff, health professionals and the staff of the Berkeley Health Department.
8. We would approach Emmett Jones (director of health and human services for the city) and an appropriate Administrator at BUSD responsible for Health Services and solicit their support.
9. We would meet again in one month (January 1989) to prepare a plan of action and youth survey.

The ad hoc committee next met January 12, now adding Matthew Mock of Berkeley Mental Health, Nancy Rubin, BHS Social Living teacher, and Steve Lustig, retired Berkeley School Board member and also a high school parent. As the committee still lacked a structure, Marc Sapir continued as temporary chair and secretary and presented a proposed agenda. The committee formed a subcommittee of Labat, Rubin, Mock and Sapir to develop the student survey. The finished survey was presented back to the committee on February 16. In addition at the January meeting we agreed:

1. That the clinic should be sited at the high school for maximum accessibility.
2. That age range of youths to be served should include 7th–12th grades.
3. That the clinic should focus on psycho-social health with physical health a second focus.
4. That this clinical project should become a major asset in coordinating existing efforts of the City and BUSD (programs such as mental health, drug abuse prevention— DAP, UC Styles Hall counselors, school nursing and counselors, Young Adult Project services etc.).

5. That Nancy Rubin would learn about the BUSD contract with New Perspectives (an organization involved in counseling students regarding drug and alcohol problems).
6. That we would take the clinic idea before the 2x2 Committee (the coordinating structure between BUSD and City government) as an informational item for the school board. And that Sapir, Labat and Medrano would meet with Pat Endsley, a BUSD administrator, to open discussions with the district.

The meeting with Pat Endsley took place on January 13 and received her enthusiastic support—for both the general concept and the incorporation of a coordinating function for existing school based related programs. Pat suggested that we draft a proposal for the city manager and superintendent of schools to approve and raised questions about how the project would be funded. The committee envisioned in-kind support from BUSD (the location, upkeep, utilities and some shared staff) with principal staffing by the City Health Department, some funding from the city and most of the operational funding from government and foundation grants. Pat agreed to join the committee.

Fred Medrano then took the concept back to Emmett Jones for approval. At the February, 1989 committee meeting, Shyaam Shabaka of the city presented Emmett's invitation that the planning committee become advisory to his office on developing and implementing the school health center, following the "Implementation Guide for school based clinics" which Claire Brindis had provided. Later the committee was re-titled the "School Based Clinic Planning Committee". Emmett then went to superintendent of schools, Dr. Andrew Viscovich, and obtained agreement for Pat Endsley to represent the district and co-lead the committee along with Marc Sapir. Laura Anderson, Fred Medrano and Shyaam Shabaka were appointed by

Emmett to represent the City and Vera Labat, Javane Strong (as well as Pat Endsley) were appointed by Andrew Viscovich to represent BUSD. Laura Anderson became committee secretary. Other founding members continued on the planning committee as community representatives. Matthew Mock obtained support from the Children's Committee of the Mental Health Advisory Board. Pat Endsley obtained support from the school nurses and mental health personnel. And already at this third meeting the "Berkeley Teen Health Needs Assessment Survey", a wide-ranging tool with hundreds of potential multiple choice responses that looked at many areas of interest, was approved with an implementation plan. By the end of that month over 1,260 young people from 7th–12th grades had responded to this survey through a range of teachers and classes.

By the March 1989 meeting we had met with Mayor Loni Hancock and obtained her support and her encouragement to bring a resolution before the city council. Fred Medrano drafted the resolution. Also at this meeting I reported on an interesting call to New Jersey where statewide school-based youth centers had been set up. They told us that forming a community advisory board should begin now in order to obtain wider community participation early in the planning process. This was excellent advice. Often advisory boards have little power, but it would be wrong to believe that that is inevitable in all situations. We later made sure they would be a powerful force.

Pat Endsley reported on a meeting that several of us had had with high school principal Ken Sherer who also was enthusiastic and open to discussing locations on campus to situate the health center. And Vera Labat reported on a school board meeting where the superintendent had spoken of the center as a replacement for the school's nurse consultants. The committee expressed its concern that the health center could not replace the nurses, that they were a necessary complement to the services we envisioned. For at least the next two years we stood firm in backing continuation of school nurses in the schools.

Also, a timeline for funding, gaining endorsements, letters of intent, city support, project design and organizing critical service elements based upon the student needs survey was discussed and mostly agreed upon. A feasibility report was to be presented to Emmett Jones and Andrew Viscovich by May 1. A number of new people joined the committee at the March meetings, including Thelette Bennett from high school administration, Doug Perry, and Cecilia Walls, RN, school nurse consultant.

Brass Tacks

From this point on (March/April 1989), meetings occurred even more frequently and began to focus on the details of funding and grant writing, program development and publicity. We enlisted Mary Friedman and Sue Fisher of the Berkeley Public Education Foundation who helped with proposals and funding. We had great interest in integrating many different types of services into the Project such as mental health counseling, peer counselors, substance abuse prevention, using the nurse consultants as case managers to coordinate referral of students who needed outside community resources and to facilitate family issues through home visits, technical support and graduate student counseling from the university, health career mentoring, peer led problem solving and conflict resolution; and medical services including preventive services, health education, STD treatment and birth control (although the district found condom distribution controversial—even in the midst of the HIV epidemic—we helped them get past this after a year or two). A productive meeting took place between Serena Jones, the New Perspectives drug and alcohol counselor, Matthew Mock and Fred Medrano of Berkeley Mental Health and school nurse consultant Vera Labat. At this meeting, developing a unified treatment model, problems of getting teachers to refer BHS students, the lack of an assessment team for youth with problems and many other issues were discussed.

We were particularly preoccupied with gaining student representation on the planning committee. Shyaam Shabaka, Nancy Rubin and Laura Anderson worked on the appointment of three students. Students who joined the committee then were Shannon Singleton, Charletha Moor, and Ramon Garcia. Community input was also perceived of as inadequate and we agreed to contact more community groups to make them aware of the project and its concept of integrating services. At Pat Endsley's suggestion a brochure for the center was developed and three sub-committees were established on June 16—Program Committee, Community Advisory Board Development and Funding Committee.

By September 1989, the City, which had been dragging a bit on funding, gave signs of likely agreement to match $50,000 of outside funding. By then we were already committed to apply to a number of foundations to achieve funding for the match. We were also applying for a larger federal grant from the Office of Substance Abuse Prevention under Health and Human Services with the City as lead for grant proposals. We had produced an organizational chart with an oversight committee to protect the interests of BUSD and the City. Our chart placed the project's advisory board as advisory to the project coordinator, not to the City or BUSD. This was very important because it linked the advisory board to operations and policy decisions at the ground level.

A Year at a Glance

Although it seemed that things were running along quite smoothly, tensions between the City and BUSD arose. Who was going to end up paying the lion's share for the center? Then in November 1989, Pat Endsley surprised us with the announcement that, due to the project taking away too much time from her district-wide role as curriculum coordinator, she would be resigning from the committee and Murphy Taylor, a BHS vice principal, would be replacing her. Pat did continue to attend some meetings and to lend space at her office for meetings, and provide other support. However, Pat's resignation required changes in leadership of the project because Murphy did not represent the BUSD Central Administration and he did not replace Pat as co-chair of the committee either. There was some concern that this change might reflect a loss of will for the project at the district level. Without an administrator from BUSD on the front line, Emmett Jones stepped in and took over the chairmanship of the committee and became more directly involved in the committee's activities up through the summer of 1990. Under various sub-committees the site was firmed up in the B building at BHS. A renovation was planned and budgeted to include architects. Enough funding was achieved to assure the opening of the center and to gain the matching City funds, though the large federal grant was not received. Throughout 1989, planning committee members had difficulty finding a broad representative group of nominees for the advisory board. However, advisory board bylaws had been finalized s part of the several grant proposals.

By the spring of 1990, with a projected opening date of September looming, the planning committee realized that the project needed a lead project staff person on the ground to manage day to day implementation. At the committee's recommendation, the district and the City found a way to put together funds for an interim coordinator (a modest consultant contract) for program implementation prior to opening. I offered to take this responsibility and was appointed. I then left my clinical job and this also made it easier for me to find and recruit strong community leaders and advocates interested in being part of the advisory board as well as to follow through on funding proposals and to oversee our time-line for opening later in 1990.

On August 27, 1990, I presented the planning committee with the names of 16 people for ratification to the advisory board and seven others yet to be invited. The final CAB included 17 members, of whom nine were ethnic minorities, 11 were women, seven were parents of students and three were students. The original members were Shirlane Baldwin, Sherrie Carr-Palmer, Aileen Corelli, Sumaiya Gilliam, Margaret Kokka, Steve Lustig, Mona Mena, Fr. William O'Donnell, Edna Rivera-Gurley, Juditte Schwartz, Shawn Smuckler, Lisa Young, Diana Young, Thelette Bennett (representing BHS administration), Bob Kaneko (representing the BHS guidance counselors), Nancy Rubin (BHS teachers), Jim Trainor (East Campus faculty). Steve Lustig and Sumaiya Gilliam were the first co-chairs and Edn Rivera-Gurley and Diana Young served as secretaries. This energized CAB took on a life of its own.

As I had hoped, from that time on the planning committee moved to the background and the advisory board, working with me as interim coordinator, became the more important implementation and advocacy group in the project's development. In the last few months of 1990, the site renovation was completed, the programmatic elements were refined and coordinated, the initial funding was finalized and then a permanent coordinator—and soon after that a health educator—were appointed. The City sponsored a part-time nurse practitioner from its clinic. Berkeley Mental Health, New Perspectives staff, the school nurses and the high school administration were instrumental in bringing in the counseling that became an important bedrock of the program. In the end, the City of Berkeley—through Emmett Jones, Fred Medrano, Laura Anderson and Matthew Mock—was a critical force in assuring that we had the resources to open the center.

Ultimately I was a bit personally disappointed, for I had hoped to return to the Berkeley Health Department in some role that would involve my working with the health clinic; and that was not to be. However, I oriented the new coordinator and later served on the advisory board myself for about two years. Emmett Jones retired from the City and he also joined the CAB. I went back to working outpatient clinics for the Alameda County Medical Center until I was appointed the medical director of the Center for Elders' Independence in April 1992. Although I often wondered what might have been achieved with some of the creative, empowering projects we wrote into the not-accepted Federal Office of Substance Abuse Prevention proposals of 1989 and 1990 had they been fully funded, I remain pleased at how much of what we envisioned for the Berkeley High School Based Health Clinic did come to fruition through the persistent efforts of so many people working in collaboration. I had only meeting minutes and notes and a faded memory from which to construct this history, so I beg forgiveness if I have omitted anyone else who contributed. I am particularly indebted to Glenda Pawsy, long-time parent member of the advisory board, for inviting me to produce this essay.

Berkeley, CA
May 31, 2000 (later re-edited)

ON SOCIAL EVOLUTION AND BIOLOGIC EVOLUTION

Many early forms of life, such as bacteria, duplicate themselves the same way that cells in our own body organs do—by mitosis. That is, they simply divide exactly in half after copying over themselves, repeatedly forming identical twin cells (a clone). If living things made only identical copies, biologic evolution would be impossible. Darwin's concept of natural selection is based upon the idea of diversity in nature. Some individual organisms and species do better than others because they have different capacities to adapt. Differences matter. Identical twinning (homogeneity) does not create diversity.

Bacteria do not always make identical twins, however. Their copying machinery is a bit unstable. It makes mistakes, causing mutations in the genes. Hits on cells by ultraviolet light from the sun also cause mutations (which is how we get skin cancer for example), but the main reasons that bacteria change their characteristics (such as becoming immune to antibiotics we throw at them) are twofold: their copying error rate is higher than that of more complex animals and they reproduce themselves in minutes where complex animals take weeks, months or years to grow babies. Many divisions a day and relatively higher copying error rates assure bacterial (and viral) diversity and create the possibility of natural selection or adaptation to changing conditions in their environment.

While this method of generating diversity worked in the era of simple one celled organisms that could divide quickly, once that process of diversity began to evolve complex plants and animals, reproduction slowed down and the potential for diversity did too. To sustain the life of any complex animal, nature had to reduce the copying error rates of cell division. As a result, complex life forms, reproducing more slowly, would be susceptible to extinction due to changes in their environment. Nature resolved this mismatch by inventing an ingenious way to allow life to continue to expand and diversify into millions of species: sex

Sex was no small innovation, perhaps why the Book of Genesis of the Hebrew Bible opens with its warning concerning sex. And to invent sex as a means to dramatically expand diversity, you'd have to differentiate the sexes of every new species that arises so that the sexes can physically and biologically conjugate. Second you have to create a mechanism that makes opposites attracted to each other and to want to couple—repeatedly. That is, sex has to be not only enjoyable, but neurologically self-reinforcing. And third and most importantly, you have to crown sex with a cellular process that creates the diversity that is missing from the simple division of cell mitosis. That last step, meiosis, is one amazing innovation, surpassing, in creativity, the evolution of simple cell replication, DNA unwinding and mitosis. In human meiosis 23 chromosome pairs are reduced to 23 unique chromosomes in each "germ" cells (egg and sperm) of each human—halving the DNA. Fertilization of an egg by a sperm then reconstitutes a full 23 pairs. That reconstitution creates an entirely new unique genotype.

Yet, long before Nature invented and began experimenting with sex, it had already begun a different project in the background that's also brilliantly creative—weaving a fabric or network of all life forms into something like a giant web or nervous system. Diversity and speciation became the driving force primarily so that life, generically, would survive natural adversity. Various species would have to support each other in this grand design. When some people think of evolution as the big eating the small, the strong eating, or exploiting the weak, and so on, they are thinking one dimensionally, missing the forest for the trees because the inter-dependency of life forms is inherent in evolution. Ants that farm take very good care of their aphids because their lives depend upon them. Humans have learned that if they cut down all the trees without replanting them we will have no wood to build with, we will suffer from soil erosion, desertification and an overwhelming CO_2 burden and oxygen deficit.[52] Readers will have a hundred examples and the point is obvious.

If we depend upon eating fish from the sea, but we do not protect the fishery from over fishing, then fish won't survive. And to protect the fishes we have to protect the oceans from our toxic wastes and preserve all the life forms that fish depend upon. This is the nature of species interdependence and the key basis of evolution. True that in some cases the interdependence is a unidirectional exploitation of a dependent species (such as cows and humans). But in the grand scheme of life, symbiosis and mutuality was fundamental.

We can surmise that this backdrop existed before sex arrived on the scene. But sexual reproduction changed the quality and the characteristics of species interdependence as well as creating gender interdependence. The most obvious change was that within any species sex created social relationships. Whether a sexual coupling is a one time deal, a lifelong commitment or reflects some intermediate relational step on that ladder each different species has a social life. Thus, sex created the possibility of culture and society. Indeed, the

---

52 See Jared Diamond's description (in his book *Collapse*) of what happened to Easter Island's collaborative diverse tribes once they began to exhaust their natural resources due to careless disregard of good husbandry and ecological protection of those resources.

very sexual relationship which can lead some humans to hurt or even kill each other is at the heart of how and why we came to develop complex culture with mores, traditions, music, art, schools and language.

Our tendency to believe that humans are more advanced than other species avoids those realities. Perhaps it is based upon human achievements in science, technology, culture, but that conclusion is not sustained by the evidence. The reality is that all evolution has social components—that is, evolution is a socio-biological process.

Begin with intelligence—the ability to reason, plan, look ahead, use accumulated wisdom in tackling problems, build tools, make choices based upon reasoning—a mostly human trait. Successful social existence does not require that kind of intelligence. Bees, birds and ants, to give a few examples, are social animals and use sophisticated communication skills to create role differentiation and societies of varying complexity and interdependencies. Seemingly less social animals like large predators are not necessarily less capable of thought and reasoning than more social animals. But they have developed different adaptive strategies for survival. Predators overcome the problem of restricted territory by expanding their territory. Humans overcame that limitation by learning how to modify their environments as well as how to increase their mobility. People borrow from the innovations of other species and enhance them.

Humans, however, have evolved greater social designs in the larger universe than just species survival and adaptation. Human social evolution soon outstripped the biologic imperatives of species interdependence, a dangerous deviation.

THE CONTINUITY-DISCONTINUITY CONUNDRUM

From a distance, a pointillist painting creates the perception of a continuous flow of pigment whether the painting be realistic portraiture or pure abstraction. Pointillism uses the realization that our visual perception, as all human perception, has specified neurological, physical and phenomenological boundaries and referents. These boundaries and mental referents can be played with by an artist (or magician) to creatively recreate perceptual realities that actually aren't there, but were constructed as a visual deception. The process is an expansion of earlier forms of optical illusion. Currently, the seemingly unexplainable relative popularity of a ruthless self-promoting sociopathic Trump, is, I think, a form of application of this theory of deceptive pointillism. Highlighting particular points of light creates the illusion of power, control, dominance, friendliness, compassion, sympathy or whatever you want because behaviorist applications have become very advanced. Nevertheless, manipulating perception is really about the manipulators' understanding how our neurophysiology allows for the gaming of the human mind.

No doubt, problems in socially constructed human reality are complicated. But untangling that complexity—and indeed understanding the real world process known as entanglement—might help shine a light on how humanity can pass beyond the self-destructive limitations of our present social evolution.

AN UNDERLYING UNIVERSAL FORCE: ENTANGLEMENT

Physicists describe four forces in the universe—the strong force which binds atoms, the weak force which holds us together and explains the Earth's molten core, electromagnetism (the relationships between electric forces and magnetic forces), and gravity. These four forces interact to govern the realm. However, problems deriving from measurement interference irregularities required researchers to come to terms with a surprising and still poorly understood phenomenon they call entanglement. It defies the expected prior rules of physics. The observations and the idea of entanglement is that subatomic particles can break into twins with opposite spins and thus opposite polarity (magnetism). No matter the distance that these twins are separated after formation, the characteristics of one (like their angular orientation and spin) always remains the opposite of the other. Somehow every one of the twins is in a fixed relationship to its twin from their birth. If they run into each other they will self-annihilate. Because the relationship is not distance dependent these interactions don't conform to the way that gravity weakens as the inverse square of the distance between two masses. Moreover, observations suggest that this entanglement causes a kind of synchronicity or harmonious behavior in which the twins are collaborative even though they do not actually message each other in any obvious way. Apparently this phenomenon is not so recently discovered since Albert Einstein called this "spookiness" and he believed that it meant that there are forces at work that even quantum theory cannot accommodate with its probablism because of the distance-independence of the partnership. Today physics says that the fixed complementarity is also time-independent and so doesn't change in one direction or the other in time. But today the relationship is believed to fit well with quantum physics.

Surprisingly, perhaps without any attributable connection, these observations (of synchronicity and entanglement) find parallels in the behaviors of many living social species here on Earth. I can't imagine how these two apparently distinct phenomena might be connected but it is, nonetheless, worth noting parallels between the forces in the inanimate and the animate world.

In his book, *Musicophilia* (p. 229 hardcover), Oliver Sacks writes of music and social synchronicity (a form of group social entanglement):

"drum circles are widely known in the Tourette's community... (Before the drumming began) I could see eruptions of tics...rippling around the thirty-odd Touretters there—but once the drum circle started, with Matt leading them, all the ticcing disappeared within seconds. Suddenly there was synchronization and they came together as a group performing in the moment with the rhythm…Music here had a double power: first to reconfigure brain activity, and bring calm and focus…and second to promote a musical and social bonding with others so that what began as a miscellany of isolated, often dis- tressed or self-conscious individuals almost instantly became a cohesive group with a single aim—a veritable drum orchestra under Matt's baton."

And p. 237:

"Every culture has songs and rhymes to help children learn the alphabet, numbers, and other lists. Even as adults, we are limited in our ability to memorize series or to hold them in mind unless we use mnemonic devices or patterns—and the most powerful of these devices are rhyme, meter, and song."

And p. 243:

"There is certainly a universal (human) and unconscious propensity to impose a rhythm even when one hears a series of identical sounds at constant intervals (as neuroscientist and drummer John Iverson has pointed out)."

And p. 244–5:

"Anthony Storr, in his excellent book *Music and the Mind*, stresses that in all societies, a primary function of music is collective and communal, to bring and bind people together…in an actual binding or 'marriage' of nervous systems, a 'neurogamy'."

". . .I observed this when I took my patient Greg F. to a Grateful Dead concert…The music, the rhythm, got to everyone within seconds. I saw the whole vast arena in motion with the music, eighteen thousand people dancing transported, every nervous system there synchronized to the music. . .I found myself unable to remain a detached observer. . .and soon lost all my usual diffidence and inhibition and joined the crowd in communal dancing (moving, stamping, and clapping)."

What does this phenomenon mean? What does it imply about the relationship of culture to biology, and the relationship between the individual mind and the idea of a collective or social mind? And, if anything, about the continuity-discontinuity conundrum, about sub-atomic quantum particle entanglement, or even dark matter or dark energy?

We do not necessarily have to believe in ESP or telepathic brain wave influence to understand how rhythmic synchronicity operates on animals, for it is hypnotic. The fact that we humans learned in the 20th century how to polarize light to create synchronous waves (then lasers with higher focusing power) is physical evidence to show that focusing and filtering of natural scatter phenomena is a powerful force readily available to us. Yet the synchronization of human groups and cultures, thoughts and intentions, even of the entire species through rhythm goes back at least 100,000 years. This implies an evolutionary benefit—whether genetically occurring or learned. That benefit may be as simple as the fact that humans living in groups larger than families could better defend and provide for themselves through shared responsibilities and role differentiation or the fact that synchronicity provides, through the group, a sense of individual well being, support, connectedness and joy. But regardless, synchronization demonstrates that humans became an innately social and a highly intra-dependent species back in evolutionary time. That may be the basis upon which all human culture developed. Thus the notion of "social entanglement" has great evolutionary impact.

Political-Economy and Social Entanglement

Nevertheless, as much as synchronicity operates in the rap of a hip-hop artist or the pulsation of an amazing drum solo, today it is also a force that is easily seized upon and employed to manipulate any culture, group or society by demagogues—a Hitler, a Trump, a Jim Jones, a Pol Pot, or, really, anyone seeking dominance. This appropriation of autonomy expanded through modern culture with the rise of capitalist relations, the social science of behaviorism and behaviorism's applications to marketing—whether that be marketing of products, ideas, politicians, Orwellian groupthink, fanaticism, religion or otherwise. The entire sphere of marketing—including mass communication—has today been molded into an intentional control idiom based within the paradigm of behavioral synchronization.[53] This is doubly fraught.

First, behaviorism operates upon the knowledge that humans, having evolved from other animal species can be induced to respond to stimuli like animals who lack as much reasoning capacity as we have. This is achieved through simple techniques of forcing choices based only upon externally imposed rewards or punishments. If you want to control people's behavior you might imprison them for violating a law or rule, but there are simpler social means easily available that are more powerful, such as social ostracism or social approval, satiation or addiction, deprivation of food, shelter, health care. If you can make smoking a social group-approving behavior, for example, kids that don't smoke will be rejected by the group at an age when group approval is important for ego development. Here the force pressing the youths to smoke often arises outside the group from the marketing strategy of the cigarette companies. Such applications of social behaviorism existed long before they were taught in the business schools of our greatest universities. However, since the epoch that began around the beginning of the 20th century, they have become a dominant force in most forms of social communications

---

53 Arising from the evolution of BF Skinner's behaviorist writings expanded by the work of Albert Bandura at Stanford.

media. Titillation and arousal, the stimulation of various hormones of our endocrine system have become the attractants used to homogenize human behavior.

Consider this proposal: enhancing manipulative conforming potential poses the greatest threat to human survival and biologic evolution on Earth. Taking over the protective and salutary potential of social synchronicity, behaviorist modeling actually suppresses the intellectual and social discourse which is vital to human culture and society. That results when so much of life and mind are occupied by the stimuli of and responses to external social conditioning. While our natural sciences are encouraged to promote product development and utilitarian technologies, the protection of broader creative endeavors and other intellectually based human functions (I'm reminded of Tolstoy's question, "What is beauty?"[54]) are not only being de-emphasized but the latter are quaintly pigeonholed as being the realm of cute antiques. Theater, art, museums, novels, newspapers, even in-depth investigative journalism, intellectual discourse and debate become relics, losing their impact upon culture, class or mass psychology.

When we attend a multi-screen movie house we note a clear segregation (self-segregation) of blockbuster action and horror films appealing to the young on the one hand and those less financially successful films called "arts cinema" that mostly appeal to dwindling audiences looking for intellectually provocative, problematic and challenging cinema. Younger people are targeted by films whose main content is excitation and hormonal titillation and games which tend to be modeled for their intellectual vacuity.

As our country moves progressively toward the outlawing of diversity in the way that Hitler's Germany did, the collective human

---

54 See his monogram: *What is Art?*

mind is de-rationalized as those who challenge that de-rationalization are attacked as deviant. Most people can still see that without our humanity and empathy (our "humaneness") we are no longer truly "human", but much more than moral suasion is being removed from culture. Our ability to make conscious, reasoned social choices as entire nations and cultures is also being biologically restricted. In the McCarthy era some philosophers began pointing out that this process can lead to the death of intellect itself.

The reductionism of the market and its behaviorist models already dominates world culture. This will attenuate human evolution (if it continues unchecked) by appropriating the forces of social entanglement and social synchronicity which are fundamental to the biological world itself. As a result, sociobiological forces lose their innate function as protective and supportive social phenomena. The atomization of human life on Earth finds its reification in the phenomenon of "survivalism" which assumes that the very worst aspects of intentional human discontent will inevitably reign supreme as each against the other (misnamed as "social Darwinism"). Such an outlook, when normalized, becomes tautological and potentially apocalyptic.

Not a determinist, I believe in human free will and that the ability to reason can expand even in the face of antisocial challenges. Among the reasons to believe that social "entanglement" (and synchronicity) can retain their biologically imperative function is that contemporary science theory—as previously mentioned—is recognizing that entanglement/synchronicity may be a fundamental physical phenomena in our vast universe. There may be a reciprocal relationship to social synchronicity.

IDENTITY—THE ROLE OF
MUSIC IN BECOMING WHO I AM

As a child of nine or ten living in suburban Northeast Yonkers, NY, I imagined myself as a composer and orchestra conductor. I loved music so much. But there were telltale signs that I wasn't sufficiently driven for such a career. Much later, after moving to San Jose with Sheila in 1973, not having played my bassoon in a decade and needing some money, I sold the instrument my father had given me as a high school graduation present. My dad was upset, though his death that year was surely unrelated. He said, "If you weren't going to play it you could have given it back to me."[55] But a few years later, I felt a deep need to return to music, picked up a used bassoon from an ad in the paper and then played bassoon in the West Valley Community Symphony. Toward the end of my year studying epidemiology (1986–1987) at the School of Public Health I joined the University of California Berkeley Symphony which needed a second bassoon.

Years after that, in 2008 I got a hankering for the chance I had missed to try composing and took a class in piano at the Berkeley Jazz School. But my only compositions are the 20-plus songs I've written.

---

55 Having been father to two stepsons, two daughters and six grandchildren I am able to appreciate how he felt about this. At the time it just seemed that, once gifted, it was mine, period. But that bassoon was more than an object of monetary worth to Dad.

WHAT IS MUSIC?

I felt music in my soul—perhaps in the soles of my feet also. As I say, I thought I wanted to be a composer, a conductor and a musician from as early as I can remember. But the love of music is not something unique. Almost everyone lives by and for music and particularly rhythm. Though we don't fully understand why, there is no human culture on Earth that doesn't have music. And yet a biologically driven purpose for music remains obscure, even though its ability to evoke joy and the soothing of the troubled mind is quite apparent.

In the preface to his book, *Musicophilia*, Oliver Sacks writes that, "Given the obvious similarities between music and language, it is not surprising that there has been a running debate for more than two hundred years as to whether they evolved in tandem or independently—and, if the latter, which came first. Darwin speculated that musical tones and rhythms were used by our half-human ancestors during the season of courtship, when animals of all kinds are excited not only by love, but by strong passions of jealousy, rivalry, and triumph—and that speech arose secondarily from this primal music. His contemporary Herbert Spencer held the opposite view, conceiving that music arose from the cadences of emotional speech. Rousseau, a composer no less than a writer and philosopher, felt that both had emerged together, as a singsong speech, and only later diverged—paraphrasing: there is much evidence that humans have a music instinct no less than a language."

My view: for a social species music serves as a non-verbal language bridging the space between individual being and social being. Language also resides in that space but music, a most universal human language, may be the superstructure, the broader scaffolding, that enabled verbal language to be constructed. After all, every language has its own rhythmicity, intonations, and modulation. Music serves, and probably served, as a fully malleable and experimental experiential realm in which to develop the nuances of language, while bringing people together in social harmony. Music is, in itself, language, and yet phenomenologically music is pure feeling with intellect more an adorning feature. Despite using mathematics in composing, Bach—in my opinion—understood this idea better than some 20th-century 12-tone composers. Thus his music lives on in the hearts of hundreds of millions—from baroque to classical to jazz enthusiasts—while whole-tone music (12-tone) appeals to only a relatively small subset of humanity. The difference, I surmise, is that Bach was able to place his compositional mind at the intersection between the "feeling" of music for the listener and the intrinsic internal design and structure of music. He tuned his creations to the evolutionary truth that music has served us as a socializing force.

THE DEATH OF HAL CARLSTAD

My friend Hal died a few years back. Hal was 82, which sounds like a ripe old age to die on. But Hal wasn't ripe, old or ready to die, though he'd been slowed by a heart valve gone floppy. An avid walker and gardener, he'd had his activity cut back too much to suit him. Even at 82, lean and tall—still about six-foot two—Hal cut a handsome figure. He'd a long angular Norwegian face and a friendly visage; still plenty of hair and bushy gray eyebrows. He was so alive still that his death seemed only an unfortunate incident in his life.

Hal put his trust in his doctors and, to the end, he believed that they did the best they could for him. He told me that up front and assertively in the ICU at Kaiser Hospital Oakland two months before his death and two months after his surgery. Were he here right now he might even scold me for suggesting they/we failed him. He didn't want me to get too much involved with it.

It's a bit of a contradiction, Hal seemingly such a trusting fellow. I say contradiction because he proudly told people that he'd been arrested about 180 times in civil disobedience actions for peace, civil rights, human rights and so forth throughout his adult life. Obviously he didn't trust everything or everyone to do a righteously good, honest job. He was outspoken, if soft-spoken, and had an infamous outgoing message—a two-or three-minute rant against US imperialism's predations—on his telephone's voicemail.

Hal was a retired secondary school teacher from Berkeley's Martin Luther King Jr. Junior High School where he taught science. He was an expert botanist and a dedicated gardener. And, well read and contemplative, he knew a lot about a lot of things. I'm sure he was a great teacher—kind, supportive, humorous.

Hal owned a home in Kensington where he lived with his partner, Cynthia Johnson. It's a nice old house—not real large, maybe three or four smallish bedrooms—here in the East Bay Area just a block below Kensington's small commercial area on the Arlington, overlooking the Bay. They took in a couple of borders. I'd been at a few meetings at the house. When Hal died the family sold it; and they put Cynthia out of her home. Hal surely would have objected.

I felt that Hal and I were more than friends; I would say we were good friends. We had extended conversations and I had driven the two of us to some protests together. Along with my wife Sheila and another woman, Connie, we got arrested in 2003 at the headquarters of KQED, the Bay Area's largest PBS station (TV and radio) when there were big protests against the US attacking and occupying Iraq. That arrest incident is an amusing story because we weren't part of the Iraq protests that day. We were demanding fair coverage of Palestine's plight under occupation—but we got our charges dismissed by being lumped together with hundreds for protesting the US war on Iraq. Perhaps I'll come back to that some other time. Cynthia, who is probably 20 years younger and survives Hal, is a real spark-plug. She can't stop herself from being involved in about 15 activist causes and activities at the same time. She talks so fast and frenetically that she sometimes loses herself in her words. Observing her is like watching a hummingbird buzz around the yard, praying it won't smack into something hard like a window. She and Hal centered their political and faith lives in the Social Justice Committee of the Unitarian Universalist Church at Cedar and Bonita in Berkeley, where they are both famous. Actually Cynthia is well-enough known around to have got herself elected to the station board of KPFA, the non-profit left-wing station that founded the Pacifica Radio Network.

Hal had told me that he was going to have a heart valve replacement as an elective surgery. I was surprised. He was still getting around fairly well. I hadn't even noticed shortness of breath, but it had become troubling to him. He said that he was declining more than he could handle. Shortness of breath on even short walks was intolerable to him; and the Kaiser doctors thought, due to his otherwise excellent health status, that he was a good candidate for successful heart valve surgery even at his age. And that his heart would soon give out if he didn't. Unhappily, I didn't learn that his surgery had taken place, performed by Kaiser surgeons at the Summit Hospital in Oakland, until about six weeks afterward, when Cynthia told me that Hal had just been transferred to the Kaiser Hospital ICU if I wanted to visit him.

From a technical "outcome" standpoint, the heart valve surgery itself had been a success. Not only did Hal survive the operation but the valve was working well afterward with his cardiac output much improved. But something else had gone wrong. Hal awoke after surgery and was lucid, but for some unknown reason his breathing was too weak to self-sustain and so they could not take him off the ventilator. He lay there in the bed wide awake, clear-minded, able to communicate by writing messages with tubes coming out of his nose and mouth and penis. This had gone on and on and on and finally, unable to discharge him to home or rehabilitation, Kaiser had transferred Hal back to their own ICU team aiming for slow, progressive progress.

Having cared for my own frail hospitalized patients from 1993–2001, I realized immediately, even before I visited Hal at Kaiser Oakland and had more information and observations, that his chances of surviving this hospitalization were diminishing by the day. For most of us at that age, a lengthy hospitalization can become a death sentence regardless of the reason for the hospitalization, and regardless of how excellent the technical level of care may be. Hospitals are a dangerous place for the elderly. And the intensive care unit or cardiac care unit is even more dangerous. In his case Hal was also in grave danger because of all these tubes and machines attached to and penetrating him.

But Hal didn't die just yet. The process of his dying, being neither sudden, nor gradual, but protracted and convoluted, took a lot out of Cynthia. She had a bad time trying to deal with what happened, what was happening. But she wasn't alone. Hal's kids too; and to some extent the grandkids. And Hal's many friends, including me. I warrant that this essay is about my own connections to Hal as much as it is about Hal's life apart, but I'm writing it as a tribute to Hal's humanity, his spunk, his wry sense of humor and wit, and his determination to soldier on through life's thick and thin. That death was claiming him was not particularly of his own doing, but, then again, it kind of was. It was not like some act of God; I don't entirely blame his doctors or the teams of nurses and other professionals that worked with him either. This story describes how human frailty in the guise of progress can get beyond our control; how Hal's medical care transgressed upon the human element in caregiving and went astray. I'd love to find someone to blame in what happened, but it's just not like that.

Also, I won't second-guess the judgment on either the doctors' part, nor Hal's about having the surgery. He knew there were risks, but he was willing to take them to achieve a better quality of life and some longevity. That's both brave and reasonable. Nevertheless, there is plenty of data to show how and why the longer an elderly person is hospitalized, the greater the chances that they will not survive. Among the reasons are these: bedbound patients, like astronauts in space, lose muscle tone and mass quickly; they become weak, they have trouble standing and walking, and become prone to falls and fractures. Within less than a week a person confined to a hospital begins to show deterioration in their mental state, loss of vital protein (albumen) in their blood, and anemia. The risk of blood clots forming in leg veins and lungs is measurable. Confusion, weakness, as well as care that focuses more on the technical side of tasks that must be regularly done for and to the patient rather than "with" them, means that their psychological state suffers, and mental deterioration from sensory and social deprivation cannot be well tended to, even with sweet, quality nurses. The longer someone is in the hospital the fewer the visitors during hours of visitation they receive as friends also grow weary. In the intensive care units there is particular isolation, less getting up to stretch or walk, less autonomy, more physical dependence and a more sterile, uniform and monotonous environment. When you keep an elder in bed their breathing effort declines, lungs are less expanded and they become prone to pneumonia. Hospitals are also the carriers of more deadly infectious organisms resistant to antibiotics, and these can spread to other parts of the body than the lungs. After two weeks, a growing proportion of people with catheters in their bladders begin to become infected.

But I believe that the underlying factor that saps one's lifeblood is the loss of autonomy, the sense of who we are—who I am. All these factors are at play even in people who are not that sick to begin with. Within a week of hospitalization most elders are considerably frailer than when they first entered; and are at risk of nursing home placement when they are discharged.

In Hal's case the situation was particularly depersonalizing. He was not only restricted to the ICU, but was aware he was unable to eat for himself and had both a breathing tube and a feeding tube down his throat. Though Hal initiated most of his breathing, the machine continued to do much of the work, forcing air into him. Throughout his stay in the Kaiser ICU of more than a month Hal remained fully alert, aware and able to converse by writing messages. He told people what he wanted. He asked us questions about the outside world. He commented on politics. And he assumed he would get better.

I don't know if his survival and return to normal life was in the cards, but something then happened shortly after my second visit to Kaiser that wrecked his chances of that. The doctors decided, based upon his reasonable cardiac output and his ability to stay off the ventilator for a half hour here and an hour there that they would try letting him eat. I wasn't there when it happened but they put some food in front of Hal and, contrary to usual practice, no one helped him or monitored him that first day. Typically a speech therapist will be the person working with stroke victims who have lost or weakened swallowing ability and cough/gag reflexes. After that a nurse takes over the responsibility. But Hal wasn't a stroke victim and the usual protocol was not strictly followed. Hal started gagging, may have aspirated some of the food and this led to a panicked response by the medical team. They decided that Hal did not have strong enough swallowing capability to be allowed to try again. They decided not to pull his feeding tube from his throat. Eventually they placed a stomach tube through the abdominal wall (a-not-uncommon procedure) in a sign that he might require long-term tube feeding. They decided to keep Hal as dependent as he already had been—now for the past eight or nine weeks. The error that the health care team made was not fully supporting and monitoring Hal's early attempts at swallowing. But instead of simply coming to terms with that relatively minor error and starting over again, they backed off (I say minor because Hal was still cognitively intact and thus he had some ability to protect himself in the situation; he was not like a stroke patient who had lost the ability to cough, and so his swallowing weakness was not the result of central nerve damage but related to disuse). The Kaiser team, it seemed, was more worried about what bad things "might" happen after that episode than thinking about what "was happening" to a depersonalized, dehumanized Hal.

The health care system in our country is technical, highly technical. Technique is great if you've benefited from a liver or kidney transplant or some electrophysiologic studies and such, but the problem is that the sicker we get, the more technique and technology gets into the act; and the focus of most experts is their technical ability. That doesn't always make sense. I've taken care of many people at the end of life; people whose deaths were usually not preventable. Helping people come to terms with death is a particular role that you learn in geriatric and hospice work (I've done the former, not the latter). But as Lonnie Chavelson wrote in *A Chosen Death* some people are also ready to live and soldier on even in the face of the worst of conditions and poorest odds of survival. Sometimes the people who are dying do most of the life-teaching for us, I have to admit that. Some of the important lessons I learned about death and dying were taught me by humble people who were dying themselves.

While I was on the staff of Alta Bates Hospital years before Hal died, I served on a utilization review subcommittee responsible for evaluation and prevention of medical errors and untoward incidents. In the case of my friend Hal, I thought his death preventable, and yet there were no gross medical errors; everything was a judgment call. The problem is that some causes are deeply embedded in the culture of our medical care system—the business of medicine. It's that culture that has to change. Our medical culture is focused on data and measurable outcomes. But outcomes, though they happen to real people, are not actually the people at all. They are facts and figures, data and summary data, stripped of any humanity just as computers strip information of its qualitative identity.

As Hal's friend, I tried—without acting too authoritative or self-important—to bring my understanding of geriatric care (and Hal) into the equation of how my friend should be treated. I had realized from the moment I first visited him, that keeping a Foley catheter in the bladder of an aware adult without urinary tract obstruction was a convenience of typical ICU care that could not be justified. That was one tube that needed to be pulled out immediately so he could pee when he wanted and needed to. If he temporarily had some incontinence, they could use pads or adult diapers. Then, once the episode of gagging and minor aspiration had occurred, I tried to convince the Kaiser team that they had to try again <u>soon</u>, and repeatedly if necessary, with better supervision. I can't remember if the family conference with the ICU director was my idea, Hal's family's or that of the Kaiser staff. But in any case Kaiser staff were fully cooperative with having the conference. Hal agreed but didn't attend.

Though Hal repeated his confidence in the Kaiser specialists, I was not so sanguine about what was transpiring. Because I did have the backing of the family and Hal's permission, I participated in the conference as a sort of curbside medical consultant. I pointed out my concerns about the bladder catheter, suggested effort to walk Hal more regularly, and encouraged improved efforts to get him off the feeding tube.

It's hard to imagine how much of our autonomy, independence and life spirit is sapped by being unable to eat or taste food. Our body suffers also. I remember a stroke patient, Fred, with mild-moderate dementia who had a gastric feeding tube and who lived with his mother. An essay about Fred is in my unpublished book, *I'll Fly Away*. Like a rambunctious youngster, Fred would sneak downstairs after his mother went to bed and eat food from the refrigerator. In fact, although he had a few episodes of minor aspiration and even an aspiration pneumonia once, Fred's ability to break free of the terrible dependence on stomach tube feeding probably gave him more quality of life than anything a medical team could do to help him. Being mischievous also made him feel a more autonomous person.

The problem in Hal's situation was that Hal didn't want to push the envelope. He was sure that the Kaiser doctors knew what they were doing, knew what was best; he didn't understand the importance of his own self advocacy with them. What I understood was that the difference in perspective (between myself and the Kaiser specialists) was not one of technical expertise—he had some of the best intensive care specialty doctors. The difference was my geriatric understanding of the toll that was daily being taken upon his mind and body which would be unable to withstand these insults much longer without cracking.

As it happened the good Kaiser ICU head and his team did not resist my suggestions. They promised to do their best to address these issues. But it soon became obvious that they did not feel the urgency that I felt. They did not grasp that Hal's very survival required treating the situation as a type of emergency though in fact there was no obvious emergency, technically speaking, other than the problem of him not yet getting off the ventilator. That, we could all agree, was a serious problem; but only that. And they were working on it.

Thus, the pace and intensity of efforts to resolve the intubations, to get Hal mobilized, to remove his Foley and his feeding tube and get him walking more and so forth increased only marginally. Certainly, I was proposing that Kaiser take some risks with Hal's life. I even wanted him to be sent home within some specified time that I called "soon", even if he had to go home on a ventilator and at considerable risk. I wanted them to return some quality of life to my friend, even were he going home to die. Quality of life (QoL) parameters are—I believe—often inimical to how technical medicine views such situations. QoL parameters are thought just too subjective. The specialists' parameters of outcome success are measurable, like the patient recovers, plain and simple. That Hal's chance of recovery was probably linked to his regaining some independence and autonomy, to his self-motivation, to their encouragement—even their insistence that Hal challenge the limits—did not fit their model of how to deal with a mid 80s man who was having trouble recovering from heart valve replacement. But I knew Hal. Faced with a demand that he had hard work to do or he might die, I knew he would have done the work.

Hal did not improve, but he did remain lucid despite all the weeks locked up in the ICU with the tubes and machines. Finally, under pressure to make a move, Kaiser made the wrong move. Instead of trying to send Hal home on a vent with heavy and costly home care nursing they sent him to another institution—a hybrid between a low-level hospital and a nursing home. The place did have plenty of advanced equipment, but no doctors on site much of the time. It was a lonely place too, farther from his home. Hal was there on his ventilator, getting adequate nursing care but the strategy did not change. He became weaker and weaker. Eventually he became delusional. A week or so after that Hal fell into a delerium—a semi-coma—and then died. A victim of what? I would say he was a victim of our health care system's disrespect of life, what it is, that intangible magic. For about three months Hal maintained his vitality, spirit, personality, verve, humor, humility, strength. And then almost suddenly it disappeared as he became aware that he was dying, alone in a foreign place not of his choosing away from his home, his lover, his plants, his family. What a sadness, I think, though Hal's stoicism about his circumstance did not allow for much outward expression of that sadness. I saw and felt a terrible sadness.

Almost two months after transfer out of Kaiser, when Hal died, sequestered at that facility, I did not go back and tell the Kaiser specialists I told you so; why didn't you pay attention to me? Because the truth is that they know so much more about technique than I do that I would seem to them an outsider, almost a non-physician, almost a commoner who doesn't understand their world and its importance to the patients they serve and cure. But the truth is that Hal's chances of surviving depended upon Kaiser doing things differently. Working harder with him as a person rather than a collection of systems, taking the risk of him dying at home with less technical support than the place where he did die; spending the money that individualized care requires. In some perverse way Hal understood me to be more a frustrated friend and political comrade than any kind of "expert" whose intervention might save his life. He did not fight back himself against this system of wrong rules, nor unleash me to challenge them more aggressively.

It's not that I know Hal would have lived had we forced this issue. Of course I don't. What I do know is that the quality of the rest of his life—whether he got better or not, lived a week, a month or years—his ability to be himself was taken away and he needed it, even if only so he could die with dignity. And that is what technical medicine, like so much else in this modern capitalist, market-driven world, robs from us: our human dignity. And so I pined for Hal.

Some time after Hal's death a memorial was held in his honor at the St. Joseph the Worker Catholic Church in Berkeley. The former head priest, Father Bill O'Donnell had been a lifelong staunch activist for human rights and a friend of Hal's with many arrests. Bill led an activist parish. He was one of the great liberation theologists. Bill had died unexpectedly while sitting at his office desk during the previous year. The church was packed with many hundreds of people who came to pay tribute to Hal and recount his exploits, his humor and his valuable life. Many of us spoke. It was a fitting event. Hal should have been there to see it. (December 4, 2012.)

THE FALSE PROMISE OF POWER
USURPS HUMAN AUTONOMY

US Major General Smedley Butler confessed to terrible things he had done. That was back in the 1930s. His exposure of his life as having been wasted as a hit man for big money—the Banks, United Fruit, American imperialism—leading invasions and taking over governments of so many countries for so-called "American interests" is truly remarkable (if you've not heard of him, put him into your search engine for details). But there is another side to that story—often the mighty don't recognize how much autonomy they lose by their assumption of power. Such is the story of Napoleon as emperor which Leo Tolstoy unfurls in *War and Peace*. When I became a public health officer (in Berkeley and then San Mateo County) in 1987–1988 I learned the lesson that Hamlet understood about the incompatibility of power, autonomy and democracy. I learned why titular authority, largely a facade for a heirarchical system, caused Shakespeare's Hamlet to refuse to ascend the throne. I thought I left Berkeley to do wonderful things in public health as a county health officer in San Mateo, then only to discover I was serving as the pawn of an x-cop in his fight with his boss, Margaret Taylor.

PART VI
Closing the loop

PALESTINE, OH PALESTINE!

This is the world as we've made it: The myth of a Palestinian state

The confusion over the viability or non-viability of a Palestinian state (known as the two-state solution) is never-ending. In actuality that is not mainly the fault of Israel's apartheid state-terrorist regime. The Israelis have done the least of any player in this great world tragedy to advance that confusion, doing so only when forced to appear open-minded by others. More often the Zionist state makes it quite clear that it won't accept a Palestinian state. In 1947–1948 it was the British and French with backing of the US and the Security Council of the UN that disingenuously sought to impose this dual-state idea into the breakup of British and French colonialism. Certainly the Palestinians got little or no say.

Moreover, it was an idea long in development in diabolical imperialist thinking. "Neither of the two national ideals permits of combination in the service of a single state," concluded Britain's Peel Commission.[56] In recognizing the decline and fall of their empires by the time of WWII, the British (and later the French in Indo-China) created the idea of the "two-state solution" out of whole cloth, first

---

56 In its final report of July 1937.

for India, then for Vietnam and Palestine. They were developing the ideology of neocolonialism (controlling nations and their labor and natural resources at a distance without colonial administrations) with a political theory based upon increasing the internal tensions and crises within newly independent regions and nations so that they could not become truly independent forces in the world political-economy. Economic dependence was later advanced through the IMF, the World Bank and other investment mechanisms (today through discriminatory sanctions as well). Britain left India in permanent crisis by fomenting riots and warfare between Muslims and Hindus and then claiming to solve the crisis with the formation of Pakistan in 1947. To kindle the flame they created Kashmir as an intermediate zone that Muslims and Hindus could fight over forever. The partition led to the displacement of 14 million people. And like the UN/US plan for Palestine today, Pakistan was formed of two separate pieces of Indian territory that, being over a thousand miles apart, a rising of resistance in the very poor East to Western Pakistan's rule would lead to the formation of Bangladesh.

In one sense the Jews who formed their guerilla armies in Palestine (Irgun and Stern Gang) were wise to Britain's intentions—even if thankful to have the Brits' colony handed to them on a platter. Though earlier agreeing to partition when they were a weak and small minority, the Zionists later resisted the idea of the two-state solution which would have granted a large portion of the colony to the indigenous Palestinians. Instead the Zionist militias targeted first the British to get them out of the way, and then advanced to the slaughter of Palestinians and ethnic cleansing of almost all their villages known as the Nakba, or Catastrophe. Later Israel would claim that the Palestinians had rejected their generous offer of land for a Palestinian state, but the Palestinians had never accepted the idea of the British Peel Commission report aimed at expanding immigration and land grabs and control by Jews fleeing persecution in

Europe—a Jewish state being formed from their lands. Moreover the settler colonial state of Israel had never accepted the idea either. After the Nakba the idea of a separate state was even more absurd to Palestinians: They were being asked to agree to give their lands to a military invader group, a Fifth Column, which had just spent a year massacring their women, children, and elderly with pogroms not unlike those Jews had suffered in Eastern Europe before the Nazis.

The unilateral declaration of Israel's independence was the Zionist answer to the UN's call for two states, side by side, living in peace. Moreover, the two-state solution was never consistent with Zionism's full ambitions either. And it doesn't conform with the role of states in the world—in regulating commerce, migration, finances and defense. It's like supposing that somehow the US could have been induced to give up manifest destiny and hand over the western half of the country to the Indians to form their own United Nations nation.

Similarly, had Israel allowed a Palestinian state, the Israel-Palestine partition would have led to the same endless confrontations and wars that India and Pakistan have engaged in, except that in Palestine, Israel would have easily cut off Palestine from outside trade and travel, which it has done, effectively, in any case. Like today, Israel would still have attacked and invaded at will. In other words, the two-state solution was a Euro-American ruse that the UN fronted. It was a cover for establishing the Zionists, principally European Jews, as a beachhead to replace direct colonial rule with a different type of settler colonization, a throwback to the days of settlements of the New World and South Africa. That Zionism has not always played by the great power rules the US and Europe sought to impose should not be surprising. Though it can be blamed for its many crimes against the Palestinians, Israel cannot be blamed for that. After all, why would Jews (Israeli Jews or any Ashkenazi Jews the world over) trust any of the great powers after suffering the Holocaust to which the nations of Europe and the US turned a blind eye while the slaughter was in progress. Nevertheless, European crimes can never justify the Zionist regimes acting like Nazis toward the indigenous Palestinians or Israel's consistent support for some of the most ruthless, brutal and reactionary regimes in the world—from apartheid South Africa to the death squad dictatorships of the Americas. But their propaganda offensive does explain why many people endlessly hope for a "two-state solution".

The entire Zionist enterprise is based on a different premise —Eretz Yisrael (a Jewish-only state from the Jordan River to the Mediterranean Sea). The bankruptcy of that goal is enough reason to envision Israel eventually joining the world community of nations as an integrated nation with a new name, a real constitution[57] that guarantees rights to all citizens and affords all those who live under its government the full rights of citizenship, internationally recognized borders, the right of Palestinian return and the end to Jewish-only settlements.

But Israel, like South Africa and the colonial regimes before them, must first be brought to its senses through economic, political and cultural isolation and then be required to reconstitute itself as a democracy with full rights for all. If Jews can have Aliyah (automatic citizenship in Israel by birthright as a Jew), so should Palestinians who were forced off their homelands. Their children in exile are entitled as well.

Yet the most important point is this: the whole idea of two states side by side was a myth from the beginning. People all too often can be taught to buy into such myths and to think they hold promise. In this case that conclusion defies history's logic. Endlessly we who support Palestinian rights point out that a Palestinian state would be made up of isolated Bantustans without access to the sea or to out-

---

57 Israel actually has no constitution and no explicit agreed national geographical borders.

side commerce except with Israeli permission. We point out so many other things like the siege of Gaza with many thousands murdered; the internationally condemned walls and the Israeli intent to maintain military control up to the Jordan in the West Bank. And yet some people persist in trying to come up with ways to allow Israel to be a Jews-only state, some "plan" that might be acceptable to apartheid Israel and achieved through peace talks. What utter rubbish!

In South Africa, Botha negotiated with Mandela when he was still imprisoned at Robben Island. When Netanyahu or some other racist reactionary murderous Israeli leader finds himself or herself "born again" and impelled to begin to negotiate with the imprisoned Barghouti (or some other Mandela equivalent) allowing him/them to engage in political activism again, we will surmise that times are changing. When Israel swears that it will stop assassinating Palestinian political leaders—PA, Hamas, Jihad, Hezbollah or anyone else— and will stop arbitrary imprisonment and holding thousands without charges, and will cease its political efforts to always divide the Palestinians against themselves, using the PA as Kapos, then, anyone who brings forward the idea of a separate Palestinian state rather than full political and human rights for all Palestinians will be ridiculed.

Until then, there is no solution. But at that moment a two-state solution will amount to nothing more than proposing that reactionary Zionism remain in power. The way to end the captivity of any captive people—Black slaves, Indians (US indigenous), Palestinians—is to assure their full equal rights and opportunities of citizenship, including the right to land, political equality, maintainance of their own language and culture. After slavery, US Blacks achieved those rights for barely a decade before Reconstruction was overthrown here. The overthrow of Reconstruction is the strongest evidence that the US itself never attained more than a paper democracy. American Indians never got those rights either, but instead were granted inferior second-class status (supposed control over the reservations/bantustans where they were settled). That is approximately what Palestine is offered. Have we learned nothing about taking the fight for rights through to completion? The problem of greatest importance is not some abstract idea about the right to self-determination under a separate but unequal state, but how to assure that any revolutionary process achieves the full guarantee of equal treatment and justice for any oppressed people.

I have experienced Israel "on the ground". Have seen how we Jews became executioners of our own humanity, squandering the wondrous positive potential of social mind and social evolution while the un "civilized" world tolerates still another apartheid state.

RETRO POLL: WE DROP INTO
PUBLIC OPINION RESEARCH

George W. Bush and Dick Cheney's War on Iraq was another replay of the phony Gulf of Tonkin incident in 1964 that was cooked up to get Americans to believe in the necessity of a war against and the near total destruction of Vietnam. Again our government was stirring up public chauvinism for war under the rubric of the moral supremacy of American exceptionalism and bold lies. Although I participated in a number of anti-war demonstrations against the Iraq invasion, I envisioned little chance that we would stop Washington from carrying out the commands of those demons who forecast America's "new American century" as the crowning glory of American power and imperial world dominance. We were trapped[58] in an endless loop of "democratic" lingo fronting for the most egregious form of totalitarianism and domination: wars of aggression.

My angst drove two different tendencies within me. One was that fantastical and utterly romantic idea that I might help communicate the fraudulence of the coming war to the nation by writing my novel. I melded the facts of the government charade, along with slightly changed names of diplomatic figures into the fabric of this Jewish silly tale based in the well-known "Wise Men of Chelm" stories by two legendary Jewish storytellers, Sholem Aleichem (Sholem Rabi-

---

58 As we are today in 2022.

novitsh), the Russian-born greatest of Yiddish storytellers, and Solomon Simon, author of "The Wise Men of Chelm" books.

The second tendency that drove me to desperation was my long-standing awareness that US media—from newspapers to TV news, to cable news, to radio, to public radio and TV—are not in the least neutral or objective organs of information. They promote capital-ist ideology and relations and, in particular, American superiority (exceptionalism and national chauvinism, both "liberal" and "con-servative" varieties). American mythology is so highly sophisticated, having been fine-tuned under the rubric known as "free press" going back to the very Declaration of Independence. How was it possible otherwise to therein declare that all men are created equal and yet deny the very humanity of the slaves and even legalize their subjuga-tion as property in Article I of the Constitution? Yes, America's elites have been more sophisticated than most empires in how they conceal dishonest motives, their misanthrope and plans. They've always used the artifices of an idealized reality to conceal deceits, such as giving credence to the nonsense that Saddam Hussein (indeed a dictator) was involved in 9/11 or developing nuclear, biological and chemical warfare weaponry.

Such themes are tools used to oversimplify how Americans should think and analyze information: the promotion of zero-sum sectarian "religious-like" logic through which the exploitative nature of class social relations do not become self-exposing. What jumped out at me in particular in 2002 was the growing media dependence upon public opinion polling as a weapon to create thought conformity and deceive people about what "most" Americans think.

This led to the creation—in a collaboration with University of California pulmonologist, Warren Gold[59] and community college

---

59 Warren Gold is emeritus professor of medicine at University of California, San Francisco School of Medicine, where he was director of the pulmonary lab and specialized in asthma.

lecturer, Mickey Huff[60]—of a new opinion research organization. Retro Poll would be—and did become—a combative though honest and revelatory opinion-polling operation in 2002, conducting eight nationwide random sample polls through 2007 that surveyed both knowledge and opinion on important public issues in each poll. We correlated people's factual knowledge base to their views showing that disinformation, not values or ideology, is the main driver of people's opinions. We ran these polls twice a year and posted our results and our polling exposed how opinion polls are conducted to fabricate a sense of coherent majority views on critical topics that are not real. We published analytical articles on our web page which was managed by our volunteer webmaster, James True, a long-time Southern civil rights activist and graphic designer who lives on the East Coast. Our findings were cited by Ralph Nader when he ran for president and our methods were copied (without attribution) by the University of Maryland's Opinion Research Center. In October 2003, Mickey and I published an essay ("The Public Opinion Polling Fraud") in *Z Magazine.* Though Retro Poll went belly up in 2007, the website remains, now under the sponsorship of the Media Freedom Foundation (at www.retropoll.org).

---

60 After the retirement of Project Censored's then director Peter Philips, Mickey Huff went on to become its director (PC is a national academic collaboration in which students investigate and critique the most censored stories of the year. It's based at Sonoma State University in Rohnert Park, CA). Mickey is presently tenured professor at Contra Costa Community College and professor of social science, history, and journalism at Diablo Valley College where he co-chairs the history area and is chair of the journalism department. He is also president of the Media Freedom Foundation and is lecturer in sociology at Sonoma State and recently lecturer at Cal State East Bay in communications. He hosts the Project Censored Show on Pacifica Radio's KPFA, 94.1 FM.

THE MAD AS HELL
DOCTORS OF 2009–2011

"It is I, Don Quixote, the Lord of La Mancha,

My destiny calls and I go…"
(opening lyric from Man of La Mancha*)*

In 2009–10 I joined a group of Oregon docs and other health workers to tour the US and then California as the Mad as Hell Doctors for Single Payer Health Care (MAHD). The project was imagined by Adam Klugman and Gary Jelinek and was co-led by retired radiation oncologist, Mike Huntington and emergency physician, Paul Hochfeld. We produced spirited multi-media events from coast to coast that engaged energetically with audiences/patients and also put their sad stories of health care denial, with and without insurance up on YouTube. We did dozens of TV, radio and press interviews and became local phenoms wherever we performed (over 60 locales). I was a regular panelist in one part of our show. Here is text of my typical four-minute MAHD panel talk:

"Almost every clinic I work these days I see patients being evicted from their homes and I can do little to help them. I've been practicing primary care medicine in California with working class, mostly minority patients for 39 years and so it makes me mad as hell to wake up every morning knowing I'm part of a medical care system ranking 37th in the world according to the World Health Organization's composite indicator for health outcomes; moreover, that to rank 37th we spend about 8,000 dollars per person per year, twice as much as the second-most expensive country. I'm particularly mad as hell that in a supposed democracy our Congress refuses to publicly debate the obvious value to us all of a Medicare for All program. Taking something 'off the table', as they did, means removing our democracy. And just weeks ago in August we saw the Democratic Party leadership here in CA block a vote on SB 810, single payer legislation, although we know it had the votes to pass—for a third time. It's obvious that the money is calling the shots so Wall Street Insurance companies can continue their exorbitant profiteering as people suffer.

"Back in 1965 this country's greatest civil rights leader, Martin Luther King Jr., speaking before the Medical Committee for Human Rights Convention in Chicago said: "Of all forms of inequality, injustice in health care is the most shocking and inhumane. '" Dr. King was pointing out to healthcare workers that health care is a right that is linked to other civil rights struggles. Yet we have let the idea of healthcare as a right lie fallow these 45 intervening years. I've got to ask this: can we afford to believe we will win this rational and reasonable reform, this public right, by merely writing, e-mailing, petitioning or educating our elected officials? As Martin King's comment suggests, don't we have to rejuvenate the civil rights movement across California and the US, envision a coordination between electoral and non electoral efforts, and most importantly, link this vitally important reform with other people's fights against injustice and for their rights, such as the immigrants rights movement, the right to have a union, the right not to be murdered by police while Black, unarmed and innocent, the right to be freed from custody unless charged with a crime, the right not to be on a government assassination list. I'm here for single payer health care but I do believe that we can and must turn the face of the Medicare for All movement outward into the minority communities and that we here can forge a commitment to fight for a collaborative justice for all, using every means available, as the great American civil rights movement did. My charge to you is that you work to assure that when we return here next year, our audience is half people of color. If we can do that we will no longer need to worry about Teabaggers (ed: referring to the Tea Party in Congress) or any other sand that is thrown up in the air by billionaires who control the media to blind and confuse the public. Can you do it? Si se puede."

MUTUALITY AND A
COMMON SENSE OF BETRAYAL

I met Sheila Thorne about a year or less after she had divorced Ned Harper. They had gotten together as Stanford undergrads before I entered medical school. When she married Ned, Sheila suspended her Stanford studies and they had lived in Albuquerque, with their two sons, while Ned attended grad school at the University of New Mexico. His coursework completed, they moved to Rio di Janero, Brazil for a year and a half as Ned tried to do research for his doctoral thesis. That task became more or less impossible because of the US-backed military coup that overthrew the Brazilian government.[61] Sheila remembers tanks in the street and that Ned's work was stymied, libraries inaccessible. After about 18 months, she moved back to Palo Alto with her boys in tow, then to Menlo Park. She finished up her Stanford BA having taken some courses at New Mexico—and divorced Ned.

Although she claims a prehistory, in my mind I didn't actually meet Sheila until late 1971 when I moved down from South Francisco to a house I had rented with a friend. Coincidentally, that friend, David Ransom, had been one of Sheila's housemates after she and Ned split. Though Sheila's divorce is not my business to write about, she's said it was a long time coming. By the time I met her the boys, Shep and Joel, were 11 and six.

---

61 It later turned out that Ned's faculty advisor at New Mexico was CIA-connected.

Once situated in the Redwood City house with David, I was having a sort of fling with a young woman, Mary, who roomed at Sheila's home down the road a piece in Menlo Park. Mary was also a member of Venceremos. She was an impetuous youngster, about 20 I think—to my 30. I recall that she was studying karate and in a fit of rage over something one day she had kicked a wall and broken her foot. I was not a witness nor contributor to that event.

I doubt that Mary was particularly fond of me and our "friendship" lasted no more than a month, but she let me into her bed a few times. Because of that, late one night I climbed into her bedroom through the window beside the locked front door. When I got into bed with her she successfully heaved me onto the floor—I can't say it was a "rude awakening" since I wasn't asleep at the time, but she probably thought I was being rude. She was quite strong apparently. I think that was before Mary broke her foot, because I don't remember a cast when she tossed me. Awakened, Sheila thought the whole scene was pretty funny. (Some years into our marriage Sheila threw me onto the floor once or twice herself.) Though never literally thrown "under the bus", I guess I was the "throw him on the floor" type of guy, despite my six feet and then 168 pounds. That seems to be one aspect of my MO.

I remember that I was taking particular notice of Sheila by then. She had a calm, friendly demeanor, sitting in her rocking chair in the living room. She was pretty; she was sexy in a stealthy way; she seemed calm, mature, and her sons were a trip. When I was visiting Mary I bonded with them even before I got much involved with Sheila.

At that time Sheila was going with a fellow who was pretty obviously not a permanent fixture in her life any more than Mary was in mine. Robert was a recently released ex-con. He was a handsome, tall, soft-spoken African American fellow. When I heard that Sheila and Robert planned to drive across the Bay for Thanksgiving to our mutual friend Eleanor Levine's home, I asked if I could join them—

Eleanor had recently ended a relationship. Eleanor had no objection, so the three of us went over across the Dunbarton Bridge in Sheila's 1969 Volvo station wagon.

It may have been late that particular night that I realized that I was falling for Sheila and I knew that Robert was about to disappear from view, literally speaking. She was, besides attractive to me, smart and literate and we had our common strong beliefs and opinions. She was exceptionally well read, a literature buff in the English language. She was a leading political figure in Venceremos. She was working on the line in a Philco Ford electronics factory and was determined and courageous in her advocacy for justice. Sheila had and still has a ferocious determination and a temper to match. Everything about her drew my attention. In the end she chose me as a partner (as much as I did her) though I never figured out why. I think maybe it was that she saw the absurdity of this young doctor who was so foppish, silly in the extreme, climbing through that window, an ordinary person who made no bones about his desire to be a loving stepfather to Shep and Joel. But you'd have to ask her about that.

I asked her out in December and by mid-January I had moved into her home—now the four of us and Mary. My time in Redwood City with David Ransom and my female Shepherd, Cocaine, was so brief that Dave (who in retirement moved back to California from the East Coast) does not remember it occurring. Sheila, however, remembers staying over there one night, which may be when we decided I would move in with her.

Trying to write about the next 49 years with Sheila Thorne has had me hogtied. I let it lie fallow for some months and it's ended up here. It's such a big and complicated subject and I don't want to simplify and turn it into a passing landscape or betray its uniqueness or how we've managed and mangled our way through. All personal relationships are unique and yet much of our daily sharing with friends and acquaintances amounts to superficiality if not supercil-iousness, e.g. "How ya doing? Good, thanks" and "Have a nice day." Now in 2021, 49 years is 61% of my life on Earth and about 82% of my adult life, after all.

We loved, we hated, we fought, we reconciled, we judged, we forgave, we collaborated, we accused, we admitted, we hurt, we salved, we supported, we undermined, we lied, we denied lying, we deceived and denied that, we deceived ourselves, we protected ourselves and we protected each other, we rejected each other and we stayed true to our trust, our truth and our bond, we steadfastly asserted our independence and our individuality and yet we clarified out ties, our need for mutuality, support, collaboration, love and our belief in an ethical and just world for our kids and for everyone. We held together like magnetic north and south, polar opposites—like those entangled particles I wrote about earlier. One of the most amazing things is how our extremely different personalities, styles and backgrounds blended us into a unit that was constantly in loving conflict with itself. Our styles of engaging with and mediating the world are different in the extreme.

Sheila and I got married in 1974. We were then living together over two years. It wasn't what you'd call a shotgun marriage since no one gave a damn that she was almost nine months pregnant at the time. However, there was a gun involved and a priest as well. We'd had no particular intention to get married, having both been divorced (in my case twice). We just decided to live together, to move to San Jose and to have a child. Having my first daughter squirreled away to Ohio by Carrie (and Lee) gave me an itch to have a child with Sheila. She already had two, her two fine boys. But she had once hoped for a daughter. *Wouldn't a daughter be wonderful,* she thought. The first time we got pregnant she miscarried in the first trimester. Early miscarriages are a common occurrence. The old terminology is blighted ovum, suggesting that the pregnancies aren't viable from the get-go.

But Sheila had also been working at a factory where she and other women sometimes leaned over a vat of vaporizing trichloroethylene (a solvent later outlawed because of its potential for cancer, birth defects, and miscarriages. It's also been used as a general anesthetic). Her miscarriage, coming as it did early in pregnancy, may have been coincidence. But the TCE vapor was so real that the workers were required to wear a hanging belt or harness to assure they didn't become stuporous and fall into the vat. Health and safety standards? Not.

But the second try went right along until politics butted in. While a leader in Venceremos, Sheila had been asked by a member—an adult—if she could buy them a handgun when she was going to a gun show in Vallejo. It seemed innocent at the time, but unbeknownst to her, that gun wound up as part of[62] the stupid prison break and guard murder that I have described previously. When we learned that the gun recipient was one of the people involved in that event, we began to have big worries about potential liabilities: what if that gun's purchase were traced back to Sheila? What if she was arrested and gave birth in jail? With no legal father/guardian, might the authorities seize our child and put her in foster care? Terrible scenarios cluttered our minds. And from this derived our sort of shotgun wedding.

Our angst was receding as we planned a simple civil ceremony in San Jose. But true to our romantic spirits we thought, *"Let's at least involve a movement, clergyman."* So we sought the help of the well-known priest at the Sacred Heart Church[63] in the Latino Gardner community not far from the city center. Father Moriarty was well-known for his strong advocacy of farm worker rights and support of

---

62 Definitely not the murder weapons, but it was there.

63 I would later spend three years as the medical director of the Gardner Community Health Center housed at the same Sacred Heart Church (1980–1983).

the UFW boycotts which we were involved with. "Be happy to marry you, he replied," looking at the big-bellied Sheila, "but you know I can't do it in the sanctuary since you're not Catholics. My office will suffice. " Ok? " "Certainly ok, " we said.

Having obtained the marriage license paper from the county clerk, we got ready for that simple ceremony—a Catholic priest to marry a Protestant and a Jew. But the night before we were married we had one classic row (though not our first). Sheila threw a hissy fit at something I said or did and said she didn't want to marry such an asshole and there right before my eyes she took up that marriage certificate and tore it into tiny pieces (I do mean tiny) and threw them on the floor. It took me into the wee hours of the morning, teary-eyed, to tape the thing back together; but by the morning our plan had been restored. I think we raised Father Moriarty's eyebrows again as he perused and signed our marriage certificate. To this day when she tells this tale to friends, Sheila ends with: "How could I walk away from a guy who cared so much, staying up half the night repairing the damage. I knew then he'd be faithful."

Cesar's ghost haunts
Donald Trump

Yeah, kids, I knew Cesar Chavez. I worked for him, but I had no special relationship with the leader of the most important rights organization still surviving by the mid-1970s. Though a doctor, I was just a union functionary. I write to share my thoughts about why the union lost most of its membership, contracts and its power as the force for workers' rights in California agriculture. It was once a bright and shining star, but only the shell remained by the early 1980s.

When I joined the UFW staff, I was told to drive down to Keene, California, in the foothills East of Bakersfield where the UFW had moved its headquarters (called La Paz), be interviewed by Cesar and get to know others in the union's inner core. Among the people who I met and became friends with during the two days I stayed at La Paz was a middle-aged woman, Maria Rifo, a Chilean exile. It was the time of the dictatorship of Augusto Pinochet who the US (via Henry Kissinger and CIA) helped place and keep in power. A couple of years before I met Maria, the democratically elected socialist (and physician) President Salvador Allende was deposed and killed. Tens of thousands of Chileans were tortured, imprisoned and thousands killed, although the military coup had been organized to look like a popular insurrection. The torturers cut off the hands of the famous Chilean singer/songwriter beloved to the people, Victor Jara, before they murdered him. Maria Rifo had played a role within the Allende Socialist Party and now here at La Paz she was again playing an important role in the editing and production of the UFW newspaper, *El Malcriado* (the ill-mannered). She talked about the situation in Chile and the importance that *El Malcriado* was covering foreign affairs like Chile and Vietnam, that would help forge worker understanding and international unity. We became instant friends. Maria also introduced me to Cesar's two handsome German Shepherds, Huelga and Boycott, of whom Maria was particularly fond. A picture of Maria Rifo cheek to cheek with Huelga is taped on the wall in front of me now—or is that Boycott? I was at that time 33 years old and Maria was perhaps 50. I guess her age based upon her death in Santa Rosa at the age of 99 several years ago. I lost touch with her long before that.

Maria Rifo and one of Cesar Chavez' German Shepherds (circa 1976).

Jumping ahead to October 1978, when I was separated from the union, we are close to the end of the many purges in the UFW. By now, Cesar Chavez has, most recently, fired the many doctors and staffs of four of the five National Farm Workers' Health Group clinics (at Delano, Coachella, Calexico, and Sanger). I was the last doctor and last medical director at the last UFW union clinic open. And then I was also fired and our Salinas staff was let go. This was one of the self-made disasters for the union and its farm worker supporters who had a great affinity to the union through the clinics.

We in Salinas had all come to realize the inevitability of our clinic's plight and our forthcoming separation after the Coachella clinic staff over a year earlier wrote to Cesar that they would not follow his order to stop giving birth control to farm worker patients. All of our clinics provided family planning. From time to time Cesar would declare this against the Church teachings and the "workers' religious beliefs". Of course, the workers themselves sought birth control at our clinics and he knew it. Margaret Murphy, herself a former nun, taught us how to deal with such presidential edicts—say nothing and ignore them. Like the legal department that was now being disassembled, Coachella didn't stick with the MO. They decided they should "defend" the farm workers' right to family planning by telling Cesar to back off. And after Cesar closed Coachella, he then turned his wrath on Dan Murphy—as loyal a Chavista as I'd seen—and the rest of the Delano staff, accusing them all of being anti-union communists. This was not the first or only sign that Cesar was heading full speed for a precipice, with no way for anyone to stop the matanza (a figurative massacre). It was close to the last.

In this difficult period, many staff, including leading UFW national organizers, a co-founder, cultural workers and volunteers had already been put out. Ultimately, Cesar attacked several key ranch committee leaders and local staff organizers because they advocated a slate of alternative union board members to his hand-picked candidates at the 1981 union convention.

I was gone by then, serving Latino communities in and around San Jose in community clinics through mid-1986 when I went back to school at UC Berkeley. With a public health degree (1987) I was appointed the acting public health officer for Berkeley. Two years later I initiated and co-led the committee that created the Berkeley High School Based Health Center; and then in 1992 I became first medical director of the Center for Elders' Independence in Oakland (CEI), where I provided care to disabled elders and supervised our other care providers for almost a decade. Had I control of destiny none of that would have occurred and I would have retired from the UFW at a ripe old age.

I was still working at CEI in July of 1999 when I received a letter from Paul Henggeler, a history professor at the University of Texas-Pan American, who wrote that he was researching a book on Cesar Chavez and the United Farm Workers (UFW) union. Professor Henggeler had already spoken with dozens of former UFW volunteers and staff and read thoroughly the Union's comprehensive archives then located at Wayne State University in Detroit. Henggeler called because my name came up in the minutes of a UFW board meeting. Paraphrasing, Henggeler related Cesar saying approximately, "I don't get this doctor. He sends me nasty letters critical of our policy decisions, but he also does whatever we ask him to do for the union."

Many of those contacted, including myself, were at first reluctant to talk with Paul Henggeler, concerned about a potential hidden agenda that he might not reveal to us. Though I was critical of plenty that had happened when I worked for the UFW I was not of a mind to discuss those things for a book unless I thought the book would help, not harm, the farm workers' movement stirring up old animosities needlessly. But Henggeler assured people that he was a "New Deal (Roosevelt) Democrat" who was very much pro-union and wrote me the following: "I admire Chavez and firmly believe that he did more to help the farm workers than any person in American history. But I am a trained historian and as such I offer assessments of my subjects based on evidence. Consequently, I am sometimes critical even of my heroes if the evidence brings me to such conclusions…In some places this work will indeed be critical of Chavez."

(Quoted from Henggeler's second letter to me—August 29, 1999—urging that I contact him and agree to be interviewed.)

After reading reviews of Henggeler's earlier book, *In His Steps: Lyndon B Johnson and the Kennedy Mystique* (1991), I agreed to talk with him to help elaborate an honest picture of the UFW and Cesar. I shared not only my own views (in a few extended telephone interviews lasting over an hour each) but sent him documents that I had saved from my years with the union, including memos from Cesar and letters I had written to Cesar and the board. By that time more than a few former UFW staff had already helped Henggeler.

In late 1999 Paul Henggeler told me his book would probably be published in two years. In 2001 and 2002 I called him or e-mailed him a couple of times and found that he was still hard at work on it. He told me that he had important "loose ends" he needed to track down, but he was "getting close" to the end. As the years went by and the legend of Cesar Chavez, as such things go, grew to heroic proportions, rivaling Zapata, Martin Luther King Jr., Gandhi and others, no book was published.

Meanwhile, apparently stimulated by Hengeller's work and his contacts to former staff, LeRoy Chatfield, the once-priest, who had become Cesar's personal and loyal assistant, got the idea of developing a historical documentation project based upon the comprehensive experiences and views of everyone who ever worked with/for the union. (LeRoy left the UFW about the time I joined.) It would be an unrestricted, uncensored, "people's history" of that very turbulent and complex era in the growth (and decline) of a powerful movement for farm workers' rights in the US. LeRoy named his project the Farm Worker Movement Documentation Project and his website can be found here: https://libraries.ucsd.edu/farmworkermovement. The website went up on the Internet in October 2005 with a bang. A few months later LeRoy estimated that, at current hit rate, the site would receive a million visits by the time it was one year old.

As a result of visiting the website, reading many essays there and with LeRoy's assistance I re-contacted a few former co-workers from my UFW days. From one of these, Kathy Murgia, I learned, in early 2006, that not only had Paul Henggeler's book not been published, but Paul had suddenly died of a heart attack at the age of only 48 in 2004 or 2005. His wife had held his "almost completed" work for some period, but then surprisingly decided not to publish it or seek someone to finish the project. Instead she sent the full manuscript to the present union leadership, relatives of Cesar Chavez (Cesar was by then deceased well over a decade—having died in April 1993). I was told that she did not keep a copy. Henggeler's book, which surely would have provided interesting historical perspective on problems within the union, was never seen or heard of after that.

I was hoping to read Henggeler's analysis. I had not known of Henggeler's death. And by the time I sat to write this essay's first draft years ago, Paul's many years of research and writing had been apparently expunged from history. On the other hand, I did read extensively the recollections, reminiscences, good times and bad times, opinions and so on, on LeRoy's huge farm worker movement website and then shared the essay of my own experiences.

In 2011 Frank Bardacke published a huge outstanding 740-page people's history: *Trampling out the Vintage*—Cesar Chavez and the two souls of the United Farm Workers (Verso). I began drafting this current essay before reading Bardacke's excellent and comprehensive work, but inevitably much of his investigation informs my own understanding and subsequent editing of this piece, though my own emphasis reflects my own particular perspective. I'm hopeful this essay may help clarify the historical context.

The UFW arose, flourished and declined in a period of tumultuous transitions—from the civil rights and anti-Vietnam War movements up through the 1970s. It's critical to reflect upon how that American history interacted with the UFW. The 1970s was a period of American preparatory reaction that is now in full bloom. By the mid-70s imperialist/capitalist retrenchment had taken a serious toll on progressive movements for justice in the US and worldwide. The UFW was, in fact, the last major independent political movement pillar standing in the face of a government onslaught against the rising wave of activism. Much of that onslaught against activism was propagated by the COINTELPRO campaign of FBI Director J. Edgar Hoover. Unsupportable provocations, infiltration, surveillance and surreptitious attacks on Civil and Human Rights organizations was widespread.

The UFW and Cesar Chavez were an important part of that broad social justice movement that was attacked, but was somewhat insulated. After the downfall of Wisconsin Senator Joseph McCarthy's anti-communist witchhunts, and the successful 1954 Supreme Court decision outlawing school segregation in Brown v Board of Education, social justice movements began to transform both politics and culture in the US—from the end of the Korean War up until the Nixon resignation. The rise of the great civil rights movement and then the anti-Vietnam War movement immediately followed on the heels of the anti-communist Crusade events. So did the appearance of the SCLC, the United Farm Workers union, Black Panther Party, SNCC, CORE, SDS, the GI Coffee House Movement, the underground press, the American Indian Movement, urban riots and a major rebellion in the US Navy which almost crippled the US military.

A charismatic, inspiring and insightful leader, Cesar Chavez was a man of great historic importance. Yet because of that, Cesar's followers—both the uncritical and critical—assume that Cesar was the master of his own destiny and the UFW's history and trajectory. Wasn't it the idea of Cesar with Fred Ross and Larry Itliong (AWOC) to pull the Mexican farm workers (of the National Farm Workers Assn) out of the fields in support of the strike by Filipino laborers

(Agricultural Workers Organizing Committee—AWOC) in 1962? Didn't that decisive action create conditions for merging the Filipino farm workers movement and the Mexican farm workers movement into one joint struggle (the UFWA), and sweep aside the drag on that development that the AFL-CIO then represented in the fields?

From that reality, however, it becomes hard for people who knew Cesar to believe other than that he made such, often difficult, choices by his own free will and his insightful understanding of what was best and effective—choices of magisterial importance to the benefit of farm workers. I don't believe that to be an accurate portrayal of the history. Instead I believe that arguments over Cesar Chavez' personal legacy (the good and the bad) tend to blur a broader discussion of the constraints that history placed upon the UFW struggle by 1975 (when I became a regular UFW doc).

Whomever was at the helm of the UFW by the time that I joined its staff in 1975 would have faced impenetrable challenges. It was because Cesar was the powerful leader he was, however, that he was able to temper and for a while ameliorate those challenges. Then these events became tragic under the weight and wounds, sometimes self-inflicted, that brought Cesar and the UFW to their knees as Cesar labeled so many in and around the UFW enemies. Those who focus on Cesar's mistakes highlight his hubris in decisions he made which (by 1976) were leading the UFW toward its ultimate decline. Examples include his declaration (supported by the Executive Board) that undocumented workers were unreliable due to status and should be deported rather than organized into the union; his purges of staff he considered insufficiently loyal to his orders; his banishment of co-founder Tony Orendain; his requiring Gilbert Padilla to seize the Texas UFW office from Tony and the Texas organizers; his forcing out Luis Valdez and El Teatro Campesino; his dissatifaction with the *El Malcriado* newspaper which, although finanically independent, was another piece of the soul of the movement he disassembled, and so forth.

In reality, the UFW began to transition into an almost revolutionary force in America, an organization seemingly capable of representing all farm workers in the US while also molding them into a political movement to be reckoned with under una sola union. And yet the Left in America was being beaten down at that very moment.

At certain points in history and in each of our lives, choices can become very limited. For example, once the US government decided to make an anti-Soviet example of Ethel and Julius Rosenberg, the couple were allowed but two terrible choices: confess to having conspired to give nuclear secrets to the Russians and live out ignominious lives, possibly life in prison, or not confess and face death in the electric chair. They found meaning for their two sons, for their beliefs and values, and for history by choosing to die—refusing to stay alive at the cost of their honor—but those were terribly limited choices and outcomes, irrespective of any facts of the case.[64] It's easy to see how the Rosenbergs' control of their own destiny was severely restricted once they had been indicted and the state had family and

---

64 My understanding in 2022 is that the Rosenbergs were to some extent involved in passing along some information to the Soviets. However, I don't understand how they had access. Sheila and I have just watched the very interesting fictionalized version of the life of the British woman who was not a communist but undoubtedly had very relevant information regarding nuclear weapons development that she passed to the Soviets. She was not accused until about 40 years after the war and the story is fascinating. She collaborated only after the mass murder atom bombings of civilans at Hiroshima and Nagasaki because she heard in the top-secret environment where she worked as a physicist and assistant to the chief, that Britain and the US had plans to launch a nuclear attack on the Soviet Union, unprovoked. In her trial in the 1990s, she claimed her effort was intended to prevent that nuclear attack. She was believed and she served no time in prison. The film is titled "*Red Joan*" and the lead is Judy Dench.

friend witnesses against them. But the Rosenbergs were not leading communists, only party members. It's much harder to view people we believe to be great and powerful leaders as becoming deeply trapped in that way, overcome by circumstances beyond their control (regardless of whether they helped create those circumstances).

By the mid-1970s the mass movements had quietly gone the way of Richard Nixon, but without the (Watergate) fanfare. The 60s represented an explosion of democratic energy and engagement suppressed earlier by the McCarthy witchhunts and the enforced Rightist conformity of the postwar era. The main thrust of the McCarthy era—even beyond the anti-communist legislation passed by Congress that outlawed membership in the Communist Party with the Smith Act—was directed toward the elimination of trade union militancy and the elimination of internationalist leaders within the AFL-CIO, especially the industrial trade unions in the CIO. The American Communist Party structure was then already so weakened (for reasons I will not detail here) that its leaders decided to all but disband the Party, telling its activists to leave their jobs and communities and go "underground" (in many cases never to be seen or heard from again). In part, the civil rights movement and anti-Vietnam War Movements thrived because of the Communist Party's weakness. Young people of that era could steer clear of the weakened Party's often conservative advice as we built a militant Movement. Freedom from the constraints of narrow ideological disputes (such as the Soviet vs the Chinese communists tension over how to proceed) helped energize the 60s. Nationwide, young people were studying and discussing history, politics and theories of imperialism and capitalism free from any required obedience to any external ideological formula or "Party line."

By and large the New Left was not anti-communist. Some were but most young radicals, regardless of ethnicity or class, were, like the Black Panther Party, assertively not anti-communist. In the post WWII era, Ronald Reagan became a well-known political figure as head of the Screen Actors Guild. He collaborated with the witchhunts, labeling militant union actors as suspected communists. Reagan's political ascendancy (and Nixon's also) resulted from their collaboration in the efforts to destabilize the powerful CIO-based trade union movement. The anti-communist purges in Hollywood amounted to a preemptive strike against a future internationalist character of the rising democratic cultural movement. The CIA eventually penetrated and often controlled the organs of literary culture to similarly undermine this inevitability.[65] The 1950s attack on labor derived from capitalist fears of the potential for a militant US working class uniting against American chauvinism—the fear that the working class here would adopt an internationalist posture after the war. An internationalist workers' movement could throw a monkey wrench into the plan for US dominance and globalization. The ant-communist crusade disrupted that unifying process. Nevertheless, internationalism and anti-neocolonialism became war cries of the peace movement in the 60s anyway when the US committed to preventing Vietnam from charting it's own national independence.

Whenever I hear defenders of US wars claim they aim to build democracy around the world, I recall President Dwight Eisenhower's famous statement, after France signed a peace accord with the Viet Minh. Ike said the US would not abide by that Geneva Peace Agreement France signed because Ho Chi Minh would surely win the Presidency with 80% in any democratic election and would reunify Vietnam. The US wasn't going to tolerate it. Our country killed two million Vietnamese and 58,000 young Americans trying to prevent that democratic election. And failed to stop reunification.

Meanwhile, Cesar Chavez, though the son of farm worker immigrants who himself worked in the fields as a child laborer in Arizona,

---

65 See Joel Whitney's: *Finks* (OR Books: 2016).

grew up in that period during the strait-jacketing witch-hunts. He then became a prominent political activist in the Catholic lay movement. This was the early 60s, the era of expanding struggle for human and civil rights. But Cesar's understanding, consciousness and his training as an organizer was derived from two factors: his deeply religious beliefs in his power to impact history and in using the pro-imperialist AFL-CIO leaders who had replaced the purged militants of the labor movement to achieve his aims.

The McCarthy era, Smith Act, McCarran-Walter Act were of prime importance in pacifying the American working class. Out of this environment, came a new breed of union leadership. These folks had avoided the attacks of McCarthyism, were trained and grew up believing that US domestic democracy could be divorced from any relationship to worldwide dominance and would provide a high standard of living, equality and civil rights for all, with their leadership. Their nationalism was at once clear, yet unstated. The idea that our democracy and higher standard of living requires taking away the rights, labor and wealth of other nations, was ignored.[66] Cesar was one of these pragmatic leaders and he himself had an anti-communist inclination, despite a pragmatic willingness to use communists in his efforts.

Additionally, in *Trampling Out the Vintage*,[67] Frank Bardacke claims that Cesar was from early on, suspicious of Mexican immigrant workers whose militant history included, for instance, the communist-led and government-repressed railroad strike of 1958–1959.

---

66 Given that déjà vu is a theme of my memoir, notice how the establishment of an American democracy in 1786 seems to have required the legalization, in perpetuity, of slavery—the founding myth of American Exceptionalism. This later blindness toward such connectedness may be a reflection of the parallel to how America's earlier history is likewise distorted.

67 Published by Verso, 2011.

Many immigrant Mexican workers had been schooled in major strikes and pro-socialist union struggles in Mexico since that time.

New breed union leaders in the US actually allied themselves with growing US economic, political and military power. George Meany had successfully linked the AFL-CIO to the CIA through the American Institute for Free Labor Development (AIFLD). AIFLD worked to undermine independent union organizing in nations run by US em-placed and backed dictators throughout the Americas, tying the US unions to transnational corporate interests. Cesar Chavez, who had faced discrimination as a Mexican American, though critical of the AFL-CIO failing to address and organize around real life and cultural needs of immigrant Farm Workers here, was schooled by Saul Alinsky's school for organizers in the art of mobilizing communities to develop power to better their own lives. But Alinsky's outlook and that of his student organizers in turn, conformed to the post WWII strategy of ignoring an expanding US imperialism. Alinsky rejected building working class power through international unity or even broad political power within the US The function of community leaders, according to Alinsky, was to stay focused on only the issues of their communities and not stray into larger political arenas.

Cesar's outlook was similarly defined.[68] At the same time Cesar, having witnessed the civil rights successes, had come to believe that liberal politicians in government like Governor Jerry Brown and US Attorney General Robert Kennedy would back justice for farm workers if the farm workers' movement gained a strong enough popular foothold and used the proper tactics—combining a morally driven urban support base in boycotts with strikes in the fields. Politicians would reap benefits by supporting the most downtrodden work-

---

68 I think this comes through clearly in Bardacke's *Trampling Out the Vintage.*

ers. Wasn't Martin King proving the power of this strategy? While gaining that influence required political pressure and moral pressure Cesar understood that his own charisma and charm, his ability to move masses of people behind the workers' struggle, would meet the test. Cesar was certain that he could rally substantial forces to move those in power. And he did.

Having worked under Cesar's leadership and observed his tactical skill, I am nevertheless convinced that early UFW successes led him to overestimate the independence of the UFW once the broader civil rights movement was being attacked and disassembled. Cesar had actually begun a revolutionary political movement—a powerful social force—even though he repeatedly asserted that he was not a revolutionary. Yet he knew the social character of the UFW was that of a movement (la causa) rather than just an economic union. And he well knew that this "movement" identity was fundamental to UFW success. Chavez had always understood that the union's independence from the powers that Capitalism's representatives could bring to bear against him required the UFW to remain a national political force as much as a trade union. That is why the boycotts played a key role. But, as the broader civil rights movement in the US was collapsing about us, Cesar had no pathway out of that "last man standing" position the UFW held in that Movement. There was, to my thinking, no apparent way out. Thus, he concluded that his influence with Jerry Brown and the Democratic Party, with Meany and the AFL-CIO, with the Catholic Church hierarchy all empowering the process he guided would save the day, not realizing that those ties he relied upon were the weak link that would be used to undermine, to divide, slice and dice the UFW.

Under Cesar the UFW had no problem mobilizing and uniting the workers to fight the growers and other up-front opponents of farm workers' rights such as the then-compromised Teamsters Union or the county sheriffs or Republican reactionaries. On the other hand, he ran into big problems trying to maneuver with his most powerful allies who were linked together in a web of influence designed to limit the full potential of the movement he led, by always threatening to deny the resources that sustained the efforts. Even if Cesar saw how these dependencies created problems, what choice did he really have? Forced by contingencies to rely upon these powerful forces the union progressively lost its autonomy and its inertia as Cesar was forced to turn against the desire for more democracy, autonomy and initiative coming from within the workers' movement and the staff.

Cesar could not run national boycotts or worker strikes without the financial aid of the AFL-CIO. He could not let Tony Orendain continue a broader front of agricultural battle in Texas, a right to work state, where passing a Labor Law like California's new ALRA seemed unlikely. And the Texas strikes, despite strong worker support were further draining union resource needed for the Boycott. He owed Jerry Brown and the Democrats for the ALRA-ALRB in the type of transactional relationship which often characterizes American politics, but which MLK Jr. had avoided.

But why had the AFL-CIO (when it was running the AWOC in CA back in the early 60s) not been able to achieve the unity that the UFW achieved? The typical answer is that the AFL was stuck in old models of trade union economism where strikes over wages and benefits and negotiation for contracts between employers and organized workers were the basis for struggle. True indeed, these desperate, poverty stricken migrant and immigrant workers have far deeper grievances and needs pertaining to their lives. Cesar recognized those needs which go even beyond the terrible housing crisis, lack of education, and near serf-like aspects of the life forced upon migrant and immigrant workers. He understood their need for common community, cultural needs and concerns with home country and family there. He also initially recognized, I believe, the importance of self-organization. But given his training, background, and dependence on those systemic allies, Cesar could not allow that process to mature. He was like a cowboy trying to reign in an unruly wild horse. And so he avoided publicly acknowledging the detrimental AFL-CIO orders he was getting from Meany—from that apparatus which actually hued to the sinister agenda of maintaining national-ethnic divisions and support for US imperialism—whether in the Philippines, in Latin America or elsewhere. Just as the Democratic Party core leadership has worked hard to diminish the influence of Bernie Sanders or AOC, Meany sought to tamp down the UFW to prevent La Causa from taking root around the US and throwing out the AFL-CIO International leadership altogether.

To the extent that Cesar was aware of this chauvinist divisiveness, he was not willing to lose favor by opposing it openly. He made that clear when he visited Philippine Dictator Marcos and then (for seemingly incomprehensible reasons) seated Marcos' ambassador on the dais of the union's national convention. Remember that the UFW had been formed as an amalgamation of a largely Filipino organizing committee and a largely Mexican Association. Fawning over dictator Marcos was a direct slap in the face of Filipino farm workers and their leaders on the union's board of directors. And a slap at the UFW's foundational uniting principle.

By that time a new Cesar had lost control of the union itself. Otherwise he wouldn't have sent Dolores to Salinas ranchers inviting them to fire leading ranch committee workers who had organized an alternative slate to his own for the Executive Board or forced out so many of the leaders he had worked with and depended upon.

While forming the UFW Cesar recruited to his side a strong leadership core, people attracted to the growing culture of solidarity, community and rich identification with the heritage of struggles of the Mexican and Filipino farm workers that the UFW represented. That culture was further enhanced with the integration of remarkable professional culture workers like Luis Valdez and his Teatro Campesino, composers of many of the movements still sung songs. A rich spirit of voluntarism among urban youth was cultivated by the UFW boycott movement which swept the country. Chavez' own asceticism and saint-like charisma drew in many people from the Church as well as from the growing youth Left movements that had arisen during the civil rights and anti-war struggles.

Yet the UFW, a movement of drama and idealism, was faced with these hidden obstacles. Fundamentally a movement of poor workers, this organization—even with the boycott movement—could not possibly fund a vast organizing effort built simultaneously upon strikes and boycotts in the long run. The murder of Bobby Kennedy certainly knocked one pillar out. Although California farm workers achieved protection for unionization with the ALRA/ALRB, farm workers elsewhere were explicitly excluded from the National Labor Relations Act that guarantees that right to non-AG workers. California success created farm labor perception everywhere that the UFW could rescue them also. Cesar and the union had moved into the ranks of leading civil rights organizations as a national beacon just as COINTELPRO repression was dividing the civil rights organizations and wiping out the Black Panther Party.

Hoover was not indifferent to the UFW ascendancy. As the Vietnam War came to an inglorious end with the defeat of US Imperialism, the militant movement against it and against racist discrimination was Hoover's target. King, Malcolm X and Robert Kennedy, Chavez' most powerful political allies were murdered.

Cesar remained undaunted through this period despite loss of impetus in the rest of society. His own, and thus UFW power and influence seemingly continued to expand. But the trap had been set. Was Cesar concerned that the rest of the wave of the social justice movement had been turned back, stilled and stifled? I don't know. But the underlying Movement crisis also erupted inside the union as an internal struggle over whether the UFW should focus on gaining and managing contracts or, through the Boycotts, grow a national Rights movement for justice.

This seemingly philosophical and ideological debate raged within the UFW for many years, but it actually obscured the underlying decline of the nationwide social-justice movement. Are we a trade union or a political movement was debated and debated with pragmatists and Meany asserting that the farm workers needed business unionism and a more efficiently run operation, a well functioning union that could negotiate and win more contracts, first and foremost. Some board members insisted upon the primacy of the boycotts. Cesar played on both sides. He knew he needed the boycott tactic to keep the struggle in the national spotlight and grow the support base, but at the same time he brought in business oriented bureaucrats to make the UFW more like a unidimensional trade union—intensifying the underlying contradiction. Then he unleashed repressive measures.

The union leadership was not equipped to service the simultaneous needs of both efforts, particularly as members under contract had grown to over 100,000. The UFW's needs at that moment in history exceeded its organizational and financial capacity, bad management aside. And so Cesar could be blackmailed.

When I met and talked with Maria Rifo on that first visit to La Paz I learned that George Meany and the AFL-CIO had attacked the UFW's independence. Meany pushed Chavez into a deal with the devil—we'll fund you but the UFW has to stop El Malcriado from meddling in foreign policy—and move it away from international coverage and solidarity. Or the paper must go, Meany told Chavez. Cesar attacked the paper's editors and it slowly dissolved.

Later the "friend of (dictator) Marcos" Philippines' gambit may have also been a quid pro quo from Meany.

Jerry Brown sought "favors" in return for his support. Chavez committed the union's resources, including his staff and farm workers' dues to support of the Democratic Party in general. Using critical union funds to work on the mayoral campaign of Tom Bradley in LA had no direct purpose relating to the union's efforts, nor were union members asked their opinion when they were ordered to LA, nor about that resource drain. Similarly the ties to the Catholic Church led to certain quid pro quos as well—such as the birth control controversy that closed Coachella clinic. With each compromise, came resistance from workers and staff, requiring Cesar to act more autocratically. Board resistance was meek and Cesar attacked resisters. He was moving the UFW perceptibly away from the human and civil rights agenda at the heart of both the farm workers' struggles and the national boycott movement, ironically weakening his own base of power.

As the gap widened and Cesar and the board lost the power of independent decision-making, internal dissension grew. He turned to the Synanon Cult and adopted the Synanon "Game" of pschological group confrontation and intimidation to force out critical voices. Like Trump he forced supporters to choose obedient loyalty to himself and his every decision, defining union loyalty, like Trump, as loyalty to himself personally. Staff loyalists were required to collaborate and enforce his actions against anyone who disagreed with anything he did. Within this framework the collapse of the UFW as a coherent movement became inevitable. And each time that Cesar found no way out other than to attack dissent he weakened another pillar of the union's unity that he himself had authored.

How could Cesar kick out the magnificent Luis Valdez and Teatro Campesino without there being long term repercussions? Or close the popular, coherent and vital El Malcriado? Or kick out some of the union's founders when they disagreed with his policies. How could he label some of his key leading advisors as enemies, communists? Or become friends with Philippine's dictator Marcos and bring his Ambassador to sit on the dais of the union's annual convention? Or do Jerry Brown's bidding? Or think that farm workers should not have the right to birth control on demand?

But Chavez' essentially dictatorial decisions were not fundamentally willful. They should not be so decontexualized, for they were reactive. Cesar Chavez' longing to wed his own destiny to a movement for justice for farm workers and his almost messianic belief that he could achieve that through force of will enabled his successes.

FBI COINTELPRO operations were inevitably part of the UFW decline. Having successfully done-in important organizations like the Black Panther Party and SNCC, and maligning and spying on MLK Jr., Hoover had his eye on Chavez. Some growers' launched a smear campaign labeling Cesar a communist. The McCarthyite Hoover knew that Cesar had a weakness in this regard, since Cesar was clearly an anti-communist. Hearing and seeing those oft-repeated accusations, Cesar made the mistake of trying to prove them wrong. He couldn't publicly declare hostility to communism and communists. After all, a good share of the union's volunteers and activists in the boycott movement were Leftists of one or another stripe or sympathy. Moreover, that might alienate that proportion of Mexican farm workers who had been involved in Left movement struggles in Mexico. But Cesar not only needed to prove he was anti-communist to refute the COINTELPRO-Ag Business lies, he also was hearing whispers within his trusted core (though no one has yet identified who were the whisperers) about dissenters to various Chavez decisions being part of a communist plot to undermine his leadership.

When I joined the UFW staff I knew people in many different Left organizations in California, though I was not a member of any organization when I worked for the UFW. There was little concealment by people working for the UFW of their views and affiliations. In fact, I know that Cesar Chavez had personal relationships with people he knew were communists, like Fred and Ginny Hirsch. But when Cesar decided to close all our clinics, that had nothing to do with Left politics, even though he so labeled Dan Murphy and later myself.

The coup de grace for the UFW as the highly regarded (by the farm workers) representative of workers in the fields came at the end of the 70s when, disillusioned by many of his edicts and decisions an important group of ranch committee leaders on UFW contracted farms in the Salinas Valley put up a slate of candidates for the union's board of directors to oppose Cesar's chosen candidates.[69] I believe there were 50 dissidents in that group, well known as union organizers/activists to workers throughout the union. Cesar had them physically thrown out of the Convention. Then to compound that divisive mistake he had Dolores give a list of these workers to the Ranch owners, suggesting the union would not object if they were fired. This was a recapitulation of the McCarthy era, expunging of key grassroots union organizers. When those workers sued him after loosing their livelihoods, he counter-sued for millions. Cesar was deconstructing the movement and organization he had dedicated his life to building. At that point even some of his most loyal board members like Ganz, walked away.

---

69 Details of this and other aspects of the internal struggle are well documented in Bardacke's book—*Trampling Out the Vintage*—Cesar Chavez and the two souls of the United Farm Workers.

People in positions of great power and authority are particularly susceptible to isolation, paranoia, and overestimating their autonomy. I've used the opposite examples of Napoleon and Hamlet. This may seem a paradox, but the sense of destiny, even in the most humble leaders, threatens to create a wedge between the leader and their followers. Opportunists like Meany, Jerry Brown and Hoover, exploit such situations, leading democratic organizations to become cults. COINTELPRO infiltration by government operatives started a war inside the Black Panther Party. I believe they exacerbated the UFW polarization.

Shakespeare so well understood and elaborated this human frailty in his great tragic plays. Paranoia results from the mismatch between being all powerful, yet feeling suddenly powerless. Cesar E. Chavez was trapped in this paradigm, but he was neither the first nor the last great charismatic leader to be so damaged. From Othello to King Lear the phenomenon is predictable. Sub-commandante Marcos of the Mayan-based Zapatista movement suggested an alternative "Mayan" model of leadership: "lead by following". Empower and train the common people to assert their collective needs, wishes and power.

Sure, collective leadership and democratic processes are messy business. But look at the alternative. The UFW, instead of looking to the workers themselves and their natural leaders in the fields to discern how to chart the union's direction, became a hollowed out shell of itself unable to find any path forward in a period of political retrenchment by US state capitalism. More recently, field workers engaging in unionizing elections here have sometimes voted for the old UFW nemesis—the Teamsters—rather than the union that Cesar built; a sad irony.

FUCKING UP

It's always convenient to blame the other side, to claim "those guys started it" for conflicts we find ourselves bound into—even when the outcome has turned out suitable enough. But, "it takes two to tango". Most fraught situations involve incompatible narratives about history and the impenetrability of a conflict. Though one narrative may be more accurate and less self serving, we need to also examine its frailty as well. In writing about the collapse of my first marriage to Irene Giobbe I suggested my role. Irene surely betrayed our marriage, falling for and hooking up with a fellow teacher, but I had given her reason to think we might not have a future with a good outcome. I had taken her for granted—assaulting her autonomy. I was a negligent partner, although my negligence was innocently born of compulsion and immaturity. However, as I told med student friends, "If our actions can shorten this war of murderous aggression by only a few weeks, we will have saved more lives and prevented more suffering, than an entire life of medical service might achieve." I won't reneg on that, even though I'm proud of what I've done in medicine for the thousands of people I've helped. Still, my behavior was selfish and ignored my partner's needs. I contributed much to the outcome and I had to live with that and eventually learn something from it. And there were plenty more lessons to come.

Though Sheila and I, by then living in San Jose's East Side barrio, left Venceremos in 1973, we were not yet through with our quest to make another world possible. We created a small study group of friends whose goal was to investigate all of the Left groups/parties that were active and see if any of these fit our conception of a working class-based party driven to achieve an egalitarian socialism in the United States.

Almost out of the clear blue sky we learned of the Communist League (CL) headed by an African American communist, Nelson Peery, an intellectual autodidact, who had fought in the Pacific in WWII as a "youngster".[70] Nels later joined the Communist Party, only to quit with 1,500 Black members around 1960. The son of a postal worker in Milwaukee, Nelson was himself a mason/brick layer by trade. His California group produced a newspaper, the People's Tribune, in English and Spanish. They were forming a nationwide communist party that would train it's members in Marxism through the study and discussion of primary writings. They were in discussion with various other groups on merging together at a founding Party Congress. In the Bay Area they were in discussion with a S.F. based organization, the League for Proletarian Revolution, when we heard of their plans. We were particularly impressed when we learned that CL was absorbing what was then the most dynamic working class force in the auto-industry, the Black-led Revolutionary Union Movement. That group began at a Chrysler Corporation plant under the name Dodge Revolutionary Union Movement (DRUM). In a major strike they had seized total control of the plant and won concessions from Chrysler, an action reminiscent of the 1934 auto sit down strikes. Thereafter the DRUM spread to Ford's giant Dearborn plant and to other automakers and plants. Earlier, when Carrie and I and the other couples moved from Northern California to Detroit, DRUM's successes and courageous actions were foremost in our minds. We hoped

---

70 Nelson Peery enlisted in the army at the age of 17 (perhaps successfully concealing his age).

to be able to work with them. Now in 1974 here was an organization, CL that was combining with the RUM leadership.

When Venceremos collapsed, I was able to attract interest in this new Party effort among about a dozen or more former Venceremos members. Sheila and I and the others attended the founding convention of the Communist Labor Party in Chicago in the summer of 1974. Our daughter, two months old, accompanied us. After the Congress, Sheila was invited to stay on (with baby) and attend the month long Party School at Nels' place. I returned to the Bay Area. Years later Sheila revealed to me that while attending that school she overheard explicit discussions about plans to dump leaders from organizations that had been absorbed into the Communist Labor Party. It was the first sign to her that the core formative leadership was playing with a stacked deck. At the time, however, both of us believed we had joined a movement that would successfully implement the Venceremos principle of majority "Third World" leadership, was profoundly dedicated to studying and understanding history and had leaders with incredible experience in working class struggles, such as in the auto plants and in the earlier successes of the American Communist Party in the 1930s. Nelson was not the only charismatic leader of this type. There were, for example, the elder Admiral Kilpatrick, the younger General Baker, the old Wobbly (IWW) lumberjack, folk hero and musical saw player, Tom Scribner. Sheila's older son Shep, despite being somewhat tone deaf, volunteered that he'd like to learn to play the saw and I drove him over the hill from San Jo to Santa Cruz once a week for lessons with old Tom. And the very kind Jerome Scott a DRUM leader, and iconoclast street beat poet and multi-language translator Jack Hirshman who became San Francisco poet laureate.[71] We were hooked. This culture felt like home.

---

71 Jack was still a self-described commie when he died last year (2021) in his sleep at 87 still in San Francisco. I attended the memorial held out doors in Washington Square Park in North Beach. There were a few hundred in attendance and more recent poet laureates that Jack socialized with; music was sung and played; his partner spoke.

Besides the UFW grape boycott movement, Sheila and I were then involved in parent organizations relating to our kids in public school—the PTAs and the Gifted And Talented Education (GATE) parent groups. It was through these that we had been effective at getting the scab grapes out of kids lunches in the 80% Latino Alum Rock Elementary School District. In working with other parents we had made many new friends and Sheila also had a sizable group of social friends and political compatriots from her unionizing efforts on the computer chip fabrication line at the National Semiconductor plant in Santa Clara.[72] We learned that, according to our friends, the biggest issue facing our schools was their unequal funding in poor minority (especially Latino) communities.[73] A California court suit, known as Serrano-Priest had exposed the injustice of rich districts having local governments implement major local taxation to augment state funding. The court order on the Serrano decision called out this inequality and ruled that the State could not allow this gross inequality in public education funding. But Serrano was being ignored. GATE parents in particular were raring for a fight on this, as we learned at a statewide GATE conference held in San Francisco.[74]

When Sheila returned from the Party School in Chicago late in 1974 we continued our participation in these school focused efforts for equal rights. Around February or March we learned there would be a statewide PTA conference in LA. The CLP leadership decided to constitute a parent group to attend the conference from mem-

---

72 At National Semiconductor Sheila was voluntarily working with and represented the United Electrical Workers Union (UE).

73 Though I continue to use the term "minority group", Latinos in California became the largest population group some years ago.

74 In 2020 that Court ruling, requiring equalization of funding, has still not been implemented in California and so the inequality in public education remains, exposing that even the SCOTUS decision on Brown v Board of Education of 1954 was being thwarted.

bers in different areas of California. I was asked to participate. I flew down to LA, joining an informal meeting of about six of us at a small cafe. I did not know any of the others well. I think I had slight familiarity with the woman who leadership appointed to direct the group. Almost as soon as I arrived I appreciated a problematic mismatch. The CLP national leadership had decided to wage a campaign in support of busing children across regions to implement integration. Some local governments and courts were implementing such programs. However, this was not consistent with the views of the progressive parents we knew concerning the problem of unequal education. They saw it as a problem of illegal inequality in funding our schools. As it happened Sheila and I had more experience working with other parents—mostly Latinos in our area—than any of the people in this group. However, the decision that we should only advocate for busing had been made back in Chicago. I suddenly found myself torn in two directions—representing the many parents we worked with on educational reform (which made perfect sense to us) or carry out the orders that were announced in that cafe. When I challenged those orders as unlikely to gain support based upon what I knew, the tension rose. After a few minutes the leader told me that she was removing me from the group and I should get on a plane and fly home, which I sadly did. The small group that I was expelled from had, to my recollection, no particular impact of note on this statewide PTA Conference.[75] But the other shoe was yet to fall.

After the group leader reported back to Chicago, I was immediately kicked out of the organization. Not content to expunge the rebel, they ordered Sheila to end her relationship with me, her part-

---

75 Though we didn't know it then, this type of top down methods would eventually cause the CLP to fail. Though some of its old stalwart members still today put out a good paper and have connections in a panoply of important working class struggles they then shrank dramatically and long ago stopped calling themselves a Party.

ner, husband and father to her three kids. If we continued to live together, she was told, she too would have to leave the organization. We both felt torn apart by these developments. Sheila did not want to leave the organization. But she didn't want to break up our relationship either, any more than I did. We reconciled ourselves to the Party leadership's decision and came up with a plan.

Since I was then only working half time with the County Health Department teen clinics, I would offer to join the Farm Worker's Health Group and be posted to the Delano clinic in the Central Valley where a doctor was desperately needed.[76] A couple of weeks later, after I had moved to Delano, Jerome Scott made a trip to the Bay Area and met with Sheila. He told her the decision to attack our family and marriage had been a serious mistake. We would never learn more about it, and the admission was too late, as this obviously had changed the trajectory of our lives, both for better as well as for worse.

Ironically, despite the way we were treated, I continued to believe in the Party, read their People's Tribune and wrote them about my concerns, such as about Cesar Chavez' attack on the undocumented. By the time that Cesar closed all the UFW clinics in 1978, I had worked very hard with the UFW about four years, learned a tremendous amount of medicine, was known by thousands of farm workers as doctor Marco and was fully integrated into the union's si se puede culture, while Sheila on the other hand suffered progressive isolation by some of the local leaders and members of the CLP.[77]

Back at the end of 1975, while working for the UFW I had moved back to our home. Now in late 1978, separated from the UFW, I asked to rejoin the Party and was accepted. Only after achieving

---

76 Margaret Murphy had already asked if I might consider doing this.

77 This despite that she was sitting on the City committee of the organization in San Jose.

that personal goal did I learn, painfully, from Sheila that she was fed up with the CLP, that she was resigning. She would also leave work in Electronics and intended to become an English instructor at the college level (she achieved that retiring from her adjunct position at San Jose State University after 15 years of teaching in the English and Linguistics departments).

Unlike what had happened back in 1975 when I was unceremoniously kicked out of the CLP, my re-entrance and her resignation became a more lasting source of personal conflict between us when she deeply resented my going to meetings and other activities out of the house with the Party. This conflict festered longer; it was particularly painful for Sheila. We weathered the storm, but in a sense it was déjà vu—like my deserting Irene for the cause again.

James Baldwin and American Exceptionalism (2019)

It is still true, alas, that to be an American Negro male
is also to be a kind of walking phallic symbol:
which means that one pays, in one's own
personality, for the sexual insecurity of others.

(From Baldwin's essay: "The Black Boy Looks at the White Boy ")

Lucky to be married to an insatiable reader, a writer with an excellent book collection, I am, for the first time, reading James Baldwin's essay collection, *Nobody Knows My Name.* Baldwin was born about 17 years before myself and *Nobody Knows My Name* was published while I was in college at Brandeis. Interested in literature and writing, though ultimately headed into the world of medicine, I took a course in American Literature taught by Mark Van Doren, a hallowed professor, one of the sons of a dean of New England literature, Carl Van Doren. Mark was also older brother to the cheater, Charles, the longest running contestant on the 64,000-dollar question TV show—until he got caught.

I loved the course. Except for a few classics taught in high school, it was really my first expansive exposure to American literature from Herman Melville's *Moby Dick* right up into the 20th century. I was very engaged in the course and wrote some good papers, then asked Van Doren if he thought I might be able to write successfully. He responded that it isn't a glamorous life at all—grueling and isolating, but if you're willing to do the hard work…hmmm, but I wasn't **that** willing.

We probably read one or more stories by Baldwin or Richard Wright. I'm unsure, but this was during the moment of the civil rights upsurge (1962–1963). I had picketed regularly at Woolworth's with our college's Emergency Public Integration Committee. Maybe we read Wright's *Black Boy*. That was indeed 57 years ago, but the centrality of Black writers to American culture was not yet well appreciated.

Now I've been reading slowly in *Nobody Knows My Name*. Baldwin's brilliance and insight deserve that. This morning I finished the last few pages of "Alas Poor Richard I"—the first of three memorial essays about Richard Wright, with whom Baldwin apparently had a contentious relationship. After Wright's death, Baldwin was asked to write a eulogy for a magazine. He wrote three. It may be that he was dissatisfied with the relative superficiality of part I and was driven to keep diving deeper until he got out all that he felt and understood about himself through his relationship to Richard Wright.

Alas Poor Richard I is essentially a review of Richard Wright's *Eight Men*, a book of short stories. I found it impossible to read Baldwin's essay without rushing to the Library to find and read Wright's stories in *Eight Men*. When it comes to the way that white racist ideology has characterized and feared Black sexuality, Wright and Baldwin's word and thought pictures portray a kind of rape of Black men. Through Baldwin, Wright's work becomes more than just compelling. Baldwin is able to create a painting that grips down to the soul, our lack of humanity, and the ensuing mixture of raw rage, violence, poignancy and outrage that true American history ought to evoke in the soul of every American. However, most American schools do not have our youths reading Wright, nor Baldwin, so we who have not lived Black don't experience the Black experience. And now in 2023 it's getting worse.

The ironies of the almost absence of Black writers in the American

Lit canon remaining even in the 1960s are abundant. For one thing, the white abolitionists—even if many were women—also came from the same New England subculture as the Van Dorens—and, in the beginning of the nation, a future president, John Adams from New England, helped the Virginia elite incorporate slavery into the revolutionary process.[78] Additionally, the later compartmentalization of Black writers as if a phenomenon apart from, denigrates American literature, just as segregation restricted the reality that Black music was and would continue to be among the most vibrant, brilliant, skillful, soulful, and probably the most intrinsically American of American music.

The historical mis-chacterization of Black America demonstrates that divisions in American culture that persist today did not arise only from within an anti-intellectual, "know-nothing" sector that Lincoln excoriated. Clearly, post-bellum revanchist treachery that began with the overthrow of Reconstruction, wasn't arrested despite the "union" success in the American Civil War. The 13th and 14th Amendments were never going to be enforced without a civil rights upheaval a century later. And so too America's white supremacist aspects of capitalist (fraudlent democratic) culture forever deny that many of our greatest creative geniuses like Baldwin were, and still are, forged in the idiomatic caldron of an Americanism that prospered from the fruits of slavery. This is not just a product of the South's slaver mentality but also of the world of Hawthorne's *The Scarlet Letter* and the Salem Witch Trials and, much later, also of a liberal and very Zionist (thusly pro-apartheid) Brandeis University. It was, I think, the workings of this American denialism within James Baldwin that drove him to emigrate to France, where he eventually came to realize that, in fact, he was American to his core and was mistakenly trying to escape himself.

---

78 See: *Slave Nation—How Slavery United the Colonies and Sparked the American Revolution.* Alfred and Ruth Blumrosen, 2005, Sourcebooks.

Baldwin—perhaps enhanced because he was gay—was particularly sensitive to constant battering by those embedded forces in America insisting that Blacks were something other—incorporating sexual predation as central within the otherification. And that otherness (which has more recently been applied to Muslims, Latinos, Asians etc.) still perpetuates the ruse that America is a white nation—though there is no such thing as a "white race".[79] The legitimizing of the slaver mentality persists today in America with Blacks being constantly targeted by police, the criminal justice system, white supremacist media and xenophobia. Our native sons (and daughters) are still targeted by a subliminal culture of extirpation and the mythical ahistorical skin of American racialist Exceptionalism. As with the human immune system, such an infection cannot be vanquished so long as the attack and the attackers are nested within the national culture and a pedagogy of historical censorship is promoted. White supremacy is a form of autoimmunity (our bodies attacking itself) gone wild. This toxicity characterizes American Exceptionalism and predicts a particular outcome from the dominant money = freedom culture: collapse, chaos, rage, death and self-destruction. Such is the meaning of the white supremacist adulation of Donald that we have all experienced.

Baldwin's focus on sexuality brought forth memories from 1987. Having just completed studies in epidemiology for a masters degree in public health, I was fortunate to be appointed the acting public health officer for the City of Berkeley, California. One of only three

---

79 As an American-born Jew, I can attest to this strange historical fact: I can be one day considered part of a mythical "white race", and the next day be considered just another outsider, from God knows what planet. This is an American version of what German Jews faced in the early 1930s—fully integrated in German society one day and spat upon and kicked down the stairs the next, ultimately sent to gas chambers. And the conscious dishonestly of such shape-shifting systemic racist states undoubtedly contributes to separatist impulses within Black nationalist thought—as Malcolm X so well enunciated.

California cities with their own health departments (usually they are countywide), Berkeley had been faking it for a while. They had a doc who signed for grants and oversight of public health functions, but his only other responsibility was working a sexually transmitted disease clinic once or twice a week, and little else. In 1987, when the city's chief of Health and Human services retired, the internally elevated director decided to rebuild an actual public health department and he, Glen Lynch, hired me as health officer to work with him on that.

I learned on the job that our Public Health Nursing Division had once run an outstanding home-visit-based prenatal program. But when one of the pregnancies had a bad outcome, the City had been sued successfully and that led to the closing of the program for fear of further liability. That is to say, hundreds of young women—generally poor, often Black and lacking regular medical services and prenatal care were once again put outside "the system". Lack of prenatal care is the number one cause of bad outcomes in pregnancy. The money based, fear based, liability culture, in an act of neglect—simply extirpated its liability problem, thus avoiding any responsibility for the institutional racism and misogyny and failures within the system most of us work and live within.

Ironically, the head of public health nursing was an African American woman, a retired career military officer who, learning of my interest in the long ago terminated prenatal program, preemptively told the city manager that I was going to interfere in her management of the nurses in her division, though I had no thought of doing that. As a newbie I had to work hard to undo her dirty work and to demonstrate that I wasn't a threat to her authority.[80] Then, six months later, after an

---

80 That working hard included sitting down with the most progressive member of the Berkeley City Council, Maudelle Shirek and her staff person, giving them a history of my civil rights and peace efforts and assuring them I was no threat to the Nursing Director.

evening session at a state-sponsored tuberculosis symposium in Monterrey, California (unprovoked I can assure you), VT came on to me and offered her affection. Taken aback, I responded, "I don't cheat on my wife," leading her to say, well at least give me a kiss, will you? Was she trying to trap me, still paranoid of my power at a higher status position in our public health hierarchy? I have no idea what motivated her advance, but in this case my memory is as clear as the clear cold winter days I remember as a teen walking down Seneca Avenue to Roosevelt High School below, a brisk westerly wind in my face.

Responding cautiously, if compliantly, I smacked her on the lips—what else might a guy do without making a scene—said good night and headed for my motel room. Had I not resigned the Berkeley position a couple of months later to take the position as health officer with the San Mateo County Health Department, I have no idea if VT and I and the department might have been able to restore that prenatal program. It would have meant bucking the entire city structure (i.e. the legal advice of the City's Counsel), so the odds were not good. But I stray.

As public health officer I too had to sometimes work that City Sexually Transmitted Disease clinic in West Berkeley near the Interstate. One afternoon a tall African American man in a long trenchcoat came in for an exam. It's a long time ago, but I think he was probably in his 40s, about six-foot two, slender and a man of the streets. He may have been homeless, or prostituting himself or had recent sex with a street walker, or none of the above. But he did need medical help. He complained of painful urination. He had a robust pussy discharge dripping from his penis—gonnorhea. What was particularly striking about this fellow, though, was not his mundane (from a medical perspective) discharge—which is to be expected in an STD clinic of course—but his member. Those racist elements in American culture which are always steeped in that deep fear of Black sexuality, purvey the notion that Baldwin relates: of the huge black phallus menacing white power (and all of "civilized society") with the threat of rapes of white women. Donald Trump—the equal opportunity thug that he is, extended the privilege to Latinos and Muslims seeking refuge in the US. It's all a bad and obscene joke. Embarrassing as well, if you think about it, to be a child of a nation where such imbecilic ideas run wild. Baldwin wrote about that white fear, and of course it's no joke at all, but a sign of that always festering infection of American Exceptionalism—a "democracy" built both on slavery and the derivative fear of its victims taking revenge. How else could any American think, similarly, that Israel, an apartheid state, is a "democracy"?

I haven't the slightest idea what the average size of penises, relative to body mass index (BMI), weight or height is for different ethnic or national groups. I've seen penises small and large and in-between from any ethnic group you might name. And frankly I have no intention to try and find out the answer—though people like Kinsey and other sexologists may well have produced such data as a product of their own (presumably non-racist) sexual intellectual fixation. To my mind, such data has no particular social value because it doesn't matter regarding either reproductive success or satisfying intercourse. To father a child, all any male requires is an erection and ejaculation to achieve what nature has designed him for. As far as female satisfaction, that's more complicated. Much of the social interest in phallic size or any other sexual characteristic is predicated upon cultural trends and the mental pictures we conjure in our own minds. If one imagines that the size of a penis has excitement potential, then it will. If a heterosexual male imagines other factors, the curve of a woman's waist to hip that differentiates her from a man for child bearing, or her face, lips or breasts, or her personality, intelligence, wittiness, or any other particular characteristic to be of personal importance in arousal, then they will be. This is the power of suggestion over the human mind, and how we perceive and conjure attractiveness. Mass culture has an out-sized impact on what we perceive to be sexy or attractive. Money promoted culture has gone viral, and often berserk, these days.

Western cultures went through a period where clothing designers and Hollywood promoted an attachment between excessive thinness and sexuality—as a result, aspiring and even successful models became sick with anorexia to survive as models. Before that, with the advent of the Playboy era it was big breasts. Today there is the selling of the "Brazil butt" and the sexuality of children. (No one involved in this marketing seems to care that all this endless sexual objectification contributes to hypersexual behavior by people more sensitive to manipulation of their limbic systems). But business school professors of marketing and their students know full well how mass culture uses behaviorism to redesign and refine brains, and how people think and feel about themselves and others.

Lately as the US population became obese, people we see on TV have tended to look more like the real us—people we encounter in our lives. Does that "new" marketing scheme reflect progress? One may at least hope, but other interpretations include: cultural "trend setters" may now be more indebted and bound to different multinational diversified food and beverage monopolies which pay for the ads that pump people with sodas, beer, legal drugs, TV and excessive calories in general; or maybe people just aren't being fooled as easily. In any case, social ideals that homogenize desires and create conformity have existed for a very long time. The powerful would have had a terrible time waging great wars without it. In the 21st century with trillions of dollars flowing, money's ability to manipulate individual desires, to sell product and ideas, to change neural networks in our brains, turns culture into self-satire. Sex is especially useful and is used to sell almost anything. Is it any wonder that we see so much male impotence around these days, given the pressure to conform and perform?

The notion that Blacks are a hyper-sexual threat to white males and their schemes of power dominance obviously didn't derive from TV in the modern era, however. That notion derives from the historically based fears of slaveholders—that slaves would rebel and might kill them and rape their women. There were, indeed, slave rebellions, and more than Nat Turner's. A lot of white slave owners died in Haiti in the revolution against the French. Well deserved their deaths were. Nevertheless, it was the projection of the guilt behind the (Jefferson composed) slaver deception—that all men being created equal, have equal rights—that stimulates the nonsense about Black men wanting nothing more than to rape white women.

This fear marvelously exposes what their white wives meant to the Southern Aristocracy—another piece of property that must be guarded and kept in line. This fear mirrors the idea that without the whip, the noose and the first police gangs, white men would be powerless to control white women as well as slaves. Presumably, their women would gravitate toward Black men and their intrinsic power (but actually their humanity, as the dispossessed).

Baldwin notes that many a young Black man internalizes white supremacist ideas about themselves from this inherently racist culture and institutions. Ironically, so many African Americans have given their lives fighting for the very nation whose underlying mantra denies them their identity as well as their rights. Muhammad Ali said it clearly enough. Though he paid a great price, having his title, his profession and his freedom taken from him, he stood his ground proudly, assuring his important place in history.

The man who I saw at the STD clinic one day in 1987 had the largest penis I ever encountered in 46 years of medical practice or in photo-art.[81] I don't know how he might have been able to have sex

---

81 e.g. Robert Maplethorpe.

with a partner at all. His member fell almost to his knee and had a circumference about that of my forearm. He wore no underwear. I confirmed that he had gonorrhea with a simple stained slide and a microscope. The treatment was straightforward with antibiotics. My hope was that he was not exposed to something worse, like HIV which was then becoming more widespread and not yet well treatable.

In our American context, writing a vignette about a Black man's penis may be construed as racist or as validating the racist mantra of the terrifying black phallus. That interpretation would reveal how "meaning" is tainted by American Exceptionalist culture. I would like to imagine that we can turn this metaphor upside down to create a productive awakening. I'm reminded that Frederick Douglas recognized the important and positive aspects of American folk song writer William Foster's contribution to the Freedom struggle. The Berkeley Repertory Theater's playbill for the musical Paradise Square pointed out that many have considered Foster a racist because lyrics of his early songs like Sewanee River and his work with Minstrel Shows seemed to glorify and extol life on the plantations under slavery. Douglas disagreed.

Obviously, my essay doesn't touch on the life of the anonymous patient with the great phallus who I superficially describe. His life story is absent, because in an STD clinic—unlike in primary care practice which is what I did most of my life—the only history required is sexual contacts to treat. Here a personal story isn't considered relevant. Unhappily, that impersonal superficiality is found throughout the over-specialized American health care system. But of course, in the real world of the money culture, this man's full story could not be more relevant, deeply relevant, as are all our stories, in both their uniqueness and their commonality.

And that is why, from my experience working with diabled elders at Center for Elders' Independence, I wrote my book of essays, *I'll*

Fly Away, and also organized *Keeping Pace,* the little book of writings by disabled elders. For, like Oliver Sacks said, it's mostly our stories that matter. This essay, however, is a riff imagined from the essays of Jimmie Baldwin, born in Harlem, where, it happens, my own mom grew up, daughter of an immigrant Polish-Jewish father. Harlem is just across the Harlem River from the South Bronx where Lincoln Hospital is located. And if one draws a triangle from the conjunction of the East River and Long Island Sound, just off East Harlem and South Bronx sits the Rikers Island prison where my dad did his student teaching internship. Mom's history in Harlem? That's a whole nother story which I know so little about.

FROM THE LIFE OF WILLIAM T (TRANSCRIBED FROM AUDIO TAPE)

At the Center for Elders' Independence Reading and Discussion Group 12/27/95: Reflections after a brief oral reading from Nelson Peery's "Black Fire" where Nels and Six become blood brothers (page 33).

I have a statement similar to that. Only I have a working situation, not the schooling. I grew up on the farm which I've talked to you all about from time to time. The farm where sharecroppers farmed. This man here is wealthy, owned a hundred, a thousand acres of the land and little houses scattered about in terse spots (that mean's good land). Every so many acres, here's a house. We lived on that man's farm. They had white attendants lived on that man's farm. And I myself, no brags or complaints, I still think of that boy today.

I was a Black boy that'd make friends everywhere I went. And I had three white boys on that farm that were lonesome seemingly. And I had seven Negroes to play with. We had a little ballgame to play on the pasture land. Well these white boys would come up and set and watch us so eventually one of them ventured out to me. And I had been playing around my house and his house for quite a while.

And he told them he wanted to join the team. The other two set back and said, "What do ya mean?" And he said, "I'm gonna ask William, could I join the team." Well I was the middle age among ' 'em, but I was the biggest guy there. I weighed 200 pounds. "(How old were you then?" someone asks Mr. U.) I was 18 years old. ("And you were 200?" A woman's laughter). Yeah.

That boy he said, "I'm gonna talk to him." And he did. And one of 'em said, "Supposen' he turn ya down." He said," "No, he ain't gonna turn me down." And he said, "Well if he takes you on, some of the rest of 'em ain't gonna like it. Then whatcha gonna do?"

"Well as long as I got William on my side I'm not gonna worry about anything." So he all up and come up among 'em and asked 'em out like we talking now. And I reached out and got him and shoved him up beside and he locked his arm around my shoulder. He said, "We're all dust farmers. We plow just like ye do, use the garden hoein and scrapin' just like ye do. Why we can't play like ye do?"

So I said, "Come on over here, Walter." The other two they wouldn't join. But they wanted to watch us. They set out under the shade tree. We had lemonade in the jars and jugs setting in a #2 washtub with ice, cold. And made 'em welcome to that. My parents and others around there, bout three or four, cut a ham. And we had it all spread out there—corn bread, whole cake, biscuits. We cut it up, slug as big as this hand (Mr. U raises a gnarled but very large and impressive hand.) Everybody had a good fill when they get a piece. But let's leave that alone and let me come back to tell ya what really happened:

I took Hamp[82] in and we joined; we had a good team. (Someone asks Mr. U: "What's his name?") Hamp. Hamp Washington. Well he tied on to me; when we broke up that game he went on home. He used to come to the house. Up there on the porch. We played jacks stone with rocks. Catch 'em up here. We had a lot of fun.

Well it got to where the sawmill moved into town. And now we

---

82 I never did ask Mr. U why he first called his young friend "Walter" but almost immediately switched to "Hamp".

lived in the country but I called it a town. Well he (Hamp) had a father that was shift man; that man was the engineer for these standard engines that buckled down on the ground, all goin' around this way with wheel and a band...Well he take care all of that and he was a fireman. He fired to keep steam going. He taught me how to fire.

Well to goin' in here we did and that mill come and it was a sawmill and they put that boy to work in that sawmill. And they didn't have no Blacks up there; they had all whites. And I'm telling ya the truth; ain't got to lie to ya, I'm gonna tell ya the truth. That company that owned that mill wasn't used to no Black people. Where they come from they had brought most them boys with 'em. But this boy Hamp they gave him a job in there through his father. Workin' on the roller bed with a overhead saw we called a cut-off saw, cut bad ends off a lumber and roll it out there to a foot marker on that wall and when they cut it it'd be an even cut, 14 feet, 16 feet, 18 feet, and then the other boys u'd runnit off down the road and off it'd go to a pile up on the side there.

Well, this boy he'd worked there about four weeks and he somehow, he didn't like the boy that was workin', we call off-bare. When he cut this lumber the other boy kick it and roll it on out. Well, Hamp wanted me there. He told his daddy, "I want William to be my off-bare for this saw." He said, "Well, we can't do it that way. All's they got in this here mill is white." He said, "Well, who stacks that lumber out there? They ain't white."

"No, those are Negroes. They do the hard work." And he said, "Well this ain't no _easy_ job. William'd be just fine. Say, look ya got two over there runnin' from this saw. And William take that lumber and run it on out yonder and take it up on the ramp and tell all the people kick it up on the ramp where it go." So his father, Mr. Luke, his father's name Luke, he looked into it and said "Well, we'd save some money." Well, he talked to the boss later and he didn't know nothin' about it. The boss, JJ White was the boss' name, he became governor too of that state. ("He did?"); he give me a job through talking to Mr. Luke. He told me, "Come by boy. Before that I always would go up there and sat around watchin' them work, but I never could get... Look, I would go up and go to Mr. Luke and tell him...I said, "I would like to get a job here." And he'd said, "I'd like to see you get a job here. We'll have to work around to it. I'm gonna tell yer daddy to don't let you keep comin' over here and standin' around like this. They wonder why you keep doin' it."

"'Cause I want a job." He says, "Well, I knows that too, but they don't, and I don't want them to jump on ya." So I just carry a bucket; that little lunch bucket I used to carry to school...with a little tin top on it. I carry that little buck with corn bread, slug a hard meat, a sweet potato and some black molasses ("Oh yeah"). I'd hang that bucket up on the side of a tree, on a nail, anything. I just stand right around until that whistle blow. When they go to dinner I go and take my bucket. Yeah, set right down, aw a little further than from here to that wall (though blind, Mr. U gestures toward the wall). They'd look at me and I'd look at them. And I'd just keep on and eat. When I'd get through I hang my bucket back up. When I go home I'd just tell my mother that I didn't get no job today.

She'd say, "Well, ya keep tryin'." She was innocent about it, ya know. I said, "Well, I'll go keep tryin'." So when Mr. Luke told me they were goin' to try to get me job, I told him what he (the boss) said. He said, "Well, that's gonna be fine. I think ya probably might get it before the week's out. I be glad if ya do." 15 cents a hour that's what they were payin'. Alright, I got that job and went to work. And they put me beside that white boy.

Him and I run that saw and that, that roller bed ran all the way out, out 35 feet. I run that thing out to where they had two other boys out there, I run it out there by myself. ("By yerself.") Yeah, I take that board and I go with it. And the rollers had little roller bearings in there they call it. They oiled them up every morning. Hamp, was his place to oil them up. They rolled grreeeeeeouwwwwww...You could cry with the board if ya didn't get up on the work, ya know.

Had to walk along; that roller bed is up about two foot high. Ya wasn't bent down and ya wasn't strainin'. Just put yer hand down on that board and away ya go ("Way ya go"—Ella C). And I carried that lumber like that for six weeks. So one day out of that six weeks we was laughin' and talking. Hamp said to me, he said, "We got to get brand new overall suits." I said, "Yeah? Well I ain't got no money, I can't get none." He said, "Aw yeah you gonna get one."

So I went on up to work. That Monday morning I come out. Hamp come up to me and said, "We called it piscetony. " It was wrapped up in a big brown. . .we called it sugar paper—brown sheet a sugar paper. I caught it this way. He said, "Go down behind the road there where just the top of yer head'll be seen and pull off them clothes." I said, "What's that for?" "Open it up, fool, and look and see." (Laughter all around the audience.) I ripped the paper back and it's a brand new overall suit. Yeah it had jumper with a blanket liner in it. These overalls, the insignia on the buckle here that said Carhart. There were some good overalls in those days: Carhart, Dixie, and another one—I forget the other one's name. But anyway, I had the best suit ("You had the best suit," echoes Mrs. Barfield). Yeah. Well, I went down and put that suit on, look liked my leg fit me just right, wasn't too low to fold up, none a that fold and I had on a good pair of old hobnailed shoes and that made me dressed up when I had good shoes on. And I come up out a there and them white folks looked at me—the company servant to them—they looked at me and they all had a big laugh.

"Come here, boy." Turned around me and looked at me. They wouldn't hit ya know; they'd take a hand and catch ya here on yer shoulder and push it back. "Get on out there and go to it." (groughly). "Well, you earned that suit. Now go on out there and earn yer day's pay." "Thank you, sir".

Went out there...we worked there about 10:30. Well, ya know we wasn't working any over 10:30 when that boy, my best friend, pullin' that saw and cuttin' that lumber and he started singin' one a them little cookoo songs. Ahooaaahahooaa. You could hear him hollerin' out there for miles. That boy could sing. He called of some kind a way. And he cut that stuff and turned himself around, and swung around playing. And he caught that saw and it went yeeeoowww, and went back. And when he turned around he turned it loose with power. Let it go, ya know. The weight'll snap it back. And that thing snapped back. And that doggone saw come right on back out when he turned, it caught that arm. Cut that hand off. ("Cut that hand off?") Cut it off.

And went in his jumper. (He had his new suit on). Went up it like that. Tellin' ya all what happened. It split that man's arm—bone—all open; fillet on just like that. He hit the floor and screamed one time. And I was right up under him. I grabbed him—I tell ya all the truth—I got this judge it. ("You picked him up?") I didn't pick him up. I got him on my knees. I put my hand under his head and I had it to my chest screamin' all the while. Well they heard that screamin' but they didn't pay no attention.

Then they turned around to look and see. Then everybody come. Had 15 men working that mill. All of em' come. Said, "Pull him off of ya, pull him off. He gonna bleed to death. And he gonna bleed like that with him." So they tied him off up here (gestures to just below his shoulder). Still didn't do no good. ("Cut that hand off," Mrs. Barfield) (Yeah, cut that hand off. And cut that arm up just like you split a watermelon. I was right down there hanging on to him. When Hamp come to hisself and stopped cryin', he threw that other arm around this back a mine and he said, "You're with me, huh?" And I said, "Yeah, I'm with ya."

"Thank God. I'm hurtin', but thank God. Tell them to get me out a here." They all standin' on over us now.

Boss man come and he said put him in a car. And they took, and run him on out a there and check into, named Brookhaven. ("That a hospital?") Yeah. They took him to Brookhaven and they took that bone on out, right out of his shoulder. They didn't lose no time, they took in out. It was split open and they took it out at the joint. And Hamp stayed in the hospital seven weeks.

And when he come out he come out askin' for me. Well, they put me on that saw. Hamp came by and he said, "Let me pull it one more time?" I said, "No, Hamp. I don't want ya to do that."

Well, they all saw him standing around me. They saw me talking to him. And after a little time they come on down. Said, "What's the matter, William?" I said, "Take Hamp away from here. He wants to pull that saw again." I said, "I don't want him to pull this saw no more."

He said, "Well, if you say he not pullin', he don't pull it." And he (Hamp) cried. Got on that shoulder right there, he cried. God, I wish I could see him right now, here with us. And he says as long as he lived and the mill's runnin' anywhere, to give him a job.

Yes, I stayed with that man four years, with that mill. And when it cut out, they moved away. And when they moved away they moved out here to Eugene, Oregon—some big timber. And my partner told me not to come 'cause I was not experienced to work in big timber. Boss said, "Well, he can learn."

"As long as we're getting all that other equipment anyway. This carriage and stuff is too small. We'll try and get stuff to handle that job." So he did. He got a 22-inch shotgun beam. 22 inches is a pipe that big around. With a piston in it works just like the piston in an automobile. Well, that thing had a shaft, 30-feet-long shaft, right down this track. Hooked that to the carriage. When they turned that steam on and moved that lever, that thing run on just about like that. Could hear that thing singin' like...yeeaaooooooowwwwww. It done cut on 20 feet long.

You run right back; and they had a seat made just like you got here; with a cushion in it. Strap around it and you buckled that man in. And the boss is up the center right up in front of you just like the typewriter. You had two little levers you matched with the air. You hit that little button. You watched and you watched your sawyer there. When it go this way you look back there; when you turn your head he was there ready to go again. This man here, Hamp, I had to tie him up, all up like that; that man's story there.

And this thing hit me now just like it was done yesterday.

Mr. William T and Ms. Ella C at the CEI reading
and discussion group in 1995 (photo by the author).

TRAVELIN' ON

Well, I am a lonely and a lonesome traveler x3...
I been a travelin' on. (by Lee Hayes of the Weavers)

In 1980, six years after Sheila delivered our daughter Joanna into this world of trouble and joy, we decided to take a grand six-week European trip that would include Spain, a train ride across Southern France to Florence, Italy, then a train trip from Torino (Turin) to Warsaw, Poland and ultimately a flight into Moscow for a three-week tour of four distinct areas in the Soviet Union. My sister, Judy, was happy to add Joanna to her gaggle of three daughters for the summer. Nineteen eighty was the year of the summer Olympics in Russia. We weren't particularly interested in attending the Olympics. With our political backgrounds, we wanted to see what was going on in the Soviet Union first hand and experience some of the history directly. Additionally, my father's father was born Russian and I had studied Russian and Russian literature at Brandeis. And the Olympics had incentivized trips to Russia and the Soviet Union.

We signed up for a three-week tour with Anniversary Tours in New York City which had a history of well reviewed tours. Unfortunately, by late December of 1979, after a successful pro-socialist military coup in 1978, the Afghan government was beset by internal conflict. Additionally, Muslim based guerrilla tribal sects, some of them lead by notorious mass murderers, drug and war lords, like Abdul Rashid

Dostim and the leader of an Islamic army, Gulbuddin Hekmatyar, had grown noticeably bolder in attacking the government. The dominant government faction in the faltering government sought Soviet military support. The resulting Soviet military intervention ultimately lead to the US arming and training the fundamentalist Muslim military force led by Osama Bin Laden. It would become Al Qaeda. Sending sophisticated military equipment like shoulder held anti-aircraft and anti-tank weapons to Osama and other terrorist factions,[83] eventually blew back against the US on 9/11/2001. Nonetheless, the Soviet Union would become bogged down trying to fight against the guerrilla forces, just as the US had been in Vietnam and just as the US now intends for the Russian Army in Ukraine. The US labeled the Soviet debacle in Afghanistan, the Soviet Vietnam. The ensuing demoralization in the Red Army and the public probably contributed to the collapse of the Soviet state a decade later.

When the Soviet Union first sent 100 thousand ground troops into Afghanistan in December of 1979, President Jimmy Carter decided to punish them with a US boycott of the upcoming summer Olympic games. In a year Carter would be voted out of office, replaced by Ronald Reagan, and the US boycott of the Olympics would amount to little more than a slap on the wrist. Closer to home the US would then promote and support the Latin American "dirty wars" of the 80s that disappeared thousands. And later American military interventions in Afghanistan, Iraq and Libya after the 9/11/2001 attacks on the World Trade Center and the Pentagon— wars in search of a worthy enemy.

---

83 Dan Rather, with CIA connections, was able to report on CBS news directly from the military camps of these Mujahadeed fighters, who the US now dubbed "freedom fighters". The "freedom fighters" went on to later be responsible for the horrendous September 11, 2001 attacks in New York and Washington, DC. And so they were transformed from "freedom fighters" to democracy hating terrorists.

Under Reagan and Bush Sr. the US persistently armed and financed the various tribal and religious extremist factions in Afghanistan to fight the Russians. The various factions of Islamic Wahabi fundamentalism, rural tribal backwardness and anti-Soviet and anti-socialist discontent forced the Russians out of Afghanistan, leading to the Taliban taking power. Under the younger Bush presidency (2000–2008) the US would attack and itself occupy Afghanistan in the longest "US war" in our history against the Taliban. The American invasion was carried out under the guise of getting the terrorists responsible for the 9/11 attack (not to oust the Taliban). That excuse, however, followed the long and sordid history of US governments' fabricating a necessity to overthrow governments all over the world.

It's not news that as bad as the oppressive Taliban rule was (and is again) for the people of Afghanistan, particularly the women, the forces that the US energized to attack the Russians were the most ruthless and dangerous to a coherent society there; US concern for the Afghan people was as much a pretense as current US claimed concern for Ukrainians.

The Afghan events were all looming in 1980, when Carter declared the US Olympic boycott. The result was that every other person who signed up for that Soviet tour withdrew. We decided, instead, that if the Soviets would give us visas we'd just go on our own and make our own tour to the same cities and republics of the Soviet Union—Moscow and Leningrad in Russia, Kiev in Ukraine, and Tbilisi, Georgia. The Soviet Intourist agency obliged, authorized our visas and arranged guides for us on some days in Moscow, Kiev and Tbilisi.

In late spring we flew into Madrid and spent a week there—I remember only the famous Prado museum and a beautiful park. Then we headed to Barcelona the capital of the very independence minded Catalonia state. Catalonia has its own distinct culture, language and history dating back to Roman times. As a state it developed earlier than and distinct from the Spanish nation. It is also home to an out-sized proportion of the natural resource wealth of Spain. A beautiful and grand city on the coast of Northeast Spain, Barcelona faces the Mediterranean sea. We visited for a few days and have returned there several times for longer stays in recent years.

From Barcelona we boarded a night train heading for Florence, Italy. Shortly before reaching the French border the train passed through a long, seeming to me mysterious, and endless tunnel. On the other side in France there was a rest and bathroom stop at a small station. The open doors to the bathrooms faced outward toward the tracks. I disembarked and entered the men's room. Along the wall was a concave ledge about four inches wide that ran downward like an inclined plane or a Hot Wheels car track. Men lined up and peed onto the ledge and gravity moved the urine along. I joined the crowd. It wasn't until I was in the act that I noticed that after traversing the wall, making a right angle turn at the corner, the ledge, at the end, poured and dripped urine onto the floor at the feet of the right most urinator(s) and sought a drain. In essence men were peeing on themselves despite the initial appearance to the contrary. The absurdity of this bathroom caused our first jocular consideration of writing a travel book entitled "Amazing Bathrooms of the World" (we never wrote nor photographed them but often joked about the book on our travels). The women's room had its own notoriety for one could see from the train into the chamber where women squatted over holes in the tiled floor.

Through the French Riviera at night the train ran, then entered Italy and traveled south to Pisa, turning eastward to Florence. In Florence we had a room in a classical and very impressive private home, on the north side of the river/canal. The friendly woman owner made us feel like honored guests. The ceilings were like 12 feet high and the front doors along this street were massive, like those of a majestic marbled palace; hers not unlike the neighboring attached houses.

After a week touring in and around Florence, our plan was to board a train from Florence to Bologna to the East and then change to Turin traveling back Northwest, then after a day in Turin to take a train through the Alps to Poland. However, political genies were out of the bottle and had no intention of leaving us be. Arriving at the train station in Florence we learn that Rightists had just bombed the main train station in Bologna (which had an elected communist city government).[84] How bombing a civilian train station might be an important political act I failed to understand. But by then we had had the Weather Underground bombings in the US that were similarly symbolic acts of rage whose purposes I couldn't fathom, so who was I to make judgments about these Rightist Italians, even if I was partial to Bologna's reform-minded city government? Our train was only delayed some hours.

We arrived in Turin at its impressive rail station to news that the ongoing rail strike by Solidarity against the government in Poland had taken on a broad anti-government political character. All Poland's trains were stopped indefinitely. Undaunted, we decided to fly from Turin directly to Warsaw. The only flights available were with the Polish Lot airline. We'd never heard of it. We flew on an old, small two-propeller plane (maybe a DC 3), a bit shaky, whose maintenance we had no way of ascertaining. It would fly over the alps; but despite trepidation and a little trembling by the plane, it got us to Warsaw without incident.

Originally I had hoped to visit Poznan—where my Uncle Ted Roszak was born and raised—and the city of Krakow with it's mag-

---

84 At the end of WWII the Italian Communist Party was transformed from a key element of the anti-fascist resistance to something like the Labor Party in England. They were in favor of progressive reforms, but mainly limited their activity to electoral efforts and working within the system. They lacked an anti-capitalist program, yet even in 1980 they had strong support in some areas like Bologna and were at one time a major force in the Italian Parliament.

nificent architecture on the way to Warsaw, but now that was out. We would stay in and around the Warsaw environs only for a few days. I particularly wanted to visit one of the Nazi extermination camps, and had decided we'd avoid Auschwitz and visit the death camp at Treblinka. Treblinka, about an hour or so outside of Warsaw by road, held no pretense of being a "model work camp" by the Nazis (as they pretended at Auschwitz with formation of a prisoner culture including a Jewish symphony orchestra to show off to international visitors). Treblinka was solely a killing center. People were killed en mass as soon as they got off the trains and buried in mass graves. The site holds a museum and a remarkable cemetery for the victims. The tombstones are in the form of abstract art—anonymous jagged rocks seemingly erupting from the earth, not far from the station where people disembarked and were killed.

The downtown old center of Warsaw, demolished by bombing during World War II, was rebuilt to old specifications after the War. In a macabre way it reminded me of the "old towns" in contemporary American cities, re-constructed as part of gentrification. My mother's father Max Gustin, a Polish Jew, had left Poland back in the late 19th century. As we walked through the old town I imagined Jews from rural shtetls long ago traveling to the city center with goods for trade, their walking through and experiencing the very same place. I was thinking of this feeling when I wrote The Last Tale of Mendel Abbe—Sonny Bush and the Wise Men of New Chelm.[85]

Sheila recalls that we hired a driver or cab to drive us out to the death camp at Treblinka. I recall having the driver stop on the way so I might talk with a farmer tending his field right next to the road. I was never a great Russian speaker in college, and it was 18 years since I'd studied Russian, but I could carry on a rudimentary conversation in

---

85_http://marcsapir.net/books/The%20Last%20Tale%20of%20Mendel%20Abbe%20syn+6%20chaps.pdf.

Russian. Although Poles and Russians tend to understand each other and Russia clearly had much influence in Poland's governance and culture after the end of WWII, the farmer shook his head and said he didn't speak or understand Russian. That "nyet" was then repeated several times in the few days we remained in Poland. We concluded this was probably due to resentment of Russian dominance.[86]

In the few days we were in Poland we were approached several times by men on the street in Warsaw offering black market exchange rates for dollars. We took this to imply both that there was significant poverty and that the authorities were lenient, more or less allowing the open illegal money exchanges. Worth pointing out: when this is allowed to occur widely in any country it will do much damage to that nation's economy through the inflationary pressure that the cheapening of their money creates. One of the easiest ways to try and disrupt a socialist state's economy is to stimulate and promote the illicit money exchange market. Not only will prices rise as the value of the Zloty (Poland) or other national currency declines but businesses will prefer customers who do business in stable international currency such as the dollar.

In Moscow we did not get hassled by exchange rate black marketers though we were asked if we had jeans to sell twice. And a man approached me at the Intourist hotel restaurant offering to buy the

---

86 Over the years, whenever we travel outside the US one or both of us have tried to gain (or already have had) some minimal language competency in the countries we visited. Sheila had no Russian to contribute, but she speaks French and Portuguese, we both speak Spanish, and I tried (without remarkable success) to learn a bit of Greek and Vietnamese. When I went to Palestine with the Middle East Children's Alliance I had hoped to learn some Arabic, but that never happened. Friends told me it was difficult and I didn't follow through. Ironically, although I attended Hebrew school as a child and can read in the Hebrew alphabet my understanding of Hebrew is no better than my understanding of Arabic—i.e. almost nothing.

watch I was wearing right off my wrist. I smirked and held the watch up to the man's face. I had bought it in Moscow when my Casio went down. It had hands on a nice green background. He sheepishly retired.

Aside from the deeply moving visit to the Treblinka death camp another "moving" experience I left Poland with did not manifest until we landed in Moscow. Shortly upon arrival I developed abdominal cramping, some nausea and diarrhea that was unsettling but not severe. It persisted, however, and was making tourism not much fun. The modern Intourist Hotel in downtown Moscow had a clinic for guests so we took an elevator up to the penthouse clinic level. Two doctors were in attendance. I would be remiss if I didn't note that both were beautiful young women. When I told the physician who interviewed me the history, including where we were coming from, she asked if I drank the tap water there at restaurants—I had. Their public system is contaminated with Giardia she responded. We have very good medicine to treat you. We see this all the time, they said and the two physicians smiled at each other knowingly. She confirmed the diagnosis with a sample on a slide—something I would do myself more than once back in the US with new immigrants from rural Central America. What my doctor didn't say was that Moscow itself had also had an outbreak of Giardia from contamination of their public water supply. I didn't learn about that until Warren Winkelstein's epidemiology course at Cal on 20th-century epidemics in 1987. Giardia wasn't an issue during our tour of the Soviet Union once I was cured, but I suspect the Russian outbreak may be the reason that the young doctors knew the diagnosis right off.

The medicine they gave me was furizolidone which cured me. That was my first episode of Giardia, but I have managed to catch this infernal, though rarely serious, flagellated parasite several more times in my life. Before Giardia lamblia became endemic in the waters of California's wilderness we, as summer backpackers, used to drink lake and stream water either without purification or with iodine treated water, for that kills most pathogens. Giardia was spread, however, throughout the wilderness in the US by deer and other animals and through human contamination of lakes.

My next bout of the nasty bug came in Bishop, California right after we came out of backpacking in Humphreys basin in the Eastern Sierra, the territory of the Paiute Indians. After a week in the wild we usually celebrated at a restaurant. This time it included hamburgers and fries, milk shakes and other rich food. I got immediately sick and had to struggle to drive home through Yosemite and back to the Bay Area. After the Poland-Russia experience with this bug I learned that furizolidone was not an approved drug in the US. I was later treated several times with metronidazole (Flagyl). I also learned in later years that in rural Central American, where people's water supply is contaminated with Giardia, a carrier state can be established in which the infected person becomes asymptomatic.

Back in Moscow we first visited a science exposition that I'd heard about in advance. Perhaps naively I was impressed by some of the medical instruments that were in general use in their health care system, such as ultrasonography and focused beam radiation equipment for cancer treatment. There were exhibits regarding space exploration and many different technical fields. I was then under the belief that Russia had an egalitarian socialized medicine system in which all citizens had equal access to the best medical care the Soviet Union had to offer. As we talked with Russians during our three weeks we learned that there were actually two tiers in their system of health care (perhaps not as badly stratified as in the US where some cannot get care, but unequal nonetheless). Members of the Soviet Communist Party had access to different clinics and physicians, better equipped to provide a higher level of care, easier access, less delays. We wandered around Moscow at our leisure mostly without any guides or chaperons. Walking through the Lenin Mausoleum in

Red Square was kind of ghoulish—we stood on line with hundreds of others filing through to see the preserved body of V.I. Lenin which had been lying there on display almost a half century. He looked stiff and tired.

When facing the Mausoleum there is the large Museum of the Revolution on the right side of Red Square which we were interested in touring. Almost as soon as we began I struggled trying to translate the captions to the exhibits. Noticing this, a young man came up to us and asked if we were tourists and could he help by translating for us. He was about 18 or so and quite friendly. He spoke good English and we welcomed his help. I think his name was Peter, but it could have been Sasha, Vladimir, Boris, Misha or anything else given the weakness my memory for events 40+ years ago. Somewhere among the prodigious overflowing files of my life—the accumulations of this admitted pack rat that I am—there is a postcard or letter from him, but I'm not up to searching just to get the name right, so let him be Misha. He spent considerable time helping us through the museum.

After touring the museum we got his name and address and when we moved on from Moscow I wrote him a postcard thanking him for helping us. I also did something foolish. Misha had told us that his father was an official in the Soviet Communist Party—not high ranking but he held some position. I wrote in my letter that we were afraid of America's never ending malign intent toward the Soviet Union and asked that he tell his father that I thought that they needed to strengthen their party's popular support to be able to block destabilizing efforts by the US. A week or ten days later, during the fourth leg of our tour we were in Tbilisi, the capital of Georgia, the hilly city of beautiful tile murals. We were the only patrons at a restaurant upstairs in the hotel when two men walked in and sat at the table right next to ours. Shortly they leaned over intruding into our conversation uninvited. One of them asserted that it was nice that we cared about peace with the Soviet Union, but that we should go back to the US and fight for that goal, rather than giving advice to them. He implied that I had involved myself in Russian politics—which I worried might be close to an accusation of spying. Apparently my letter to Misha had been turned over to KGB or some other security people and we were being warned that we shouldn't be getting involved in Soviet politics.

I felt duly intimidated and realized that they were tracking us fairly closely, though most of the time we were sightseeing on our own without a chaperon. Thinking about how they saw us, I surmise that the Soviets didn't know what to make of an American couple who came there on tour despite the Boycott put in place by Jimmy Carter. What were we we up to?

Joseph Stalin was a Georgian. I had asked to visit the small village and his birth house which is about a two-hour ride from Tbilisi. Intourist arranged it for us, but it was the first time that we seemed to have obvious KGB or similar security personnel along with us. We went out in a big black limo with a driver and another suited fellow sitting shotgun. We took a picnic and when we asked, on the way, to stop to have the bag lunch we brought the two of them left us alone on a little hillside and went off apart, diligently trying to appear innocuous and unobtrusive, which made them look ridiculous. That was an amusing experience for us, but I suspect that our chaperones were bored stiff with their assignment. I remember nothing particular about the little house where Stalin was born, but I don't remember much about the little house in Guanajuato, Mexico where Diego Rivera was born either. I myself wasn't born in a little house, but in a small Jewish hospital in Brooklyn. And not being a person of particular note, the place where I was born was torn down and no longer existed a good half century ago. I should report that I have left a trail of torn down structures (like the Wayne County General

Hospital and that house in Menlo Park) in my wake in several other places as well. I take no responsibility (or pride) in this.

To get to Georgia we flew from Kiev, the capital city of Ukraine.[87] We felt secure in the Aeroflot planes we flew on from Leningrad to Kiev and to Tbilisi. At that time Aeroflot had a good safety record and was a reliable airline. Their planes were of Russian design and manufacture from two different companies and had interesting design contrasts and flying practices to what we were used to. One of the Aeroflot practices involved pilots throttling up the engines in a test in preparation for take-off. Though I don't know that it actually mattered it seemed reassuring. Later, Aeroflot deteriorated dramatically and suffered quite a few deadly crashes. The international flights we flew in and out of the Soviet Union were very "classy", undoubtedly to impress foreign tourists. It was like flying first class with lots of room and there was an area where we sat around a small table with complementary champagne and caviar. We were duly impressed.

Domestic flights were the opposite. Not only were they more crowded with less room but there were no flight attendants. On the flight to Georgia, however, the passengers were decidedly more gay and joyous than typical Russians. These were Georgian commoners, obviously not from the elite political class. Domestic flights were affordable for most people. They had brought lots of food and drink aboard and they were sharing all around, including with us. But, despite the great company, the trip to Tbilisi got rough. Flying over the Caucuses mountain range we ran into a front of heavy storms with lightening all around us and high winds battering the plane. In fact the pilot and air-controllers decided the plane should land and we descended to a small airport on the Black Sea seashore—it may have been at Sochi. On the way down, as the plane was being thrown around

---

87 In March 2022, most people now know Kiev as Kyiv and that it was the original target of the Russian invasion of the Ukraine.

furiously I probably looked green and very worried for the Georgians around us began to console us. Don't worry, we are going to be fine they assured us (in English). It happens all the time, they said.

This was far from the last time that we would be on flights in other countries where our plane felt like a toy being played with and tossed around by mother nature, but it's the only time I remember the passengers joking about it as a group.

Aside from these brief events: the hills surrounding Tbilisi, a ride on a tram and some beautiful tiled murals (a Georgian specific art form) I remember little of Tbilisi. However, I have another very personal earlier Soviet Union story in sad contrast with our 1980 trip. My mom was an avid enthusiast for ocean cruises. Her affinity for cruises began when there were no trans-Atlantic plane flights. Her parents often took transatlantic trips on the great vessels of the day—Cunard Line's *Queen Mary* and *Queen Elizabeth*. As I noted in the Cadillac story, Max was pretty ostentatious in his behavior. Whenever Max and Sally headed out from New York, they'd throw a big send-off party on board the ship. Mom and Dad probably took a cruise to Europe for their honeymoon; also for the Spanish civil war project in Belgium that I've written about.

Among the books my mom published, one, **Children with Learning Problems—Readings in a Developmental-Interaction Approach**, is a collection of essays by leading thinkers and practitioners (from Anna Freud to Erik Erikson to Noam Chomsky to A.R. Luria) that she co-edited with her colleague, Ann Nitzburg. A.R. Luria, an internationally prominent neuro-psychologist was based in Moscow where he ran an Institute. From interactions with Mom, Luria invited my parents to visit the Institute in Russia/Soviet Union. She jumped at the opportunity and planned a cruise to Leningrad[88]

____

88 Now St. Petersburg.

and a visit in Russia. Dad's father was an emigre from what is now Byelorussia. Dad had never been in that part of the world, despite their trips to Europe, so he welcomed the opportunity as well.

They traveled on the Russian cruise ship, Lermontov, from New York to Leningrad and they had a great time on board. Dad was by then settling in well to his teaching job with children with mental illness at Hawthorne Cedar Knolls School. But as the ship arrived in Leningrad there was some distribution of tickets to events on shore—perhaps the Bolshoi was in town or something like that. Not wanting to miss out on the opportunity, Selma—pushy as she was—butted in line in front of a man who spoke up in a nasty tone of voice, telling her to butt out. Dad was offended that his wife was being rudely treated—despite the fact that Mom was in the wrong. He told the fellow to leave her alone; or maybe he asked for an apology. I have only mom's sketch of what happened. The man became belligerent and what began as a small dispute got intense. Perhaps there was pushing. At that point my father grabbed his chest in pain. It was the onset of his third—and fatal—heart attack.

Bob got onto shore but collapsed and was taken to a hospital in this spectacular city he would never actually see and walk through—though Sheila and I would do that seven years later. Mom stayed by his bed as they kept giving him shots of morphine and nasal oxygen, but his pain did not abet. By evening she was told that visitors were not allowed to stay overnight and she had to leave to a hotel. The next morning Mom arrived at the hospital to be told that Dad had died overnight. She did not get to say goodbye to him. She may have taken this blow quietly, or she may broken down or started screaming at the staff. I have no idea, but Soviet officials became very worried about this death of an American in their hospital, and an inconsolable wife who had not been allowed to be with her husband. Might they, the Russians, be suspected of something untoward? The result of their concern was that for several days they refused to release Dad's body for transport back home and Mom had to involve the US embassy. When I arrived back in New York for the funeral, the body had only just arrived and was in a sealed case.

I think my dad's death in Russia was ironic. Recall my writing that my parents, for perhaps many different reasons, had strong feelings against the Soviet government—under Stalin in particular. They clearly didn't want me to become a communist on any account though they had many friends who had been communists. Yet they went to visit the Soviet Union without much hesitation. To me it seems like an Edgar Allan Poe story. In the end, their worst nightmare was visited upon them as the endpoint of that supposed-to-be idyllic vacation visit to Luria in Russia.

By 1973 coronary artery bypass surgery (CABG) for severely obstructed coronary arteries, severe angina, and heart attacks were being widely performed in the United States. The procedure was first performed in 1960 but a large number of cases weren't done until the late 1960s. Less intrusive stents had not even been invented. I imagine that the Soviet Union's physicians had not done very many of these procedures, although CABG might have become available for Party elites. It is conceivable that the Soviet doctors and officials were aware that this American visitor who stepped off the boat at Leningrad with an MI might have been offered a CABG had he been in New York. This is all speculation. Maybe they were paranoid about the never ending hostility of the United States. I don't blame them for dad's death.

Years later, after calming down about all she went through in Leningrad/St. Petersburg, Mom admitted to me that she felt guilty that she had caused dad's heart attack and death by trying to get in line in front of that man. In the end though, such things in life are often about "that man", don't you think? My parents relationship was not without tumult and contentiousness, but love—and men being what they are—when "push came to shove" Dad behaved like a chivalrous knight—and thus he died. Oy vey!

CALL ME ISHMAEL

I spoke with Mark Van Doren, the Brandeis American Literature professor, during his office hours toward the end of his course in 1960—1 asking him if he thought I had the chops to become a writer. I had written several papers in the course by then which he had graded as A's. I didn't tell Van Doren that I had begun writing a tale riffing off the opening line of *Moby Dick*. He made sure that I didn't think of the writing profession in some romantic fashion, explaining how hard a life it is. He wasn't unsupportive, just reality basing. Still trying to escape from the undisciplined youngster I had been, I never got beyond a few pages of writing on this project. But I ran across that handwritten piece among voluminous disarrayed materials within the last year only to now find it "unsearchable". I don't know where I put it. Indicative that.

"You can call me Ishmael…if you want, though it's not my name," is how my story began. Now, 60-odd years later, my narrative approaches its ending. Ishmael, of course, is Melville's narrator who impeccably and determinedly relates every detail about the whaling ships, life on them for the crew, the science and techniques of the whalers work and their killing, interweaving all that with the tale of the monomaniacal captain, Ahab, seeking vengeance on the White Whale who caused the loss of his leg on an earlier expedition.

Moby Dick was published in 1851. Leo Tolstoy's *War and Peace* was first published as a complete novel in 1869, though the tale is set in

1812. Melville's and Tolstoy's worlds, their great novels' subject matter, their class perspectives, the culture from which they arose, their overarching metaphors can seem so distinctly different, yet I think they fit together like two pieces of a giant jigsaw puzzle, or like the inseparable and attracting opposite poles of a magnet, or the complementarity of a subatomic particle that has split into two separate yet somehow connected entities with opposing spins. Such fit rests in their being perfect opposites that need each other to be whole. In a way that is how I see my 50 years with Sheila Thorne, although such a perspective treats only the dimension of complementarity.

Even by the 1850s, before the American Civil War, Melville recognized that the incipient monomania of capitalist development—this new form of the human quest for permanence and dominance—had within it the seeds of self-destruction, a totally rational irrationality, and thus the captivation of the soul. Was not Ahab's fixation on the memory of the great White Whale akin to what I have related regarding behaviorism—external conditioning of the human mind, the bending of our emotions through influence on our limbic and conscious selves—particularly this transforming of the most evolutionarily necessary of positive feedback loops—fixation on sex— into an unquenchable quest for things and power? Less than two decades after Melville's publication of Moby Dick/The Whale, the Russian Count, a teacher and student, with humanist sensibility and a brilliant mind, pointed out how that quest turns to social suicidality exemplified by Europe marching off to war in Russia behind Napoleon—he as monomaniacal as Ahab.

Obviously my own cynicism and that of many these days has become a big part of our human problem. We are a species that has great potential to determine its own destiny yet in déjà vu form we often bow down to leaders who lust for power. Repeatedly those running the show are our worst representatives who abdicate responsibility for social solutions under the pretense of pragmatism. Perhaps the collective human spirit will yet prevail. Maybe we are stymied because Marxists fell into the idealist trap of "historical inevitability" and sequestered themselves in their frame of mind. But, unlike technique, social progress and positive evolution are not inevitable. The work, the struggle, the cultural joy and enrichment, the organizing from below must be enjoined, particularly as today the future of human civilization and life's evolution on this planet are at great risk. We live our lives on two separable plains or planes—the plane of the mind and the plane of the act. They ought to merge holistically through culture. But we remain creatures living in a world of illusion and allusion, reflecting the capacity of our minds for metaphorical thinking, not just doing. That is indeed a miraculous feat of nature. Dreaming and hoping and praying beings are what we all are, all because of language. Yet, it may also be our ending.

I find myself indebted to Elzie Crisler Segar the inventor of Popeye the Sailor Man for these wise words: "I am what I am, and that's all that I am." In my decades of providing primary care medicine to tens of thousands of working class patients of every age, gender, ethnicity and nationality I've tried to respect folks and be responsive and responsible. I've sometimes been called a "micromanager" (often a pejorative in a manager, but sometimes a worthwhile "defect" in a doc). I believe I helped and supported many, though I'm sure I was imperfect in this aspiration. And for the rest of it, I've had my say—including indulging in these many pages—miraculously without spending any time in a dungeon or on a wrack, and done did some things that I take pride in.

"You know, Sancho, my friend, we've done our share of jousting... yet in my dreams those damned be-knighted windmills just keep blowin' in the wind, evermore." "Take solace, mi don, windmills are, after all, not such a bad idea."

Marc describes his memoir to Jorge Luis Borges, the renowned
Argentinian writer, who was unfortunately not alive at that time
(photo by Sheila Thorne at a Buenos Aires restaurant with wax display).

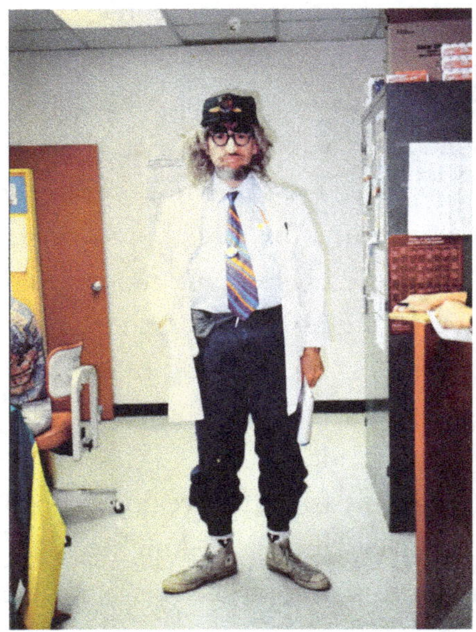

Halloween at the Oakland Central Clinic on
October 31, 1991 (photo by Cecilia Asercion).

THANKS

Thanks to grandson Moises Sapir-Uribe, Oliver Sacks, Bruce Franklin, Steve Masover and Peg Miller for encouragement of my writing, technical advice and helpful comments. Likewise to all those friends and family—unnamed here—who have said they can't wait to read the book (whether or not they meant it, it has still meant a lot to me). Particularly, I thank those who contributed kind words for the back cover. I am, as always, especially indebted to my partner, Sheila Thorne for putting up with the exigencies of my endless, sometimes quixotic, projects and personality—this being only the latest venture—over our 50 years together. We have stressed each other to no end and yet she's hung in there with me, as I have with her, loving her magnificent oft-published short stories, parenting, gaming, gardening, cooking, hiking, climate action and surviving our daily crises.

I also thank Iram Allam for her kind and consistent collaboration in the formatting and type-setting of this book; the inimitable Eric Drooker for his, as always, wonderful art in front cover design; also Miguel Cervantes, Herman Melville, Leo Tolstoy, Shakespeare, Kurt Vonegut, Don Delilo, James Baldwin, Tony Morison, Leslie Marmon Silko, Richard Wright, J.M. Coetzee and countless other writers in the English language for inspiration from their brilliant insights into the human condition. Because narratives, fictive as well as living, are the life blood and font of human intellect, imagination and creativity.

Most books have long lists of acknowledgments. Am I a stand-alone? Most of those mentioned collaborators are dead and only became collaborators in my own head (with the exception of Oliver Sacks); thus the human dialectic of historical continuity lives on.

Retired family, community, public health doc and activist, Marc Sapir, writes plays, essays, fiction. His satiric novel about the second Bush war on Iraq (*The Last Tale of Mendel Abbe—Sonny Bush and the Wise Men of New Chelm*) was self-published (2004). Marc lives in Berkeley with wife and rotating grandchildren.

website: marcsapir.net
e-mail: marcsapir@gmail.com